Attachment and family therapy

Attachment and family therapy

Patricia Crittenden, Rudi Dallos, Andrea Landini and Kasia Kozlowska

Mc
Graw
Hill
Education

Open University Press

Open University Press
McGraw-Hill Education
McGraw-Hill House
Shoppenhangers Road
Maidenhead
Berkshire
England
SL6 2QL

email: enquiries@openup.co.uk
world wide web: www.openup.co.uk

and Two Penn Plaza, New York, NY 10121-2289, USA

First published 2014

A catalogue record of this book is available from the British Library

ISBN-13: 9780335235902
ISBN-10: 0335235905
eISBN: 9780335239337

Library of Congress Cataloging-in-Publication Data
CIP data applied for

Typeset by Aptara Inc., India

Praise for this book

"This book is a tour de force! The authors have contributed one of the most significant theoretical developments within the family systems field for some time. Their book is part of a blossoming movement to integrate attachment theory with systemic theory and practice. They offer a powerful explanatory alternative to a DSM based description of distress in children and families that not only offers a compassionate, causal framework for the development of problems in families but also provides clear guidance for tailored assistance and intervention with children and their families."

Arlene Vetere, Professor of Family Therapy and Systemic Practice, Diakonhjemmet University College, Norway

"I have long looked forward to this book and it in no way disappoints, combining as it does engaging clinical material with a clarity of conceptualising that has become regrettably rare in the world of contemporary family therapy. Crittenden and Dallos bring alive the remarkable explanatory power of the DMM in a synergy with family systems therapy, to produce a readable therapeutic guide that is truly more than the sum of its parts."

David Pocock, Systemic Family Therapist and Psychoanalytic Psychotherapist, and Trainer in independent practice, UK

"This book presents a much-needed shift from infant-mother attachment to consideration of the wider family and professional system – including Dad! It offers an accessible, thoughtful and at times provocative approach to helping families struggling with a wide range of problems including those where children have autism or ADHD. The emphasis on assessment as a means of formulating an intervention plan, rather than diagnosis and prescription, is particularly welcome."

Steve Farnfield, Senior Lecturer and Director of the MSc in Attachment Studies, University of Roehampton, UK

We dedicate this volume to the families who have shared their distress and hope with us, enabling us to help other families through sharing their experience.

Contents

About the authors

Patricia McKinsey Crittenden is a developmental psychopathologist. During her doctoral work under Mary Ainsworth, she began to develop the Dynamic-Maturational Model (DMM) of Attachment and Adaptation. She pioneered video-feedback with maltreating mothers in the early 1970s, ran a family support centre, trained as a behavioural and family systems therapist, was the Director of the Miami Child Protection Team, and consulted to family courts in several countries. She has developed a life-span series of assessments of attachment. In 2004, she was given a Career Achievement Award by the European Family Therapy Association. She has published more than 100 empirical papers and chapters, as well as several books, and is the founding Chair of The International Association for the Study of Attachment.

Rudi Dallos is Professor and Research Director on the Clinical Psychology Training programme at Plymouth University. He works as a family therapist using an attachment narrative therapy approach which he has developed. His recent book publications include: *Attachment Narrative Therapy* (Open University Press, 2006), *An Introduction to Family Therapy, Third Edition* (Open University Press, 2010) and *Reflective Practice in Psychotherapy and Counselling* (Open University Press, 2009).

Andrea Landini is a child and adolescent psychiatrist. For two decades, he collaborated with Patricia Crittenden in the development of the Dynamic-Maturational Model. He teaches the DMM and its assessment methods internationally, has published many articles and edited volumes on the DMM. He is on the faculty of several Italian schools of cognitive and family systems psychotherapy.

Kasia Kozlowska is a child and adolescent psychiatrist at The Children's Hospital in Sydney, Australia, Clinical Associate Professor of Psychiatry and Paediatrics and Child Health, and Clinician Researcher at the Brain Dynamics Centre, all in the University of Sydney Medical School. She has published numerous papers, particularly on the topics of mind – body interactions, treatment of children with somatic symptoms, multimodal approaches for complex presentations, and the integration of DMM and systems thinking into clinical practice.

Acknowledgements

Most of all we are appreciative of the families whose stories form the basis of our understandings and help bring our book to life. In addition, we gratefully thank the following people who have helped us in many different ways: Clark Baim, Chip Chimera, Robert Duschinsky, Charles Nelson, McKinsey Pentland, Verter Pregreffi, Trina Robson, Nicola Sahhar, Blanche Savage, and Arlene Vetere.

Introduction: The rhythm of life: cycles and changes

What this book is about

This is a book about how people adapt to the challenges of their lives and the ways that mental health professionals can assist them when they are in trouble. Conceptually, it is a book is about the interconnectedness of life processes within and among individuals. These processes are multi-layered and reciprocal, with communication occurring both laterally and vertically through the layers and across individuals. It is a book about complexity, but an ordered, comprehensible, and functional complexity. To address the complexities of life – of survival and reproduction – we gather together an array of systems theories, from genetic and epigenetic to neurological, psychological, relational (dyadic and familial), and cultural. From these theories, combined with case study evidence, we will derive an approach to treatment that combines ideas from attachment and family systems.

Interpersonal neurobiology

Within that array, we focus most intensively on the bridge that connects one person to another in ways that shape the neurological development and functioning of each (Siegel 2012). It is at this point, where two minds converge in time and topic, that brains are shaped. This is the transfer point in childrearing, where the parent's genetic and experiential heritage coalesces in protective behaviour directed toward a specific child in response to the child's signals. The parent acts and the child's brain is differentially activated, leading to a situation-specific response. Across cycles of similar interactions, the child's brain is shaped, adapting the child to his or her unique family context. The parent is changed as well.

Such processes are also the transfer point in psychotherapy, where the therapist affects the patient's or client's mind and is, in turn, affected by him or her. Repeated across innumerable interactions, the cumulative effect of these interchanges shapes children's emerging neurological structure, parents' changing neural structure, patients' modified mind, and therapists' potential to respond sensitively to patients. Remove the cycle of interactive connections and brains do not change.

It is as simple – and complex – as that. The brain is the interface between the body and the context. It requires a reciprocal chain of input/output exchanges to represent this relation. Of all the exchanges a person has, those in attachment relationships have the most impact on the early organization of the brain. 'Attachment' refers to both the protective relationships among family members and also the cyclical chains of information processing that underlie interpersonal behaviour. It also describes the relationships between therapists, functioning as transitional attachment figures, and their patients.

In this book, we consider the conditions that promote or hinder adaptation and well-being among family members and between therapists and the people who come to them for help. Both attachment theory and family systems theory have strong traditions of analysing moments of human connection to discern patterns of behaviour. We draw on both traditions to understand how behaviour is organized and can be changed.

In accord with current usage and historical derivation, we use both the term 'patient' and also 'client' to describe people who receive mental health treatment. The term patient', from the Latin *pati* (to suffer), refers to a person who is suffering. Later it was applied to people seeking medical treatment. Most people who seek mental health services are in a state of distress and suffering; mental health professionals seek to reduce this suffering by working together with their patients to generate change. We retain the term 'patient' to capture this aspect of psychotherapy. The term client also originates from Latin (*cliens*, to listen), thereby referring to a person who is at the call of another person. Later the term came to mean customer, i.e., the person who 'called'. Recently in health care settings it has been used to emphasize clients' competence to articulate their needs and make choices about their treatment. Although this reflects growing respect for those who use health services, it also over-estimates the ability of people needing mental health services to describe their problem accurately, i.e., to issue the call, and to evaluate treatment options. Were there a term that captured professionals' respect for people who suffer from psychological and interpersonal problems, we would use that term. Instead, whenever possible we will use the terms child, family, person or individual rather than talking about clients or patients.

Diversity

Because every human life is different, this is also a book about diversity, but diversity in the service of universal goals: staying alive and giving safe passage to the next generation. There are as many ways to fulfil these functions as there are combinations of people and contexts. Yet, in the midst of unique individual differences, certain strategies are organized again and again. Something about our human make-up interacts with common variations in our experience to yield a small set of universally human strategies for protecting ourselves and our progeny. Too often, however, variations are seen as aberrations (cf. Gernsbacher 2010). One task we set for ourselves is to explore the adaptiveness of self-protective and progeny-protective strategies in their contexts. We consider three forms of adaptation: short-term, long-term, and mental health (Ainsworth 1984).

Our aims

Why did we write this book? We think that, together, attachment theory and family systems theory and therapy can yield a more comprehensive theory of human adaptation that could improve treatment. Attachment theory and family systems theory were both inspired by John Bowlby's emphasis on systemic interpersonal functions, the evolutionary biology of survival that underlies attachment, and the importance of working thera-peutically with families instead of individuals (Byng-Hall 2009). Yet for half a century their leaders have pursued separate priorities leading to different understandings of what is best for people.

Attachment theory, initially taken up by researchers, took an empirical and positivist approach. Repeatedly, the data indicated that desirable outcomes were associated with attachment security (Type B). Type B is best; security is the goal. However, most of the early research involved safe, middle-class, white infants and families living in advantaged countries. When it was discovered that less-advantaged subgroups in these countries or dominant groups in other countries had fewer securely attached children, it was assumed that intervention with these groups should focus on security. Little attention was paid to what these insecure individuals were doing; instead those with behaviour that was not described by Ainsworth were assigned to 'disorganized' (in what became an ABC+D model of attachment). Unsurprisingly, such groups often protested, arguing that attachment was a culture-specific idea that was not relevant to their culture. For them, attachment felt like a 'one size fits all' theory that didn't fit them. Insufficient inquiry was directed toward understanding the effects of differences in family or cultural context and how these might affect secure attachment. In spite of a wealth of sound research and valid assessments, at its worst, attachment could seem elitist, judgemental, and inflexible.

Family systems moved in the opposite direction. The variety of families made it impos-sible to define what was best for all families or what characterized a 'healthy' family. Rapid social change in the late twentieth century elicited a non-judgemental attitude toward minority groups, new roles for women, single parent families, divorce, homosexuality, and cultural variation in general. The postmodern period was upon us: All attitudes and beliefs were seen as having value; there wasn't a universal 'best' nor an absolute 'truth'. Without examining the context any more than had attachment theorists, family therapists yielded the authority to prescribe what was best for others, focusing instead on each per-son's perspective as personally valid. (The exception was cases of domestic violence and sexual abuse where family systems theory accepted the need to protect women and children from male dominance.) Compared to attachment theory, family therapy seemed rudderless or, more accurately, to have too many rudders to steer the boat effectively.

As is true for most dichotomies, both sides have some of the truth. Both Pop-per (1963) and Kuhn (1962) have criticized positivism as being too certain of what is true. There has been an emergence of a more relativist position (critical realism) that acknowledges that empiricism is necessary even though most information is altered by the observer's implicit values. In short, this argues that realities exist, but we can only know them through our personal interpretative lenses (Robson 2002: 624). The goal then becomes stating hypotheses that can be refuted rather than expecting to prove ideas (Popper 1963). For example, the data are clear: Mental health and happiness are associ-ated with security. But when the context is not safe, Type B may not be the best, i.e., most adaptive, strategy. The non-secure forms of attachment (Types A, C, and A/C) might be more adaptive under conditions of danger than Type B. Concurrently, this process needs to be seen as embedded in social understandings of who and what humans are (Kuhn 1962). These post-positivist ideas undergird the approach to psychotherapy that we offer.

This is where the Dynamic-Maturational Model of Attachment and Adaptation (DMM) has tried to function as a bridge. It acknowledges some universals, and chief among these are the evolutionary imperatives of protection from danger and production of the next generation. On the other hand, *how* one achieves safety and reproductive success may be tied to the context and to the relationships among people in the context. Because contexts and relationships vary greatly, different interpersonal strategies might be more or less adaptive, even within a single family. Such an approach respects all strategies, without yielding the ultimate goal of promoting protection and reproduction. It also recognizes that both safety and danger (e.g., domestic violence and sexual abuse) are found in families and, it is there, in families, that protective and reproductive strategies are organized. This complexity of understanding creates tension between the desire for security and happiness and the reality of dangerous contexts (from families to cultures) that might require non-B strategies to promote survival.

In sum, both attachment and family systems theories have made substantial contributions to understanding and healing human suffering, but each has limited itself by holding fast to tenets that occluded important information. Attachment theory has delivered sound empirical data and validated assessments, but sometimes at the cost of ecological/cultural validity and with premature judgement of what is good for specific people. Family therapy has focused on clinical action in the diffuse world of troubled families, often giving up empirical rigour and clear guidelines for action in favour of clinical creativity and range of applicability. By integrating the two theories within an evolutionary understanding of the ultimate need to survive and reproduce, we hope to reduce these limitations and to increase both our understanding of human dysfunction and also the precision of therapeutic responses available to professionals. We think the time is ripe to unite the strengths of these two traditions, that is, to join theory and therapy, rigour and range – and to set the whole in the context of adaptation to diverse and changing circumstances. Specifically, we offer a synthesis of developmental ideas and assessments with family processes and effective treatment techniques, all directed toward fostering the development of the next generation.

In this book, we explore the connections among several systemic theories, particularly as they affect therapeutic work, by offering an account of development across the life cycle that embeds individual differences in universal aspects of dyadic and family experience. The Dynamic-Maturational Model of Attachment and Adaptation (DMM, Crittenden 1997) is our starting point. Though originally drawn from the Bowlby–Ainsworth theory of attachment, it has extended the construct of attachment to include sexuality and reproduction and to describe more fully the complex pathways that development takes as it is shaped by the challenges and dangers of life.

Connecting concepts

We employ a variety of concepts over the course of the book, but want to highlight four processes that are central: knowing, communicating, organizing, and change.

What is known and how it is known

Information is the key to adaptation; without good information, people cannot attune their behaviour to their circumstances. Information comes in many forms from genetic and epigenetic to non-verbal (both thought and enacted) to spoken and written. Information can be innate or acquired by experience, both directly and through communication from others. It can be known implicitly or explicitly and it can be known in different ways at one time. Moreover, information can be false, or merely distorted, or true for the past, but irrelevant to the future. Discrepant information can be held within one person or among different people.

Without meaning, information does not affect our functioning. With meaning, it predisposes behaviour. However, attributing meaning to information is always a unique, self-relevant process that occurs in a brain that is defined by the state of the self at the time of making meaning. That is, the attribution of meaning always combines aspects of the external context with aspects of the self to yield a self-relevant disposition to act. But we get ahead of ourselves. The important points here are that 'information' combines external 'reality' with person-specific internal states and these are real as well. In doing so, information becomes unique for each person. This is adaptive because it both protects each person maximally and also confronts each person with alternative understandings. Sorting out what is known and its predictive accuracy is crucial for survival and that requires discovering and resolving discrepancies.

Acquiring and using information are a fundamental process that is refined by both neurological maturation and interpersonal experience. Because humans are born with little awareness, we are dependent upon attachment because attachment connects mature, conscious parents with immature children. That is, survival in childhood depends on the quality of the information and that is tied to connection to a stronger, wiser person, an attachment figure.

Communication of what is known

Communication occurs between individuals and also as an internal dialogue. Survival is promoted when there is both an interpersonal dialogue (e.g., non-verbal signalling, conversations, texting, publications) and also an inner mental dialogue (e.g., in reflective thought, dreams, and preconscious forms of knowing, including somatic forms). Moreover, exchanges between interpersonal and inner dialogues invigorate both, in a dynamic exploration of meaning. The degree to which each individual can express information and understand the communication from other people is relevant to both survival and successful reproduction. When communication omits, distorts, hides, falsifies or denies information, either information that is transmitted to others or information received from others, the probability of personal and interpersonal dysfunction is increased. As with knowing, communication changes as a function of development.

Organization of information and behaviour

Humans do not act randomly, nor are they at the mercy of behavioural contingencies. To the contrary, human behaviour is systemically organized, like a weather system or a school of fish or ... a family. Information provides a basis for action, but is not itself action. Instead, information is *organized* to represent the relation of self to context (both people and places) and the organization *disposes* the individual to act. Information-generating systems that communicate are self-organizing systems based on feedback. This is true for the functioning of our genes, internal organs, families, and cultures. Everything is in a dynamic systemic relation that yields fluid organizations that function to protect us, protect our partners, and protect our progeny.

Because mothers are the irreducible, universal context at a child's birth, it is not surprising that the organization of the infant–mother dyad has implications for survival. A half-century of attachment research demonstrates that the quality of infant–mother attachment is central to the infants' survival, development, and adaptation. But mothers have other priorities, other children, and a need to protect themselves. Thus, in a family context, there are many needs, conflicting priorities, and diverse dispositions to act. Survival is promoted when the family system has and communicates sound information about the state of each individual. Because family members and life contexts are constantly changing, adaptive families modify their organization as their members grow and change. Life is defined by constant small adaptations. Families that focus instead on protection from past dangers run the risk of maladaptation.

Change

Change is central to knowing, communicating, and organizing. Nothing is absolutely constant, but neither is life unstructured and random. Safety depends upon a complex and dynamic interplay of self with others and with the environment. That is, there isn't a right way to live, nor is today's way necessarily best for tomorrow. At the same time, there are regularities in what is safe and promotes safe reproduction that are sustained across families, cultures, and generations. Complexity, change, and attunement to new conditions promote adaptation.

We propose that complex and flexible self-, partner-, and progeny-protective organization develops best within families that communicate accurate information clearly and frequently. Further, we propose that most intra- and interpersonal problems involve lack of dynamic flexibility in what is known, how it is communicated, or how it is used to organize protective behaviour. Although, in the short term, rigidity can be protective against danger, it is usually maladaptive in the long term. As usual, there can be a trade-off between current needs (to stay alive) and long-term adaptation (to promote the fitness of the next generation).

Some examples

Feedback and regulation of arousal

Bowlby proposed that a sensitive parent and dependent child interacted in such a way that the child's level of arousal would be kept within moderate limits. Although Bowlby thought that 'security' was the best means of achieving moderate arousal, he also pointed out that, in the face of danger, changes in arousal were adaptive (Bowlby 1982). DMM theory takes Bowlby's notion further by recognizing the complex relation between patterns of arousal, patterns of self-protective and reproductive behaviour, and context. Arousal is both the body's response to environmental demands and also somatic information about the meaning of the context for the self (Damasio 1999; Porges 2011).

When a threat requires action, the sympathetic system is activated to rouse the body into flight or fight. If the threat cannot be resolved, the old parasympathetic system may be activated, causing metabolic and behavioural shutdown or 'freezing' (Porges 2011). Once the danger has passed and the environment is safe once again, the individual shifts back to a more calm and positive physiological state. However, if the environment remains unsafe, the distressed individual shifts between states of sympathetic arousal, sympathetic burnout, and activation of the old parasympathetic system; such states are associated with a broad range of physical, emotional and behavioural symptoms (Chrousos and Gold 1992; McEwen 1998; Porges 2011).

Conceptualizing arousal as somatic information about current and past danger or opportunity for sex that can be communicated to others and used to organize self-protective and progeny-protective behaviour gives clinicians a better way to understand and treat individuals with dangerously high or low arousal.

Looking at triangles

One of the most enduring ideas to emerge from family therapy is the notion of triangulation (Kerr and Bowen 1988). Minuchin and his colleagues (Minuchin 1974) proposed a variety of triangular processes, including displacing attention to a child's problems and enlisting children in the struggle against the partner. The situation becomes complex and confusing when communication within the family is omitted, obscured, or distorted about what is going on. In such situations, children and their parents often become confused about the causes of events and their own role in family problems.

The focus on triangles can be an important bridge between family and attachment perspectives. It allows us to see a child as functioning in both direct dyadic relationships with each parent and also in an indirect relationship between them (Palazzoli et al. 1989). In effect, the child can be seen as having an attachment strategy with each parent, but having those strategies function to meet the parents' needs in their marital relationship – without the child's awareness. That, of course, is the critical point: the child lacks important information.

Family systems therapists also proposed that inflexible and misattuned dyadic processes sometimes pull in a third person to 'balance' the process (Kerr and Bowen 1988). In DMM attachment theory, this has been expanded to troubled families who reach a developmental or interpersonal impasse (based on the limitations of their information, communication, and strategic organization) that pulls in professionals (Ringer and Crittenden 2007). In some cases, it was observed that professional systems function to maintain and legitimize the dysfunctional homeostasis by diagnosing it and medicating it rather than changing it (Crittenden 2008). When a child is labelled as having a problem, such as autism, attention deficit hyperactivity disorder (ADHD), conduct disorder, or anorexia, this can distract attention from familial processes contributing to the child's behaviour.

The function of symptoms

Like Bowlby and Ainsworth, many of the pioneers of the family therapy movement (e.g., Minuchin, Palazzoli, Jackson) came from psychoanalytic backgrounds and maintained a strong interest in linking individual experience, unconscious dynamics, and 'problems' with family processes. A connecting thread was the idea of the *function* of behaviour. For family therapists, the focus was on the function of symptoms for the family; often the function was linked to maintaining homeostasis in families, i.e., avoiding change when change was required. In attachment theory, the notion of function was elaborated in terms of enduring protective strategies that could be fulfilled by any number of behaviours depending upon how they were organized interpersonally. The DMM approach to attachment and adaptation has emphasized the adaptive value of the non-B strategies and also added reproductive functions to protection.

How we wrote this book

Usually there is a sharp dichotomy between academic/scientific writing and story-telling/poetry. We intend to span that dichotomy, moving fluidly between data-precise and impersonal communication to affectively expressive and person-specified communication. Metaphorically, we want to use information that ranges from computer printouts to songs because this is the range of communication used daily by humans as they try to express and structure their experience with each other.

We hope you are not disturbed by this range. It's part of everyone's daily life as they switch from shopping lists and stock market reports to their favourite music on their iPod. But it's not so usual in academic books where facts and citations overwhelm feeling and aesthetics – even when the topic is emotion or beauty.

Life is lived on many levels: from the chemistry of genes twining together in the nucleotide dance of life to rioting mobs that appear from nowhere, shouting with one voice about the semantic abstractions of freedom, equality, and opportunity. We seek to span this range of daily human experience and expression in the hope of making our meanings clearer.

The plan of the chapters and topical highlights

Each chapter opens with a vignette of normal family life. This is intended to carry the reader back to universal aspects of the age period addressed in the chapter. This is followed by a discussion of the major developmental advances (for both children and parents) that affect interpersonal relationships. Once the universals are in place, individual differences are addressed, especially as these differences generate conflict among family members or become sufficiently extreme to endanger individuals or create a misfit between the family and the larger community. The closing section of each chapter presents one or two clinical cases. The cases usually have DMM assessments of attachment strategies; to keep the text focused, all information about the assessments and their application is given in Appendix 1 on Assessments. A crucial feature is the search, in the functional formulation, for a critical cause of the family's problems. Critical causes are 'those causes which, if changed, would lead to improvements in the other detrimental conditions and, thus, to improved family functioning' (Crittenden and Ainsworth 1989).

We have sought topics and cases that present unresolved problems; that is, if effective treatment approaches are already known, we chose a different topic. Our interest is to explore the growing edge of clinical understanding. When the perspective on the cases differs substantially from the usual understanding of this sort of problem, we offer a brief, but formal, review of the literature, together with a rationale for our perspective. Specifically, we offer novel formulations of: child abuse, autism, ADHD, bullying, and conversion disorder.

But what should I do?

Our goal is to improve mental health treatment. Recent years have seen a plethora of branded treatments without corresponding clarity as to which treatments are more effective. Further, there is not even clarity as to what mental disorders are (cf. Insel and Wang 2010; Division of Clinical Psychology 2013). In this volume, we take a new approach. Rather than focusing on symptom reduction, we place adaptation first and ask what is necessary for adaptation. The answer is quite simple: to protect oneself, protect one's partner, and protect one's progeny until their reproductive maturity.

Safety and sex: that's all there is. But oh! How complex those two little functions are. Knit together across lifetimes, they coalesce repeatedly in organizations that function and fade and take form again, newly, but always to promote the same immutable purposes. The DMM describes strategies for achieving safety and reproductive success in the face of varied threats. By connecting the rich and precise analysis in the DMM of an individual's internal states and dyadic relationships with an understanding of the complexity of families (family systems therapy, FST) and how to work with families to achieve change, we hope to assist psychotherapists to reduce the suffering and increase the adaptation of the people who seek their assistance.

Our tools are reframing problems in terms of safety and sexuality, assessing behavioural strategies for managing relationships and psychological strategies for managing information, formulating problems within the developmental capacity of each person, and selecting treatment responses suited to these parameters. Because relational issues – the quality of communication and connection with close others – underpin many mental health problems, we begin with the centrality of the relationship between the persons seeking treatment and their psychotherapists. When this relationship promotes accurate communication around the process of clarifying experience, suffering tied to the past can be reduced and maladaptive processes that harm individuals in the present can be changed. These ideas will be elaborated developmentally in this volume and then presented as an integrated whole under the label of DMM-FST Integrative Treatment in Chapter 7.

1   Birth and infancy

Life has a rhythm. It turns and turns, like a wheel. And like a wheel, it never twice touches the same ground. Where does it begin? With the birth of a baby? With the joining of the parents? With their childhoods? Their births? In the turning of this wheel, there is no beginning, neither is there an end, but each turn carries forward some of the history of what went before and is marked freshly by the land over which it now rolls. We will enter the story with the birth of a baby, but we know the baby enters a flow of lives that have already taken shape and carries genetically the accumulated knowledge of previous generations. A birth is both a beginning and a continuation. Nevertheless, the purpose of our story is not simply to show how one life develops in the context of other lives, but, more importantly, to explore universal patterns of human adaptation, processes of change that affect us all, and the way that time shapes and reveals these.

Birth

Birth and danger

Birth is a good place to begin. It is the most dangerous moment in life, a moment that is startlingly close to death. It is dangerous for the baby; many infants do not survive birth itself and the first day of life, weeks of life and even the first year of life winnow out many human infants. Only the strong babies, born into strong families, and blessed with some unseen source of luck – the random coming together of unpredictable good fortune with sound preparation – will survive. Birth is also dangerous for the mother; many mothers die in or shortly after childbirth. A woman's reach for the future carries risk for her present. A man risks his wife to have his child. The young couple risks their harmony to leap into an unknown future with a small person they've never met and in parental roles they've never filled. Their families continue – or await another opportunity. Birth is a dangerous moment in which a family might begin – or not.

Most babies live. Most mothers too. Families take shape and thrive. But there are casualties along the way. If we combine the sick and stillborn babies, the mothers who do not survive and the families who will come to child protection or mental health attention, the danger of childbirth is real, very real.

Birth reminds us that we are one in a series of species, carrying in our genes an accumulation of information from an unbroken chain of life about surviving on earth (Darwin 1925). Nothing is more physical and beyond intellectual control than giving birth; nothing is more dependent upon this innate knowledge about how to survive. However, once the biological imperatives are favourable, birth is quintessentially psychological and interpersonal.

First moments of life

Screaming and howling (both mother and son), John is born. John, Johan, Johannes, Giovanni, Jean, Jan, Ian, Juan, Ivan, Jahja … a human boy is born. In this moment, something profound occurs to his mother and to everyone present at his birth. A transformation begins, one that ties his mother to him and his father to them both so strongly that the couple will risk their lives to protect their tiny infant.

A lot has been written about maternal bonding and infant attachment, about family roles and cohesion. Out of all of this, nothing is more basic than seeing that the function of all of these dyadic and family connections is to promote the survival of a human baby – to create, one infant at a time, the next generation of humans. That this happens in a community context is important as well (Bowlby 1953). Representatives of the community attend the birth and other representatives accept the baby formally into the community through an array of naming rites. Infant, dyad, family and community: all are needed to promote survival. The attachments that develop are shaped by a complex web of family relationships, expectations based on the baby's gender, and ideas about how this baby will be similar to or different from other family members (Dallos 1991).

The mother's bond to her baby

While her baby is being born, the mother's body, her very being, is changing. Genetic switches trigger changes in her hormonal status and her body responds with new secretions, rapid physiological reshaping, and a flow of feelings all directed toward keeping her new baby alive (Macdonald and Macdonald 2010; Feldman et al. 2013). Without milk, John dies; without love, no one feeds him. Both, however, are beyond conscious control and almost always appear when they are needed. Birth releases milk production whereas looking in a baby's eyes, hearing his cry, and feeling his body against her own release feelings that tie a mother irrevocably to her baby (Swain et al. 2007; Strathearn et al. 2008; Strathearn et al. 2009).

Moreover, because birth is so difficult, cultures have devised ways to reduce the threat. Someone is almost always with the delivering woman – and it is rarely her husband. Someone wiser, less emotional, and more experienced in these things guides the process of birth: a dula, a doctor, a midwife, a friend. Without this community support, birth is more dangerous yet (cf. Crittenden and Craig 1990). That is, the birth of a child is a personal event that creates a dyad, a couple's event that creates a family, and a community event that contributes to the survival of a cultural group. The connections made in the moments that follow birth are crucial to the survival of the baby, his family, and together with other births, his community. Biology and custom come together to promote survival.

Meanwhile, fathers often feel marginalized. Whether they do and in what ways vary from culture to culture and family to family. Nevertheless, as important as men are, they become background to their pregnant wives, newborn infants, and wives after birth. They are needed, very definitely needed to provide for the safety and survival of this precious and vulnerable unit. Still, it can be unsettling to find oneself in the supportive background. Our point is that the joyful event that establishes new relationships puts stress on existing relationships. Change does not come without cost.

Nor are all births equally blessed. About 10 per cent of newborns have a handicapping condition. Some are born into families that can't feed the mouths they already have. Some come late – after the years of childrearing were thought to be finished. Some come too early. Some are welcomed with joy – and others with a groan of disappointment. Each birth makes a profound change in a family and it does not necessarily promote happiness. Of all the possibilities that become realities in the moment of birth, one of the most anticipated is the baby's gender. When John, Ian, Jahja . . . is born healthy and sound, there is universal rejoicing. Mary, Maia, Mia, Maria, Mari, Maija, Marija, Marietta, May, Marita . . . may not be so unreservedly or universally welcomed. Regardless of how one gender or the other is perceived, the family is changed more profoundly by gender than by any other characteristic (other than health) of the child. Whole life trajectories take shape as soon as a baby's sex is known.

Cycles of adaptation: the first year of life

Regulating arousal

Mary is crying. Babies cry when they need something, thus somatically representing and communicating the threat they feel. Babies differ in how rapidly their arousal escalates from a fuss to a red-faced howl. We can think of that as an individual difference – an aspect of innate, genetically influenced temperament – in a universal aspect of human functioning (i.e., intensity of arousal). Here, from the first moments of life, nature (in the forms of babies' experience-expectant innate neural pathways, universal responses, and individual differences in these) and nurture (in the forms of variation in mothers" responses and cultural practices) begin their joint input on what will become Mary's strategy for regulating her inner arousal and an aspect of her relationships with other people.

What happens next is crucial because it is the beginning of the effect of the environment on a baby's behaviour. Mary's cry functions protectively only if someone gives it meaning and responds (Hoffmeyer 2008). If Mary's mother comes quickly and picks her up, three things will happen, all without Mary's awareness but all with implications for her future development. First, being upright enables Mary to engage visually with her surroundings, creating neural pathways that connect her body position with her context (Galiana 1986). Second, Mary will begin to learn how to transform a state of distress into calm. Mary's state of calm is mediated by activation of the parasympathetic system: this both slows down the heart and also activates neural systems that enable Mary to communicate and connect with her mother (Porges 2011). Third, Mary will begin to connect her mother's arrival with feeling better.

If Mary's mother is right there, already holding Mary close to her body, so that she immediately soothes Mary, Mary will rarely experience severe frustration and the horrible state of out-of-control screaming. But if her mother is too responsive, the dyad will have fewer opportunities than other dyads to engage in interactions where mother helps Mary shift out of the state of distress – a state of sympathetic arousal – back to a calm and positive physiological state. Lacking practice, Mary will find it harder to learn to self-soothe and calm herself. She will learn less about different feeling states and how to communicate them to other people.

If, on the other hand, Mary is usually separate from her mother, for example, in her bassinette or cached in the hollow of a tree, and her mother is busy with her own tasks, then Mary awakens both alone, without her mother's body to warm and mould to her, and also at a distance in time from her mother. In that case, her mother's sensitive responsiveness becomes crucial. Will she come quickly, before Mary becomes severely distressed? Will she not come at all for some hours, leaving Mary to exhaust herself with crying until she sleeps again? Will her mother come too quickly, responding to her own anxiety, thus, picking Mary up after every little rustle or whimper? In any of these cases, the dance of mutual arousal regulation will be more awkward and less recipro-cal than if her mother were better attuned to Mary's somatic state. Put in construct terms, her mother's response will affect both Mary's temporal cognitive and sensory affective experience of the state of her 'self' (see section on contingency, p. 28).

In thinking about these possibilities, it is important to note the effect of the mother's own characteristics and her usual patterns of perception, attribution of meaning, and response. How much of Mary's movement and sounds does she perceive? Or is her mind elsewhere? Is she busy with Mary's 3-year-old brother John who is pulling the dog's ears? Does her gut cramp when she hears Mary cry? If she notices Mary's arousal consciously, what does she make of it? Does she think it is important? Is it a call to her? That requires action? Which action? The one her mother used when she was 8 and she wanted her own mother so much but she didn't come at all or the comforting one she had imagined she would offer her own child? All of these intra-personal processes occur within Mary's moth-er's mind (Crittenden 1993). An inner dialogue may occur, if there is time, in which Mary's mother consults all the relevant information that she has: her body, her emotions, past epi-sodes with Mary, books she recalls reading, her mother's words, her husband's rules, etc. Or there may be no dialogue; Mary's mother may spring into action with certainty. Mary herself has no access to her mother's mind; she has no information until her mother acts. Then Mary's nervous system responds to the sensory stimulation provided by her mother.

Both the inner dialogue and the springboard for immediate action have a common base: neural activation. We will call all these neural networks dispositional representa-tions (DRs) (Damasio 199; Crittenden and Landini 2011). By dispositional representation, we mean an activated neural pathway which attributes meaning to current sensory stim-ulation by combining aspects of the external context with aspects of the self. This combi-nation yields a self-relevant disposition to act. At any moment, there are as many DRs as there are parallel neural pathways activated by concurrent sensory stimulation. The spe-cific features of these DRs will depend on the place of the DR in the neural system; each point in the neural architecture allows for specific meanings to be reflected in the DR. As different parts of the brain become functional with maturation, the individual's ability to make meaning of sensory stimulation (as reflected in various DRs) increases. Overall, simpler DRs at lower brain levels allow less complex meanings that dispose less sophis-ticated action than DRs at fully mature neo-cortical levels, but they do so more rapidly.

As defined here, the construct of dispositional representation refines and substi-tutes for the idea of 'inner working models' by bringing the concept in line with neurobi-ology and by highlighting the transient and context-specific nature of DRs.

Learning to predict

What Mary's mother does when Mary cries provides Mary with information that Mary's brain is expecting about the effect of her crying (Glaser 2000). Nothing? Mary cries more and more until she learns that crying leaves her with escalating distress, but nothing changes outside of herself. She exhausts herself in trembling, red-faced misery and eventually falls asleep. Her mother, if she notices, may think to herself that she did the right thing because Mary now sleeps. The next time Mary cries, her mother is likely to repeat this response of not responding.

Between 2 and 3 months of age, when genetically regulated maturation first makes selective inhibition possible (Durston et al. 2002; Watanabe et al. 2011), Mary will probably inhibit her crying until she becomes an especially quiet and silent baby. Tucked in the hollow of a tree, left in a crib in a room filled with other babies, or in her own bed but with a withdrawn and depressed mother, Mary will learn that she has little impact on the world around her. She will not have the opportunity to become skilful in her capacity to regulate the vagal brake to shift between different states of arousal – calm rest, focused attention, play, eating, exercise and distress. She will not develop 'self-efficacy' in terms of her ability to communicate her emotional state to a responsive other, her ability to self-soothe and her ability to use eye and voice contact to connect intimately with her mother (Blehar et al. 1977). Mary may have difficulties in sucking, swallowing and digesting, physiological functions which depend on the engagement and disengagement of the vagal brake, and which are compromised in physiologically stressed babies (Porges 2011). In extreme cases, the absence of contingent responses will so overwhelm unique individual differences among babies that there will be near uniformity among neglected babies. Neglected children show delays in brain maturation due to insufficient stimulation (McLaughlin et al. 2010), have over-developed amygdalae and high glucocorticoids in response to novelty (Tottenham et al. 2010; Lupien et al. 2011) have difficulty discriminating emotional expressions from human faces (Pollak et al. 2000) and have high rates of feeding difficulties, which may manifest as failure to thrive (Block et al. 2005). Children raised in institutions show a constrained range of personality as compared to infants raised with responsive human care (Spitz 1946; Muhamedrahimov 2000). Specifically, most institutionalized children suppress negative affect and increase the intensity of positive emotions (Muhamedrahimov et al. 2008).

Is this inhibition adaptive or maladaptive? It depends. If Mary is cached while her parents search for food, silence might save her life. If her mother is given to angry outbursts, invisibility might save Mary from serious injury. But if she is the youngest of many siblings or one of many babies in daycare or in an orphanage, crying more vigorously and longer might get her the tiny bit of attention that will teach her personal efficacy and, maybe, even give her a chance at establishing a personal relationship with a caregiver. Adaptation is complex; it depends in part on the context.

In a more usual case, Mary's mother comes to calm Mary and see what she needs. Maybe she calls out, 'I'm coming' – or not, but either way, her footsteps come closer and then she reaches down and Mary feels hands on her body and feels herself being lifted, she hears her mother making soothing voices, and finally she is nestled against her mother's body. Suddenly there is warmth and softness and the rhythm of mother's voice and ever so much to look at over her mother's shoulder. If Mary does not settle immediately, her mother may begin to rub her body or to rock her rhythmically. All these interventions – mother's voice, mother's touch, and the rocking – provide powerful somatic inputs which function to activate neural circuits associated with emotional regulation: heart rate is slowed, the sympathetic arousal system is switched off, and the functioning of the baby's facial muscles is enhanced allowing her to attend to mother's voice and face cues (Porges 2011). Being upright, Mary's brain settles into a calmer state and Mary's eyes open wide as she looks at everything around her (Regal et al. 1983).

Mary's crying has subsided and she is in a state of moderate alertness, neither highly aroused and screaming, nor sleepily unaware. In this state, she can take in information and respond to it. In this calm moment while Mary takes in these delicious new circumstances, Mary's mother can decide what Mary needs. Changing? To be fed? Or is she just bored and they should go for a walk, around the house or down to the park? If Mary has a sibling, her mother will need to include him in her considerations. How will this affect 3-year-old John? Can he handle a moment alone or are his needs more urgent? Separately, Mary's mind and her mother's mind process the situation while together her mother's body attunes itself to Mary's, helping Mary to find and maintain that special state of alert and comfortable arousal. They are together and separate at one time, as humans often are.

Within only days, Mary recognizes the sequence. As soon as her mother's hands touch her, the neural circuits for down-regulating stress-response systems are triggered into action, and Mary begins to calm. A few days later, she calms at her mother's voice as she leans over the crib, then at the footfalls near her bed. By some months later, Mary knows, just *knows*, when she hears her mother's voice call out from another room, that mother and comfort and milk and all things good are on the way – and Mary begins to calm herself. This is the momentous power of her mother's contingent responsiveness offered in the context of Mary's own biological maturation. Through repeated use – the repeated pattern of soothing interaction with her mother – the neural circuits underpinning Mary's capacity to calm herself have been strengthened (Perry and Pollard 1998). Mary learns to predict and she uses her predictive dispositional representations to regulate her arousal, a skill that involves activation of a higher-order brain circuit (the orbital frontal cortex, the amygdala, the anterior cingulate and other interconnected regions) involved in emotional regulation, which will become more and more important in Mary's capacity to self-regulate, as she and her brain mature (Davidson et al. 2000; Ochsner et al. 2004). Mary and her mother are communicating and this dialogue about what Mary needs and what her mother will do can now move from full enactment to shared signals (Bowlby 1982). By the middle of the first year of life, Mary gives a brief cry – and listens. Her mother calls back – and Mary settles, knowing she was understood and her mother is coming.

Contingency depends upon linking in time. It is a different sort of information as compared to affect. It is 'cognitive' information about the temporal links between events (see chapter summary). As a newborn, Mary needs an almost immediate linking of her own behaviour (e.g., her crying) and her mother's response to discover the contingency (Gergely 2001). As the contingency is repeated and, concurrently, as Mary's brain matures, the time can be extended without the contingency being lost and the expectation violated (Bell and Ainsworth 1973). Mary's mother need no longer be a 'slave' to her baby. Instead she can communicate and Mary can understand and use the communication to bridge the temporal gap between her own signal and her mother's response.

This is important because many mothers *intend* to come to their newborns, but get waylaid by something else. The time between the first cry and their reaching down and comforting their baby becomes too long. The baby can't make the temporal connection and, instead of calming, the infant becomes increasingly distressed. In such cases, affective DRs take precedence for the baby over cognitive information. Mary's intense negative affect, plus her mother's own sense of urgency, arouse her mother; she hurries, trying to do everything. By the time she arrives, she is excited and Mary is distressed. She reaches down to pick Mary up, but Mary is squirming; she's somatically aroused and hard to calm. Mary's mother is rushed, her hands are too tight on Mary, her voice too fast and high-pitched, her rocking too frantic; Mary's affective DRs in the form of sensory images that Mary perceives are not associated with comfort. A struggle begins and Mary's mother feels a bit frantic and helpless against such howling and activity in her 'difficult' baby. Such mothers are not unresponsive and they don't endanger their babies' lives. Mary will be fed plenty and changed and cared for adequately in physical ways. It's just that it will be hard for her to discover the contingency, i.e., information about the temporal links between events, between her own behaviour and her mother's response.

When mothers misgauge their babies' ability to wait, the power of contingencies to shape their relationship is disrupted. Rising sympathetic arousal takes precedence, and the baby has fewer opportunities to learn how to self-soothe and calm; in the long term, such babies will be less skilled at regulating the vagal brake to differentially engage and disengage with others and with daily challenges in the broader environment. The babies of such mothers are on a cognitive schedule of unpredictable, intermittent positive reinforcement of negative affect. They will cry more than other newborns. As their brains mature, they will eventually discover the contingency, but the discovery will both be delayed and also affect their crying differently, compared to other babies. They will escalate to intense crying very rapidly (because responses have come at the point of intense crying) and they will cry for increasingly long periods, holding out for the desired response. Because crying is very aversive to adults, the response eventually comes and this reinforces the baby's expectation of needing to scream and scream and scream.

Knowing – before language

How do babies 'know' somatically, cognitively, and affectively? Infants are not yet conscious and they cannot speak, nor understand what is said to them. Nevertheless, within the first moments after birth, they are beginning to learn from their experience, especially their repeated experiences with caregivers. It is in the behavioural connection between two minds that each is shaped by the other; in Siegel's terms, this is 'interpersonal neurobiology' (Siegel 2012). Attachment is where the knowledge of one generation is passed to the next, interaction by repeated interaction. Because parents' behaviour already has predictable patterns, it has greater influence on infant's neurological development than the reverse, but both parent and child are shaping the other's mind.

One of the most powerful forms of knowing is somatic. Babies feel in their bodies what they know about their safety: this is why a mother's sensory input – her voice, her face, her smell, her touch, her rocking – is so powerful. We too can discern a baby's emotional state through the baby's body. When we hold a baby, we feel as she relaxes, stiffens, or hangs limp like an object not a living creature. Babies express intense somatic discomfort through their inability to eat, sleep, or retain food. Their bodies know what they cannot yet say.

Babies also 'know' because the brain develops in a use-dependent fashion and because babies make associations between aspects of the sensory environment and how they feel (Perry and Pollard 1998; Perry 2009). The smell of their mother, which they can discern within hours of birth, relaxes them or, conversely, can send them into the panic of fear (cf. the discussion of 'Harry' in Kozlowska 2007: 491). Such sensory images will be called 'affect'.

The way a child responds to a given association depends on repeated instances of interaction which function to strengthen specific neural circuits in the brain. So if Mary's mother usually responded quickly and sensitively to her distress, just the sound of her mother's voice will help Mary activate neural circuits associated with self-soothing DRs. When she is older, the smell of her blanket (which she associates with warmth and comfort from her mother) can comfort her, even into toddlerhood. On the other hand, if Mary has been exposed to domestic violence – perhaps her parents have shouted loudly at each other, and perhaps her mother had been hit while Mary was in her arms – then the sound of a raised human voice may activate DRs that mediate freezing, an innate fear response which involves attentive vigilance, body stillness, decreased vocalizations, slow heart rate, and sensitivity to pain (Fanselow 1994). Freezing involves concurrent activation of the sympathetic and parasympathetic systems, together with activation of the immobility centre (the ventrolateral periaqueductal grey; Walker and Carrive 2003). Sound, touch, sight, and taste all elicit imaged DRs that provide information that babies use to regulate their arousal or to activate defensive body states long before they understand any language.

Predictable sequences provide another form of information, i.e., 'cognitive' information, about temporal sequences. Even neonates recognize temporal sequences between people when it includes their own behaviour. They can even learn in a single trial if the sequence includes a somatic representation of danger (Wilensky et al. 2000; Bush et al. 2009). That is, they learn what to do to elicit responses and how to respond to others. These predictable sequences are called 'procedures' and constitute non-verbal, cognitive DRs about what to do.

These three ways of knowing (somatic states, cognitive procedures, and affective images) are very basic forms of information. They function throughout the life span. They are processed very rapidly. These DRs dispose one to act self-protectively when they signal danger. And they exist before and outside of language. Recognizing what another person knows and responds to in these three preverbal ways is important throughout life. It is crucial in infancy because there is no other form of information and no way to communicate except through somatic state, actions, and sensory images.

Individual differences: Ainsworth's Types A, B, and C patterns of attachment

By the end of the first year of life, experience with these three ways of knowing coalesce in the self-organizing patterns of perception, attribution, and response that we will call a self-protective strategy (Ainsworth 1979; Bowlby 1988). The Type A, Type B and Type C self-protective strategies (or patterns of attachment) each involve different learned patterns of perception, attributions of meaning, and responses in these three ways of knowing. The Type A strategy is based on a dominance of the cognitive, procedural DRs, and an inhibition of negative affect that together function to keep the somatic self tolerably calm, while reducing the probability of eliciting negative responses from caregivers. The Type C strategy features a dominance of expressed negative affect and a lack of cognitive prediction that keep the somatic self tolerably aroused and increase the probability that caregivers will respond. The Type B strategy uses both affective and cognitive DRs in balanced ways, associated with the most comfortable somatic states, in the expectation of a protective and soothing caregiver response.

All three strategies reflect a developmental stage understanding of information that can be labelled as 'realist' (cf. Kuhn and Franklin 2008). Infants' dispositional representations are used as if they were a direct, simple and perfect reflection of reality. The core features of this developmental stage are summarized for clarity in Box 1.1. The infant–parent attachment is non-symmetrical in power because babies are entirely dependent upon their caregivers (and not the reverse) and non-reciprocal because parents take care of babies (and not the reverse, except in cases of 'role reversal' or 'compulsive caregiving', see Chapter 2).

Box 1.1   Realist mental processes

1   *Definition*: Gaining facts/information that drive behaviour; the implicit belief is that what one knows is exactly what exists in reality.

2   *Limitation*: No process to manage discrepant information.

3   *Information type*: Preconscious somatic, procedural and imaged DRs.

4   *Executive functioning*: Infants do not regulate which DR disposes their behaviour.

5   *Individual differences*: Essentially all intact humans master this.

6   *Treatment implications*: When infants' behaviour indicates distress (especially somatic distress of a non-medical nature), the context (as mediated by parents) should be changed to generate different information about reality; guided interactive work with infants can augment this if necessary.

Fathers, siblings, and the extended family

Often this story is told as though Mary and her mother were the entire world, with Mary depending on her competent mother who doesn't need anything from Mary in return. Sometimes a single mother does care for her first child all by herself. But more often there is a father, two sets of grandparents, a host of aunts and uncles, and there may be siblings (see Box 1.2). For example, Mary's mother may need some recovery time. By picking up some of her usual chores, including care of the other children, Mary's father can ease the arrival of a baby. Or an older sibling can take on new responsibilities, becoming a mother's helper. Grandma may offer her hard-earned wisdom and an afternoon of babysitting. An uncle may be a fatherless child's 'male role model'; if he himself is childless, he may feel the genetic and affective pull of parenthood and adopt the role of a surrogate parent for the child (Trivers and Burt 1999).

Box 1.2   Attachments in infancy

• *Parents*: Non-symmetrical and non-reciprocal.

• *Non-parental adult figures and older siblings*: Non-reciprocal, with infants largely unaware of a relationship that has meaning only for the other person.

In the process, the mother and father might grow closer, seeing how they can work together and depend upon each other. The older sibling can gain new skills, skills that are relevant to becoming a parent him- or herself, and, at the same time, feel like a valued and contributing member of the family. The extended family can become an integral part of reciprocal caregiving that nurtures them all, especially in times of need. In harmonious families, the birth of a baby is a chance for everyone to grow a bit.

Alternatively, Mary's father might feel displaced by all the attention Mary and her mother are receiving – and this will make it harder for Mary's mother and, thus, for Mary too. The siblings might feel displaced and jealous of the baby. Some might sulk and withdraw, others might be disruptive. In some cases, an older sibling might try to harm Mary. Mary's uncle might come too close and abuse her. Mary's mother might resent her in-laws so intensely that family bonds are disrupted as her husband is forced to choose which family to support (Haley 1976).

The point is that that the mother–infant dyad is rarely an isolated unit (and when it is, it is a very vulnerable unit). To understand how the dyad will fare, we must consider how other parts of the family respond. This is not as simple as tracking triadic interactions; in fact, it is not triadic at all. This is the more fundamental issue of interlocking family subsystems that affect one another. Can Dad use his relationship with Mary's older sister to assist her to take on a motherly role? Can he guide his son to feel tender and protective toward his mother? Can the siblings use their mother's preoccupation with the new baby to strengthen their ability to occupy themselves in safe and fun ways; can they learn to play together with greater self-reliance? Is this their opportunity to develop closer relationships with their father and to appreciate the variability and flexibility of a father's role? If these things happen, the family grows and each member of the family grows.

In the meantime, an outer layer of relationships can also support or hinder the development of the family. An infant is part of the reproductive agenda of previous generations, and each branch of the extended family has plans about how to give or receive, contribute or evaluate, support or criticize how this infant is raised and how the parents are adapting to the new conditions. This can help or hinder, but mother–infant dyads who have no such support face the greatest risk of all (Bowlby 1988; Dallos and McLaughlin 1992). Indeed, mothers' perception of being isolated and without support affects infants' ability to inhibit a startle response as early as 4 months and endures at least until 4 months (Huggenberger et al. 2013); this suggests that the integrity of contingency processing is being affected at its inception.

When there are problems

Often we put so much emphasis on the wonderful aspects of having a baby that it becomes difficult when reality doesn't measure up. Sometimes the problem is in the baby: he has an impairment, was born prematurely and can't go home, or turned out to be a girl! Sometimes it is in the mother: she is depressed or is disabled herself. Sometimes it is in the context: the parents have a troubled relationship, they can't afford another baby, someone important just died, or it is wartime and a dangerous moment to have a baby. Strengths in the child, parents, or context might make the problem workable. For example, Mary's mother might *think* she has to manage home, work, motherhood and being a good wife and know that she cannot manage all this and fall into despair. However, if her husband understands her fear of failure and responds to it by comforting her, also making it clear that having a clean home can wait a few decades until they retire, post-natal depression might not be the outcome.

Mary's mother might benefit from the crisis by discovering how wonderful her husband really is and how much more flexible she can be than she had expected. Alternatively, her family might come to her aid, taking over some family tasks and making it clear that Mary's mother can relax and take her time, and that her feelings can be understood and appreciated. Or Mary herself might snuggle in so nicely or look at her mother so intently that, in spite of her physical anomaly, her learning disability, or her having to stay in hospital, her parents fall in love with her. So it is not simply the presence of a problem that creates risk, but more importantly, that the whole system of influences does not generate a solution.

To illustrate the sorts of problems that might be addressed by an integration of attachment theory with family systems theory, we present two cases. We begin with cases that highlight gaps in the treatment system, because that is where professionals can grow.

Discovering the unspeakable problem

Ian and Kate referred themselves to family therapy when their son Robert was 10 months old. Ian made the call and said they were considering divorce after five years of marriage. An appointment was set for six weeks in the future. The service they contacted was affordable because it was a training institute in which student trainees in marital therapy observed a master therapist (a man, in this case) working with a junior therapist (a woman) and, after the sessions, discussed what had occurred and how the treatment might progress. This was explained to Ian and Kate and they agreed. The viewing curtains were opened and the first session began.

Session 1: Establishing a contract

Both parents sat stiffly, with Robert on the floor near his mother. The lead therapist asked them what brought them to treatment. After an awkward pause, Ian said his wife was rarely happy, that she couldn't laugh and wasn't playful. Kate gave a forced smile and slipped down on the floor to play with Robert. Robert tolerated this briefly, then crawled off. Kate waited a bit, then returned to her seat. She was asked what concerned her and she mumbled something imprecise. The focus returned to the idea of her not being playful and she agreed she wasn't. The therapists struggled a bit to engage the couple with the junior therapist making particular bids to Kate, but Kate remained polite and distant. The goal of session 1 was to produce a contract that specified a problem and defined the period of treatment. Playfulness, with the underlying idea of Kate becoming more emotionally open, became the focus and ten sessions were defined. The family left with the assignment to find free moments when work and household chores could be set aside and they could play in a light-hearted way. They were to return with notes on how that had gone.

Sessions 2–9: The treatment

The next eight sessions passed quickly. The stiffness remained, but Ian spoke more and laughed more than Kate. He also sat twisted up tightly, with fidgety thumbs. He spoke of having too little power at home and that he wanted Kate to share her power. Kate said that she didn't feel powerful and only made decisions when he couldn't; she seemed subdued and not able to address this issue. Moreover, she seemed uncomfortably aware of the observation window and never looked at it. For sure, nothing about her seemed playful – and Robert was observed playing near his father in tense moments.

The discussions among the trainees centred on how boring this family was and on reaching Kate and articulating her perspective. Someone suggested seeing her alone, but the consensus was that this would break the trust with Ian. Another of the trainees wondered about Kate and Ian's history, but that was set aside in favour of working in the here and now. Nine sessions had passed with no obvious movement in the family.

Session 10: Closing the treatment

In the tenth and final session, both Kate and Ian seemed a bit more relaxed, possibly a bit relieved. They still behaved politely and answered all the questions, but it was as if they were waiting for the minutes to tick by to release them from their contract. Eventually, of course, that happened and they all parted, saying it had been a good experience; yes, things were better; we wish you well in the future; thank you; thank you. They left with Robert in Kate's arms.

The aftermath

A week later, Kate called the woman therapist; it took two days for her to return the call. Kate was agitated and her words tumbled out. She and Ian had had angry words and he had hit her and she had left with Robert and she didn't know if she could return home safely. She was in a hotel; she had talked with Ian. He was sorry, he wanted them to come home. She hadn't told him where she was. Could they see their therapists again? They needed help.

The therapist said this was quite unusual after the end of the contracted period; she would need to discuss it with the others and would call back. When the therapist called back three days later, Kate had returned home. The therapist said they had begun working with another family and couldn't fit Kate and Ian into the schedule. Kate asked to see the woman alone; it was explained that this was not possible. The therapist asked how things were going between Kate and Ian now. 'Fine, fine.' It was left at that: good luck; thank you, I understand; yes, of course; thank you; goodbye

Reflecting and reconsidering

If we reflect on what happened, it seems that the uneventful treatment had in fact been powerful – but on a schedule that didn't fit the contract. Nevertheless, ending the 'unsuccessful' treatment had brought the danger into the open. Kate had said something to Ian – and been hit for it. She'd moved out; Ian had initially said they were considering divorce. Some real issues had been laid bare briefly – and then, when help was not forthcoming, they had been hidden again with Kate saying, 'That's fine.' 'We understand', 'Don't worry', 'We understand the situation' and the call for help was ended quickly.

In retrospect, we should worry about couples who present with Type A inhibition and a politely vacuous manner, but with statements about divorce and strong signals of somatic inhibition (see chapter summary). The discrepancy was stark. Ian's twisted up body and fidgety thumbs, and Kate's avoidance of any 'real' topic suggested fear and tension. Kate's inability to laugh or play suggested she had given up. Was she depressed or simply oppressed? Since no one moaned or complained about this overtly, it was omitted from the team's formulation. Kate's urgent call seemed to convey her sense of connection to the therapists, but her timeframe and her terms were outside the contract. Kate, in other words, felt an on-going relationship to at least one of the therapists, but the therapists had moved on. In addition, it seems unlikely that Ian and Kate understood that the offered contract was not suited to their needs and that a brief course of treatment might be disruptive without providing the opportunity to repair the disruption. Possibly, having gathered no history and holding no private meetings, the therapists didn't understand that either.

We'd like to know what happened to this young family, but we don't. Long-term follow-up was not part of the service and the couple never called back. Indeed, if Kate had not called, the danger released by the treatment would not even have been known to the therapists at all. We wonder what would be revealed in this and other cases if follow-up were a standard part of treatment.

Kate and Ian's course of family therapy had seemed innocuous, but in fact it had had powerfully dangerous effects that the therapists had completely missed. How did that happen?

We focus on four issues: assumptions, assessment, cases-specific formulation and planning, and process variables during the treatment.

Assumptions

Reflecting on what happened, it is likely that both Ian and Kate and also the professionals worked on false assumptions that were not articulated and, therefore, could not be corrected. It appeared that Kate and Ian had assumed that the therapists would know what to do. They didn't consider how the therapists would discover what was needed. On the other hand, the therapists seemed to believe that Ian and Kate would be able to articulate their problem and advocate effectively for the services that they needed.

The inaccuracy of these assumptions in this case is stark and dangerously clear. But was this an anomaly or is it a pervasive problem that professionals need to address? Many problems that bring families to professional attention are not fully understood by any members of the family. Instead, they bring their discomfort, confusion, and a proximal cause ('lack of playfulness' for Ian and Kate) to the therapist. But often the actual problem is 'unspeakable' and sometimes even 'forbidden to know'. For Ian, violence against women was impossible to consider; it conflicted with all his values. For Kate, her sense of danger was too inexplicit to articulate; only after she was hit could she announce what happened, but even then she hid her fear from the therapist and, possibly, herself.

Assessment

Careful assessment of individual, dyadic, and family functioning might have prevented the family therapy from augmenting the family risk while, concurrently, increasing the probability of effective therapy. Tools like the Adult Attachment Interview (AAI) and the Parents Interview (PI) (see Appendix 1) could have enabled the therapists to find the unspeakable and forbidden-to-know problems, as well as to see how reliance on Ian to speak for the couple could be misleading in this very earnest, but troubled, young family. The use of a group of observers was meant both to support the training needs of new therapists and also to provide reflective insight into families' problems. We think, however, that crucial aspects of functioning are too subtle to be noticed in real time. In addition, many important issues cannot initially be discussed in language. Although short checklists are of some help, many adults do not know how to answer about risk.

Surely Ian and Kate would not have checked 'family violence' items. Consequently, the most comprehensive assessments should not rely overly on the content of the answers to the questions, but also evaluate how the discourse is organized within each speaker and among the speakers. This is what the DMM assessments are structured to accomplish. The time and expense of good assessment are, we think, essential for both effective treatment and also to prevent inadvertently eliciting danger.

Interpersonal and psychological treatment is very powerful at changing mental and behavioural processes. When medications are offered for these purposes, extensive prior testing of suitability and negative side-effects is mandated. When medications are prescribed, competent physicians discuss side-effects with their patients and, after the medication has been used for a short time, they enquire about the outcome. We think all forms of behavioural intervention require the same diligence (Lilienfeld 2007; Barlow 2010; Dimidjian and Hollon 2010). The medical dictum 'First, do no harm' should apply to all professionals.

The failure to assess before instituting treatment and to follow up after treatment caused danger to Ian, Kate, and Robert. Once the danger was identified, the failure of the therapists to act left a very vulnerable couple to solve by themselves problems that had escalated to being dangerous. They came to treatment because they couldn't solve these problems. Therapists have an ethical responsibility to help such families find appropriate services.

Formulation and case planning

In this and many cases of contracted family systems therapy (FST), the formulation was premature, the product of a quick and informal process that failed to generate sufficient data. We think that once the therapists had become aware that they were struggling to generate a meaningful formulation – this was clear in the first session – a more comprehensive assessment process should have been initiated (seeing each parent alone, taking a marital history, family of origin histories, and so on) to identify the problem and design a family-specific means of ameliorating the problem. The formulation should both explicitly identify discrepancies and the critical cause of danger in the family and also be stated explicitly as reflecting 'approximate knowledge' that will be updated as the treatment progresses and new information becomes available.

The process of treatment

Four issues are relevant to the process of treatment in this case. One is that, being a training programme for psychotherapy students, the ten-session plan was pre-defined for all families. This was an inappropriate plan for Ian and Kate; after assessment and formulation, they needed to be referred to an appropriate service. Second, the service plan disallowed individual contact; in cases of family violence, this might augment the danger to family members. This stricture should be seriously reconsidered by those family therapists who still use a 'family only' approach, especially in cases of violence. Once the risk of violence was discovered, the family should have been cared for appropriately until another service could take over. The third issue is the overlooking of Robert. Because he was 'just a baby' and couldn't talk, he was present, but no one attended to his communications. But babies know when their parents are uncomfortable. Watching Robert's non-verbal communication could have been informative. The final point is the importance of discrepancy. The observers identified some discrepancies (boring family refers themselves? Kate can't be reached? One partner talks, the other is silent?)

and overlooked others (calm and playful Ian is fidgety? Kate tries to reach Robert, but he moves away?). Each of these was a possible warning sign. Discrepancy is the opportunity to discover something new; it should be embraced.

An unwilling grandmother

Sometimes the birth of a baby is not a joyous occasion. Consider, for instance, Mrs Freeman's situation. Her daughter and son-in-law have had their first baby. It's a moment of joy? She has her first grandchild – that special event all her friends are beginning to exclaim about as, one after another, their first grandchildren are born. Why does she feel so angry? The early intervention specialist who comes to her home is about to get an earful on exactly that topic.

Beginning an intervention

As the worker greets the family, she immediately sees the problem. The baby's mother is smiling and smiling, wanting to show off her new baby. The mother is holding the baby unsafely – like a 3-year old dangling her doll by the arm – and the worker almost grabs the baby away to protect him. The father smiles broadly and says something the worker can't quite understand while he reaches out to the baby with a spasmodic jerk. The baby is screaming. Backing up, the worker looks at Mrs Freeman who seems to be the only normal person here. She shrugs her shoulders with a satisfied 'I told you so' look.

Mrs Freeman's daughter is 28 years old and moderately learning disabled. Mrs Freeman prefers the term 'mentally retarded' which makes more sense to her, but she knows she isn't supposed to use it. However, she has heard it often enough from the children in the streets jeering at her daughter; thinking about it makes her want to scream with anger. Her son-in-law is 30, has a slightly lower IQ and cerebral palsy. They met in an institution for older adolescent learning disabled individuals who couldn't be managed at home. Now married, they are enjoying the rights of all individuals to have sex and babies. But grandma looks like an angry, trapped animal. When the worker suggests the importance of her role in the family, she lets fly, with an explosively angry tirade: she had to give up her job when her special needs infant was born; she had professionals crawling all over her house until her daughter finally went to the group home; now the law says her daughter can marry and bring up a child, but the consequences are that the child is unsafe (Figure 1.1). Well, let the law raise the child, she wants her freedom back! All during this outburst, the parents just keep smiling, while the baby dangles precariously from her mother's arms.

No one is wrong in this family. But solving the problem is beyond the family's grasp. A little parent education is not a solution. Psychotherapy isn't the answer either. Clearly, Mrs Freeman is the only solution, but who would dare to ask her to take on her grandson and his parents after giving up her young adulthood to care for her disabled daughter?

A family/attachment approach

Families have a history of relationships with each other which shape their current relationships. But families also continually create and re-create their ways of relating: this creates potential for change. So, let's start by looking at what has just happened. Mrs Freeman became very angry with the worker. We wonder why this happened? Surely the worker had just attempted to validate her importance to this family, so why the

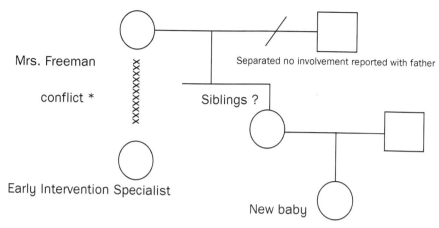

* Tension and disagreement between Mrs Freeman and the early intervention specialist

Figure 1.1   Genogram: an unwilling grandmother.

anger? We can make some speculations. It is possible that there is a history of Mrs Freeman feeling that she has not been listened to and that her feelings and opinions have been ignored. The worker may have inadvertently repeated this pattern by failing to respond to her non-verbal communication about her distress/despair with regards to her grandchild's situation, as well as her own. Perhaps Mrs Freeman perceives the worker to be enacting some 'politically correct' stance towards her daughter and son-in-law: treating them as competent adults with rights to parent a child, whereas she understands that they are more like big children and are not capable of looking after a baby. Mrs Freeman may understand the communication from the worker as manipulative, an injunction for her to continue to support her children and now her grandchild, while at the same time her feelings and plans for her own life are ignored. In this light, the worker's 'validation' sounds like an expectation that Mrs Freeman take on this caregiving responsibility, while putting aside all her own feelings, needs and plans for the future. None of this may be apparent to the worker, who may be trying to be kind and constructive and who may be using the 'professional' language that she was taught in school. However, if she were able to conceptualize Mrs Freeman's anger as a form of clear and direct communication, she would find it easier to empathize with Mrs Freeman's predicament.

What kind of a relationship has this early intervention worker got with Mrs Freeman? We suspect not a very close one. If she had, she might have looked her in the eye or sympathized as she saw how ineptly her daughter was handling the baby; this would have been an emotional communication that acknowledged the reality of the situation. We must also wonder whether the worker – or any other worker – has ever talked with Mrs Freeman about how she felt when she recognized that her daughter had a 'learning disability'? Did the worker know how many times Mrs Freeman had wept secretly over the loss of a healthy daughter, the loss of her dreams for her daughter's future, and for the relationship she desired with her? Perhaps only Mrs Freeman sees the future clearly: a lifetime of looking after her daughter, her son-in-law and her grandchild, a lifetime of trying to protect the daughter from herself, a lifetime of being a downtrodden caregiver.

A conversation about these issues needs to occur, as otherwise Mrs Freeman may cut off the emotional pain associated with her many losses and the lack of understanding that she feels from professionals. Once she is cut off from her feelings, Mrs Freeman may decide to let the government take her grandchild into care, where the outcomes for children are poor (Tarren-Sweeney 2008). Maybe someone needs to acknowledge the appropriateness of her concerns and complaints. This might free her to work within the constraints of an imperfect treatment system.

In order to make some connections to Mrs Freeman, a family therapist would paradoxically need to think about spending some individual time with her to better understand her experiences, thoughts and feelings. This would reveal some important things and raise other questions. Where is Mr Freeman? Did he leave the family when the issues around his daughter became too stressful to bear? This happens more than occasionally after a disabled child is born. Where is the rest of this family? What kind of a childhood and experience of parenting did Mrs Freeman have? What did she hope to do with her life? What has been her experience of professional systems? The answers to these questions would tell us about her hopes, fears and possible sadness about her daughter. It is possible that once Mrs Freeman felt heard and understood, she would soften and would be able to think flexibly rather than reactively. But this is not an easy process, and unless Mrs Freeman perceives us to be genuinely interested in her experiences, and unless we are able to ask these questions in language Mrs Freeman perceives to be neutral, it could easily go wrong. There is a risk, however, that asking Mrs Freeman about her own attachment history might make her even more angry: 'So you are implying it's all my fault again, are you?' There is a risk that exploration of past problems with professional systems could intensify Mrs Freeman's sense of injustice and make it more difficult for her – and for us – to leave past grievances behind.

As professionals working with Mrs Freeman, we need to reflect on our own attachment needs and experiences. As she criticizes the treatment system, it is all too easy to see her as belligerent, hostile, uncooperative, or even as impossible to work with. Are we able to 'contain' – that is, both hear and understand – her feelings and her anger without feeling overwhelmed? Two considerations can help with this process. Recognition that where there is anger, there may also be vulnerability: holding both sides of the coin in mind may help us tune into the pain which underlies Mrs Freeman's anger. This, when we find it, will be the 'critical cause' that can turn everything around. What is our own attachment strategy? How do we ourselves manage distress, anger and our need to be protected and understood? Many workers employ displacement attachment strategies in their own lives; they care for others, overlooking themselves. Do they expect others to do this as well? That seems to be the expectation put on Mrs Freeman. A conversation about tears, distress, anger and hurt may be very difficult for some professionals to tolerate. It may cause them to retreat from the emotional content of their work by turning to prescriptive semantic knowledge: offering advice, suggesting parenting techniques, and implementing behaviour management plans. Although all these interventions are all potentially useful, they are more effective when delivered in the context of a strong therapeutic relationship (Benedetti 2011), with a focus on positive change.

So our conversations with Mrs Freeman may move between articulating the difficulty of navigating professional systems and an exploration of her mixed feelings.

These conversations can draw on her responses to the AAI. It is remarkable how this interview can be experienced not as an intrusive assessment, but an opportunity to talk about one's own life while being listened to properly. The structure of the AAI removes much of the risk of interrupting and making premature interpretations or interventions while someone tries to tell and reflect on their life story.

If we can build a trusting relationship with Mrs Freeman, we can function as a transitional attachment figure for her, helping her to make the transition from angry and misunderstood mother and grandmother to appreciated and competent guardian of her grandson, her genetic future. Maybe she can discover that the opportunity to raise a happy child has been presented to her once again. Maybe the issue is reframing the situation in terms of her needs instead of her daughter's needs.

Improving service to families with infants

We began this chapter almost lyrically, but close it on a sombre note. Not all beginnings are auspicious, but all began with hope. Mental health treatment is intended as a bridge across the gap between reality and hope. We are struck, however, by the limitations on families' improved well-being that are imposed by professionals' limitations. Professionals working with disabilities and child protection often know too little about family functioning and may have too few skills for managing the complexity of family relationships. By focusing almost exclusively on the identified client or patient, they often fail to be helpful and sometimes create unintended harm.

Family therapists, on the other hand, have little engagement with families with infants. Although family therapy has a strong tradition of exploring non-verbal communication, it is focused on the non-verbal commentary that accompanies verbal exchanges. Attention should be paid to communication with infants and young children who only use non-verbal communication. After all, this is the time when families are creating the procedural and imaged structures that will shape their lives for the next two decades. Further, somatic well-being or discomfort are most visible and most easily tied to their interpersonal roots in infancy. Improve communication in infancy and many problems will be prevented.

How can this be accomplished? We think cross-training is called for. For all clinicians that includes extensive training in individual and family development. Understanding of assessment and the benefits and limitations of alternate types of assessment is also needed. Experience in formulation of family problems in a developmental context is crucial. Simply relying on the presenting problem or psychiatric diagnosis is not enough because families often cannot describe the underlying problem (if they could, they might be able to resolve it themselves) and because diagnoses are not related to either aetiology or treatment (Wang and Insel 2010; Division of Clinical Psychology 2013). Repeatedly in this volume, we will encourage initial systematic assessment, ongoing informal reassessment, consideration of the developmental status of each family member, and functional formulation of problems to yield novel solutions that use existing tools. The point will be to increase professionals' skills and flexibility in using their expertise to promote more comprehensive and effective solutions to the problems that families bring to them.

Summary of constructs and treatment principles

Constructs

1 *Attachment*: According to Ainsworth:

> Attachment is an affectional bond, and hence an attachment figure is never wholly interchangeable with or replaceable by another, even though there be others to whom one is also attached. In attachments as in other affectional bonds there is a need to maintain proximity, distress upon inexplicable separation, pleasure or joy upon reunion, and grief at loss. . . . there is a seeking to obtain an experience of security or comfort in the relationship with the partner. If and when such security and comfort is available, the individual is able to move off from the secure based provided by the partner, with confidence to engage in other activities.
>
> (Ainsworth 1993: 38)

In terms of information processing, the relationship of a protective and comforting adult with a neonate is the context of somatic, cognitive and affective learning about danger and safety. During the first year of life, this learning comes to be organized in attachment, a process for mentally representing danger and disposing to interpersonal behaviour. This process functions strategically to promote the survival of the neonate and the reproductive success of the adult.

2 *Dispositional representations*: Parallel neural pathways are activated by sensory stimulation. Each parallel pathway disposes to self-protective action that is based on an attribution of meaning to sensory stimulation. The meaning is attributed on the basis of a combination of aspects of the external context with aspects of the self, reflected in the activated neural pathway. As long as the activation lasts, it is an active DR of the relationship between self and context in that moment. Each active DR changes the probability of a similar pattern of activation (that is a similar DR) occurring in the future in response to a similar sensory stimulation.

3 *Somatic information*: Danger can be represented in the form of bodily states of the body. Discomfort, increased arousal, high muscle tone and pain are some of the somatic representations of danger. These can be ways of knowing (unconsciously or pre-consciously) or communicating (directly, non-verbally) about danger. The changes in somatic information about danger towards comfort, lower arousal, relaxation or pleasure represent safety. Somatic DRs reflect the immediate state of the self.

4 *Cognitive information*: Represents sequences of events, that is, the temporal order of events, that lead to predictable outcomes, particularly dangerous or safe outcomes. When sequences are predictable and include the individual's behaviour, they are easier to represent and learn. Perceptions recognized as part of a sequence allow cognitive DRs about *when* danger and safety are going to occur.

5   *Affective information:* Sensory aspects of the environment can represent danger or safety. Some aspects are innate (darkness, emptiness, sudden loud noises, certain tastes) and others are acquired by association with dangerous or safe outcomes. Intense, unexpected, and quick rapid perceptual changes activate somatic states representing danger whereas mild, rhythmic and predictable, and rhythmic changes activate somatic states representing safety. Both innate and learned perceptual features lead to affective DRs about *where* danger or safety are likely to be.

6   *Type B strategy:* For individuals using a Type B strategy, danger is represented and communicated using relatively accurate and unambiguous somatic, cognitive and affective DRs. This usually reflects an environment with low dangers and predictably accessible resources, allowing the adult to respond sensitively to the newborn's signals (see circular model in Crittenden and Landini 2011).

7   *Type A strategy:* For individuals using a Type A strategy, danger is represented and communicated using mainly cognitive DRs, treating somatic and affective DRs as irrelevant or misleading. This usually is associated with an environment with predictable dangers, where inhibition of negative affect promotes survival (see circular model in Crittenden and Landini 2011).

8   *Type C strategy:* For individuals using a Type C strategy, danger is represented and communicated using mainly somatic and affective DRs, treating cognitive DRs as irrelevant or misleading. This is usually associated with an environment with changing and unpredictable dangers, where shifting attention to new perceptual conditions is advantageous for survival (see circular model in Crittenden and Landini 2011).

Treatment principles

1   The birth of a baby marks the beginning of a family and a restructuring of *self-*protective strategies to function as *child*-protective strategies. When there are problems, this is the best opportunity for prevention. This is well understood by the infant intervention and attachment professionals, but in family work seems under-utilized.

2   Working in here and now it does not mean that individuals have no past that they bring to the present. Knowing about the past can inform and focus treatment, even when the treatment itself focuses on the here and now.

3   Just as individuals' strategies can blind them to other possibilities, therapists' ideologies can blind them to – or even prohibit them from using from alternative solutions to helping families.

4   In the change from 'patient' to 'client', we may sometimes have overlooked the individual's inability to assess fully their need for help. Most people needing treatment are not sufficiently clear about the problem to be able to 'shop' comparatively for services or to define their needs in a contractual form. Possibly therapists cannot do this either until they have a good history and knowledge of each person's self-protective strategy.

5   Formal attachment assessments can provide essential information regarding both history and self-protective strategies.

6   Discrepancy is the key to discovering new information and unexpected meanings in prior information; discrepancies should not be left unaddressed.

7   People coming to treatment are hurting; they are more likely to see the therapist as being in a personal relationship with them than vice versa. However, the therapist, while still protecting their own privacy, also needs to acknowledge their own personal connections triggered by the client or these will intrude unhelpfully into the process of the therapy.

8   Aftercare may be as important as the designated treatment. Sometimes the effects of treatment do not fit the contracted – or expected – timeframe. Therapists have an ethical obligation to assess the impact of what they do and seek corrective services when these are needed.

2 Toddlerhood and the beginnings of awareness and intention

Mary is 12 months old; when she looks in the toy mirror that she received for her birthday, she sees movement. At 18 months when she toddles over to the mirror on the closet door and peers at it, she sees herself (Lewis 1990). The beginning of consciousness has dawned.

At 1 year, John does something naughty and then looks to see if his mother noticed. John is aware of consequences, but only after he has acted. At a year and a half, John first looks at his mother, sees that she is looking at him – and *then* he does the naughty thing. Intention has dawned and, with it, a complex use of probable consequences to achieve interpersonal goals.

Family life changes when one has a toddler. The 'preoperational shift' marks a period of rapid neurological change that occurs between roughly 18 and 24 months of age (Piaget 1970). During this period, babies are transformed into walking, talking, charming little devils. The 'terrible twos' are a delightful period when children are filled with wonder – and anxiety. For parents, maintaining moment-to-moment balance – far less psychological balance – during this period of uneven growth and rapidly reversible changes can be a challenge. And yet … and yet toddlers are so engagingly human, so much more like ourselves than are babies that they capture our hearts.

In this chapter, we describe the developmental changes that occur in toddlerhood, then address the impact of these on dyadic and family functioning. Complexity becomes the key – complexity of psychological processes; complexity of managing multiple, interconnected relationships; and complexity of behaviour – all in a context of partial awareness. We consider the refined self-protective strategies that some toddlers organize, focusing in particular on the emergence of the 'coercive' Type C strategy and the 'compulsive' Type A strategies. We close with a clinical case about which we offer the assessments of attachment, a functional formulation of the problem, and a discussion of treatment.

Development in toddlerhood

Physical competencies

Toddlers can walk – and run. They jump and climb and reach. They don't stay put at all. These simple developmental advances change their relationships with their parents and with the world dramatically. Suddenly the world is available for exploration. With so many exciting things within reach (or just a climb away), toddlers become explorers. They try and test and learn. Their minds explode with understanding as their range of movement becomes greater. At the same time, the world becomes dangerous because toddlers cannot fully predict the outcomes of their behaviour.

To protect their young children, parents must develop 'eyes in the back of their heads'. That is, they must predict and prevent injuries. To some parents, this means child-proofing their homes to eliminate the dangers; doing so means they don't have to watch their child every moment. To others, it means combining some child-proofing with a few simple rules about safety. Other parents adapt less, believing instead that their children should learn to obey the rules. When the rules are clear and consistent, most children can adapt, but there is a cost, usually in increased inhibition and decreased exploration. However, when the rules are situation-specific, toddlers cannot predict what is forbidden and the struggle between parents' protection and toddlers' exploration begins in earnest. The signs of this struggle are increased admissions to accident and injury departments and more complaints from parents to doctors about obstreperous and hyperactive children.

Changes in parenting of toddlers (as opposed to infants) are often assumed to be based on knowledge and belief that parent education can address these. However, especially in cases of risk, they are also based on the parents' memories of their own childhoods and what they liked, disliked, or feared. Consequently, some parents want to give more freedom than they remember having to their infants to explore and develop, whereas others want to give more structure than the chaotic circumstances they recall. That is, essentially all parents want better for their children than they themselves had. Unfortunately, if their own upbringing was skewed toward risk, then, in trying to reverse that for their own children, they may overshoot the mark, creating the opposite risk. 'Pendulum parenting' (Crittenden 2008), by being an intended correction, can sometimes produce exactly the distortion that the parents cannot perceive. For example, a permissively raised parent may vow to set firmer limits, but overshoot the mark, producing a fearfully compliant child who appears well regulated to the parent. In particular, parents who have unresolved traumatic experiences from their childhoods may engage in extreme and rigid attempts at correction. They may consciously (semantically) think that they are giving their children a better experience while not recognizing that implicit memories are eliciting behaviour that is either too risky or too restrictive to best meet the needs of their children. Therein lies the danger.

With the onset of toddlerhood, parents' relationships with their young children are expanded from protecting and comforting their infants to encompass negotiating how their children can be safe without the parents always being present. Parents must add judicious discipline to their parental functions. That means that they must discern children's needs even in the context of loud expression of children's desires and decide what responsibilities for their own behaviour their child is ready to manage. If they demand too much, their child will fail – or become extremely anxious trying to fulfil near impossible demands. If they require too little, their child's growth might be stunted or the child will seek limits by pushing further toward danger. Either way, the successful parent needs to function protectively within comfortable limits for the child (Vygotsky 1978).

Similarly, parents need to accurately reflect to the child the child's emotional state, while making enough of a difference to communicate containment and mastery of their feelings (Fonagy et al. 2002). Because children are constantly changing, this zone of new learning is changing – and thus parents of toddlers need always to be adapting. Of course, once you get the hang of it, life is a dance, one with an array of changing rhythms, but precious few pauses. Toddlerhood is a good time to learn to negotiate the dance.

To manage this transition from infancy to early childhood well, parents need to account for changes in children's cognitive understanding, affective states, and communicative abilities.

Psychological changes in cognition and affect

Toddlers become able to anticipate the effects of their actions and to regulate their action in order to achieve desired effects. This capability is applied to many sorts of circumstances, each of which has implications for parent–child and family relationships. Children who have been given a rule by their parents, for example, 'Do not run into the street', can behave so as not to violate the rule. This improves children's relationships with their parents and, when parents can count on this cooperation, it permits the parents to turn their attention to other aspects of family functioning. Some children are excessively concerned to keep their parents calm; these children sometimes learn to exhibit parent-pleasing behaviour in order to calm, soothe, or satisfy their parents. Of course such children must remain quite vigilant regarding the parents' state. This can interfere with the development of autonomy.

Other children show what is possibly the most elaborate use of this new cognitive ability, using provocative behaviour specifically to attract parent attention. John, referred to in the opening of this chapter, was using his recently maturing cognitive capacity to attract his mother's attention. Children do this when they feel unsure that their parents will be attentive in the crucial few minutes when the child really needs protection. Once the attention is achieved, children of unpredictably available parents face two new challenges. If the parents respond with angry authority to the provocation, the child must disarm the anger or risk being punished. Plus, even if the parent isn't angry, the child must maintain the parents' attention. That is, how can a child both demand near constant attention and also not make their parent angry by demanding so much?

New abilities to regulate affect serve these functions. The abilities are:

1   Being able to feel one way while displaying a different feeling state.
2   Displaying part of what one feels while inhibiting display of other aspects.
3   Using 'coy' behaviour.

Coy behaviour is a set of non-verbal signals, used by other mammalian species as well (Eibl-Eibesfeldt 1979), that terminate aggression and elicit nurturance. The signals include cocked heads that bear the neck, protruding tummies, and open legs that display the genitals. These three parts of the body (neck, belly, and genitals) are very vulnerable; attack on them can result in death or loss of reproductive capacity. Their unprotected display is therefore seen as an unambiguous signal of submission that almost always terminates the other individual's aggression. This appearance, however, can be misleading. Submissive individuals often harbour very deep resentment. Other coy signals suggest the covert anger: raised shoulders, eyes that slide away from direct eye contact, half-smiles with teeth (weapons) covered, and hands raised in the 'no weapons' or praying positions. Finally, some coy signals elicit nurturance (as the price of submission): open-mouth 'feed me' expressions, bent ankle 'crippled' stances, and shy looks.

Although toddlers are gaining increasing understanding of what adults say to them and increasing their own use of vocabulary and syntax, speech does not become the predominant means of communication until about 2½ years of age. Until then, non-verbal communication is primary. This means that parents need to combine language with non-verbal signals that clarify their meanings while also making them easy for children to remember. Gestures, facial expression, voice tone, body position, and context become crucial to effective communication (Sluzki and Ransom 1976; Taylor et al. 2001; de Gelder 2006). Physical gestures, voice tones, etc. enable young children to represent information in more accessible ways than does language alone (Goldin-Meadow and Beilock 2010). Context too clarifies meaning. Consequently, reprimanding a child in the midst of a fun activity has less impact than removing him to a quiet, non-distracting context before speaking to him. Similarly, mixing positive and negative signals is unsettling for children because the feelings (i.e., affective DRs) do not give a clear disposition for action (Volkmar et al. 1980).

For example, 30-month-old Melinda was climbing up onto the dining room table to get the coloured glass bowl that she really, really liked. Her mother reminded her not to do that, saying there were only three rules in their family and this was one. Melinda shot her mother a threatening look and continued to climb onto the chair to get onto the table. After two warnings, her mother suddenly swooped Melinda up, swung her around and planted a big kiss on her cheek. Melinda pushed her mum away saying loudly, 'Don't kiss me!' Her mother then twirled Melinda around, in a way that children often enjoy, kissing her here and kissing her there while saying, 'I'll kiss you any time I want to!' Melinda continued to protest and, as soon as she was down on the floor again, she ran off. From her mother's perspective, the distraction technique worked: the glass bowl was forgotten. From the perspective of their relationship, affection was becoming confused with anger and discipline and Melinda was not learning when to obey her mother. It was probable that their relationship would become defined by an on-going coercive struggle.

Changes in attachment: the goal-corrected partnership

Goal-corrected partnerships

Bowlby described attachment in toddlerhood and the preschool years (about 18 months to 5 years) as a 'goal-corrected partnership' in which parent and child communicate about the child's safety, the parent's availability, and the plans each has for the time when they are apart while keeping the child safe (Bowlby 1982). Such communication is a feedback-regulated system in which what each says – and does – has implications for the behaviour of the other.

Because children are both using and learning language, it is crucial that their parents communicate in ways that children can understand, while at the same time, enabling them to understand more. That is, parents should try to communicate within each child's 'zone of proximal development' (ZPD). The ZPD refers to those skills which a child is ready to learn. This contains the idea that parents need to be attuned to what the child can do but to also promote change and growth in their abilities. This construct, when related to attachment, refers to the interactive balance in the toddler–parent relationship between protection and exploration. What the toddler can explore competently and safely, the parent can stay out of. What the toddler is not yet competent to manage, the parent must take care of entirely.

Competent parents let children do for themselves what they can do for themselves. They assist children to acquire new skills in the child's ZPD and they do for children what children cannot yet do for themselves and are not ready to learn at this moment.

Discovering the limits of each child's ZPD is an active process, one that requires parents' attention to their child's behaviour and thoughtful response to what they notice. Of course, children are learning and changing all the time so parents must adapt their responses all the time. When the topic is danger and safety, however, parents cannot afford to misjudge their child's skill. The safest communications about danger contain three parts: (1) a clear direction that the child can follow without any concerns regarding the child's competence (i.e., less demanding directions than the child's ZPD); (2) added information that is new, but within the child's ZPD; and (3) review of what actually happened, in the terms of what was said before. The review, while not yet reflective, establishes the process of looking back on what happened to see if there is anything to learn. In the case of toddlers, it consolidates what parents said in advance in terms of what was experienced.

If things had gone differently with Melinda, her mother would have firmly but gently taken her off the chair, turned and pointed to both the chair and the bowl and said: 'You may not do that because you might fall down and you might break the bowl and cut yourself. Let's go over here and play with [a favourite toy of Melinda].' A few minutes later, as Melinda glanced at the bowl on the table, her mother might approvingly say, 'Yes, it's a beautiful bowl, but you remember the rule: Don't climb and don't touch the bowl. Shall we look at this new book together?' Crucial to making this strategy work is mother's quick and attuned response; she does not wait until Melinda is being bad (when she would have to admonish her), but instead catches her being good, articulates what has happened, and gives her daughter attention, tied to something that is both fun and safe. Probably this means being more sensitively responsive to Melinda than is easy for her mum, but this bit of attention in toddlerhood can prevent years of struggle between them.

Interpersonal breaches and repair of breaches

Miscommunication occurs all the time! No parent has enough time, attention, and patience to monitor their child every moment and adapt their behaviour perfectly to subtle changes in children's behaviour. Instead, this dyadic dance to shifting tempos, with new steps added daily, contains ever so many missteps. These metaphorical missteps are simply breaches of harmony, moments when adult and child demand too much of one another or restate the obvious or interrupt each other or talk over each other or take inaccurate meanings from what the other communicated or – worst of all – communicate in ways that hurt the feelings of the other person. This list is long! And it is incomplete. Just reading it, we all recognize aspects of our daily adult communication with other people. Imagine the difficulties when one is still learning to communicate – and to use language as the means for communication. Breaches occur all the time, with everyone. Not only is the harm done usually very little, but learning to repair breaches is a crucial life skill (Howe 2011).

Dyads who learn to communicate clearly and then to act in a manner that is consistent with their communication have the fewest breaches (Watzlawick et al. 1967). However, though it might seem that breaches are 'bad', in fact, learning to repair breaches is an essential task. Once each partner's behaviour is acknowledged and their intentions made clear, then parent and child can communicate to re-establish their shared goals, enabling the toddler to do as he (or she) wishes while still remaining sufficiently safe. Managing this is far less complex than trying to explain it in writing. For example, the child interrupts the mother who is saying something important. Mum repairs the breach by putting her finger to her mouth – or maybe to her child's – then saying clearly what she needs her child to hear; then, when her communication is accepted, she returns to the child's interruption: 'You were trying to tell about the cat. Can you tell me again, now?' When the cat tale begins, the repair is complete.

If this sort of repair doesn't occur on both sides and with recognition of intentions, then the relationship and the trust in it are harmed. Both the Type A and Type C strategies involve by-passing resolution and finding a different, albeit less satisfactory, way of moving forward. These non-B strategies are adaptations to contexts in which 'moving forward' quickly is a priority: taking the time or communicating to achieve resolution of a specific problem might be dangerous, either because contingencies can't be changed (A), or because they are too complex to fathom (C).

For children or adults using the Type A strategy, the by-pass is usually to ignore the problem and get on with it. Sometimes, it is to make excuses for the other person's breach – and then get on with it. In either case, the issue itself and the hurt feelings it elicited are ignored – and left to recur with repeated distress. For children or adults using the Type C strategy, the by-pass is usually to avoid attending to the other person's perspective and, instead, simply repeat one's own hurt feelings. In the opposite way from Type A, the breach stays open and unhealed. In either case, the problem isn't solved (and so is left to happen again – and again), but more importantly, the toddler isn't given the tools for resolving interpersonal misunderstandings. Without conflict resolution skills, interpersonal problems will become more prominent and more destructive as time passes.

Becoming a specialist on one's own family

With their new cognitive and affective skills and their ever-increasing communicative skills, children become more aware of and responsive to the nuances of their parents' behaviour. As they adapt their strategies to these, they become specialists in the patterns of attachment used by important family members (mum, dad, mum's boyfriend, grandma, etc.). This greatly improves their relationships at home, while at the same time, narrowing their range of adaptation. Their strategies fit in their home. Move them to another home and they might not have the necessary strategies – and their world will fall apart. Many of the disruptions seen in foster care reflect not only the reasons that children were removed from their parents, but also the misfit of children's home-learned strategies with foster parents' strategies. When changing family, very, very many aspects of daily life are changing at one time and such processes almost certainly will be disruptive. Of all the times when one could move a child, toddlerhood is possibly the most disruptive at least in the short term. This is because toddlers' communication skills are limited, their ability to repair problems is limited, and they are specialists in only their own family and not yet ready to learn the strategies used in other families.

Gender

Before discussing the changes that some children make in the Type A and Type C strategies, it is pertinent to note that gender becomes an important issue beginning in toddlerhood. The awareness of the complexity of the differences associated with gender increases with age. It affects relationships with mothers and fathers through what is agreed as being gender-adequate in the interaction. Therefore, these gender-based (culturally modulated) differences in interpersonal experiences may affect the distribution of strategies among boys as compared to girls.

Changes in Type B self-protective strategies

Toddlers whose attachment figures are sensitively responsive to the toddlers' development and communication increasingly use language to replace non-verbal communication. Language is used to say what the child wants, to understand what the parents treat as important, and to find workable compromises. Moments of intense affect, however, are expressed either non-verbally or with both non-verbal signals and also language. Nevertheless, in toddlerhood, the language of feeling is usually subordinate to the direct expression of feelings.

In addition, when parent and child have been apart, language is used to bridge the separation with each person saying what they did while they were apart, thus bringing them psychologically close.

Because language clarifies behaviour, especially behaviour when people are apart, and because toddlers can make more complex predictions, the plans that toddlers make with adults can be more complex. 'Mummy is going to the store. You are staying with Aunt Margie. After I come back, we'll go to the park.' 'But I wanna go to park now!' 'Ah, I know you do. But we need food for lunch and Aunt Margie wants to play with you. Can you go get your dolly so Aunt Margie can help you dress her? I'll be back soon and then we'll go to the park.' A shared plan is made, reasons are given, the plan is revised and mum ensures that it is implemented before she goes. When she comes back, this exemplar mum will ask about the dolly and remind her toddler to get ready for the park. In this sort of sequence, the communication is clear and reciprocal, the toddler is required to modify her plan, but is guided to see that it is not a power struggle in which mum wins, but rather is a necessary step for the family as a whole. Then she is assisted to act on the new plan. Finally, after asking her toddler to delay gratification, mum provides the promised reward.

Changes in Type A self-protective strategies

During the pre-operational shift, the Type A strategy of infancy is sometimes refined into a compulsive strategy that better fits the contingencies on the parents' behaviour. This is most likely to occur when parents are very predictable and consistent and when they are either very unresponsive to the child or very demanding regarding the child's behaviour. When parents are pervasively unresponsive, children often become caregivers, thus, organizing their behaviour around fear of abandonment. 'Compulsive caregiving' (Type A3) includes both false behaviour (caregiving to the parent when care from the parent is desired) and displayed false positive affect when fear of abandonment is felt. In its softer form, this is compulsive attention; the strategy is used when parents feel more comfortable and safer when their children are actively attentive to them. In the latter case, 'compulsively compliant' (A4) children learn to meet parental demands immediately or even in anticipation of the demand. The affective DR motivating this cognitive contingency is fear of punishment or loss of parental love. The milder – and more common – form is 'compulsive performance'. In these cases, parents value themselves and their child based on the child's athletic, academic, or social achievements. All of the compulsive strategies result from fear conditioning and reflect an adaptive response to current conditions that can, in other conditions, become maladaptive (Delgado et al. 2009).

Changes in Type C self-protective strategies

The really big changes in self-protective strategy are those in Type C: both the organization of a functional coercive strategy and the large number of non-C infants who acquire a Type C strategy in toddlerhood. Type C is the most elegant of strategies. It is the perfect strategy for people who are unsure of the contingencies and, as a consequence, feel vulnerable. It is the strategy for uncertainty, ambiguity, and complexity.

In construct terms, the Type C strategy is quite simple to state: The C strategy involves both relying on one's own feelings to guide behaviour and also using exaggerated and changing displays of negative affect to influence other people's behaviour. Specifically, the strategy consists of splitting, exaggerating, and alternating the display of mixed negative feelings (of anger, fear, and desire for comfort) to attract attention and manipulate the feelings and responses of others. The alternation is between presentation of a strong, angry invulnerable self who blames others for the problem (Types C1, 3, 5, 7) with the appearance of a fearful, weak, and vulnerable self who entices others to give succour (Types C2, 4, 6, 8). The Type C1–2 strategy is a very normal strategy found in people with low risk for mental health problems and a great zest for life. Infants display the Type C1–2 behaviour and affect, albeit without its function. Beginning in the middle of the second year of life, the ability to split feelings, exaggerating the display of some while inhibiting the display of others makes the organization of interpersonal coercion possible. The Type C3–4 strategy (i.e., aggressive behaviour alternating with feigned helpless behaviour) reflects the strongest form of the strategy among young children.

Interpersonally, the coercive strategy is extremely flexible and variable – and therefore difficult to pin down in words. But, of course, it is a non-verbal strategy, one that functions to keep the attachment partner engaged. The other person must play their part of being engaged or the strategy fails. Given that parents try to meet toddlers' expressed desires, it becomes necessary that the toddler using a Type C strategy both not accept viable solutions and also keep changing the apparent problem, thus, keeping the parent involved in solving it.

All strategies are dyadic. In families, however, they are enacted in the context of others' strategies. In the next section, we consider how the constellation of dyadic strategies is organized at the family level.

Dyads, triads and family functioning

Families are made up of a multiplicity of relationships, roles, and interpersonal strategies. We have discussed some of the strategies and influences upon the development of strategies. However, strategies do not develop in isolation from other relationships. To the contrary, strategies usually develop in response to more than one person and in the context of other family members' strategies. Many children use a different strategy with their father than they use with their mother, thus, clarifying that attachment is not based in child temperament.

Intra-familial relationships

In two-parent families, children form attachments to each of their parents. Of course, no two parents respond identically and a child's relationships with them will not be identical. This is an advantage in that children learn more than one way to relate to another person. But when the parents are each extreme and different in their pattern of caregiving, children can find the situation too complex to manage comfortably. They risk showing the 'wrong' response to the wrong parent or exaggerating the strategies to extremes. Children find it easiest to adapt to mild differences between their parents that are predictable and most difficult when their parents are both very different from one another and also unpredictable (Crittenden et al. 1991).

In addition, parents have relationships to their children that enable them to fulfil several roles with regard to their children. How they manage the array of parental functions (protection, provision of food and shelter, play, learning, etc.) reflects their parental relationship. Finally, parents have a mutual relationship independent of their children, i.e., a spousal relationship. Thus, families are very complex, interdependent systems in which the patterns of relationship are often overlapping, competing, or even contradictory.

Management of bedtime can illustrate this issue. Bedtime is one of most common early sources of both fear and pleasure for young children. Toddlers need to be moved out of the parental bedroom so that the parents can sleep better and also so they can resume intimate relations without fear of waking the child. The toddler must get used to this separation and to sleeping in the dark and without the parents. In some families, one parent handles the whole process: 'Kiss your mum goodnight and let's go upstairs!' In other families, it's not predetermined who will put the child to bed, nor is the routine so predictable. Some fathers make a joke out of children's fears, perhaps attempting to ignore the fears and to distract the child. The mother, in contrast, when she puts the child to bed perhaps takes these fears so seriously that, by talking extensively with the child about what he is frightened of, she increases both the child's fear and her own anxiety, and ends up allowing the child to come into the parents' bed as he gets 'really' scared (see Figure 2.1).

In these sorts of situations, toddlers are learning to differentiate their parents and to develop different strategies for interactions with each of them: with dad you have

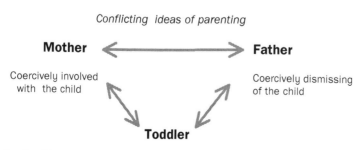

Figure 2.1 Conflicting bedtime management of a child's fears.

to pretend to be brave and tough whereas with mum you can exaggerate your feelings and vulnerabilities. Experiencing these different ways of dealing with feelings can be positive and enriching for the child. It can contribute to developing multiple strategies which can be employed flexibly with recognition that one needs to adjust and get different types of support from different people.

Although family life is changing in Western cultures, mothers are still more often central to than fathers. Mothers may, for example, keep an ear for how things are going when father is putting the child to bed. They may chide the father for being a bit too hard on the little boy (or for forgetting that the child is a girl and, therefore, needing more sensitive handling). Well, many mothers are a bit prone to seeing their toddlers as the babies they were! Parents can deal with these differences about how to manage the child's fears in a calm way, or it may lead to tension. In some cases, a mother may feel that dad is making such a mess of it that she will take over. Maybe the toddler comes downstairs again and again after the father has tried to settle the child. The father may come to feel irritated at 'being watched and judged' by his wife and become angry and/or start to retreat. No matter how big the house they live in, it is likely that a child will start to pick up some non-verbal signals that there is tension between the parents and come to feel unsafe.

How does a child make sense of this tension that exists in every family? Most children quickly learn how to behave with each parent. When they are the source of dispute between their parents, the explanation given to them can be sensible, accurate, and framed in terms a toddler can understand: 'Mummy and daddy don't agree right now about what is the best way to take care of you. We both have ideas and we're trying to decide what to do. You know how you get angry with your sister, but in a while everything is fine again? Daddy and I are like that too. So you don't need to worry. Everything will be fine. Why don't you go get your dolls and let us be alone together for a while?' Such an explanation doesn't make the tension go away, but it makes it tolerable. On the other hand, when inter-parent conflict cannot be resolved, it has effects on children. Most children learn to inhibit attention-eliciting behaviour. However, when infant negativity has been expressed strongly since early infancy, children may also show serious problem behaviour (Pauli-Pott and Beckmann 2007). In this study, temperament and dyadic strategy cannot be discriminated because the child's behaviour with other interactants than the mother was not assessed; if the child's negativity had changed when interactants behaved differently, we would interpret it as part of a dyadic process and not as temperament.

Triangulation

In other cases, the parents cannot help their children so easily. This is especially true if they themselves are not sure everything will be okay. When the conflict is perceptible, but not 'speakable', toddlers can misconstrue the situation. Because they do not yet possess language to help them represent and reflect on their experience, they may develop a sense that somehow they are responsible for the conflict between their parents. This feeling may become acute if they hear their name being used in parental quarrels. The child may attempt to use either or both a Type A or a Type C strategy in response. She might try to be very good and compliant and start to hide her fears, using a Type A strategy: this might reduce the parents arguing and conflict. Alternatively, a Type C strategy might be effective in distracting the parents from each other to focus on the 'naughty' behaviour of the child. However, there is a risk that this leads the parents to argue even more, blaming and accusing each other of upsetting the child. The short-term advantage is that the child feels at the centre of the parents' attention and the ambiguity of the immediate situation is reduced; in the long term, the child does not learn to resolve problems. This process might be alleviated by the child receiving some early diagnosis as physically ill, temperamental, ADHD or merely having a strong case of 'the terrible twos'. The emerging attachment strategies involve the child attempting to manage both the relationships with each parent and also the not-quite-visible relationship between them.

Of course, parents may be able to reflect about their differences and find ways of resolving them or explaining them to their children. However, this is by no means an easy task. If the child becomes fretful at night, he might keep waking, coming into their bedroom, needing to be soothed, comforted, and so on. The parents may start to suffer broken sleep, feel tired and become a bit irritable, work gets harder to manage and they feel something is going wrong. Furthermore, the eagerly anticipated freedom from waking up to feed the baby and the hope of the nights becoming a bit more romantic and sexual might start to fade.

If the triangulation involves parents with contrasting attachment patterns, such reflection is less likely. Instead, they might alternate between blaming the other or themselves. Alternatively, they may come to see getting help for the child as the solution and this endeavour might temporarily unite them. There are considerable risks of the child starting to become pathologized in this process, but also potential that the parents might receive some assistance regarding their relationship. Not infrequently, they might be offered parent education. This intervention carries considerable risks in that it may make them feel more inadequate, reject the advice because it doesn't address their own attachment needs, and further submerge the reasons for their conflicts and the possibility of constructively exploring these. With the authority of information from the parent education course, the parents might be less likely to reconsider their own contribution to the problems. Something more personalized is usually needed in families that already have problems.

Trauma: what parents unwittingly bring to childrearing

Everyone wants to raise their children better than they themselves were raised. Nevertheless, parents sometimes bring misunderstandings based on their own experience that will distort their children's experience. Parents' unresolved trauma is particularly challenging for children.

To think clearly about trauma, we must differentiate it from danger. Danger occurs in every life and exposure to danger is important for the development of competent self-protection. The person who has never faced danger is the most vulnerable person when there is danger. Consequently, children need to experience danger in order to learn to manage it safely. The trick is to ensure that children are exposed to only those dangers for which they have self-protective strategies or are ready to learn self-protective strategies and have the necessary support. That is, children can be left to cope with dangers for which they have ready solutions, but need support when the threat calls for new responses that they are ready to learn.

Like strategies, dangerous experiences can be processed in four primary ways: activating, deactivating, swinging between activating and deactivating, and a balanced integration of activation and deactivation. Clearly these reflect the basic self-protective strategies (Types C, A, A/C and B, respectively), but in the case of unresolved trauma, they are applied in non-strategic ways.

Parents' psychological trauma – especially when carried forward from early childhood – is often reactivated by having a small child. When this occurs, the current context is lost and a past context replaces it in the parent's mind. The parent's behaviour reflects the past circumstances, rather than the current circumstances. If the circumstances are similar, the 'trauma response' may yield a rapid, self-protective behaviour. But if the behaviour from the past was not protective or if the current circumstances are different, then the parent's behaviour will not be appropriate and may be maladaptive. In these moments, trauma-based parenting replaces more adaptive parenting. (See the case of Cecilia and Juan below.)

When there are problems

Mother's unresolved trauma and the making of a bully

The current situation

Cecilia, aged 19 years, and her son Juan, 16 months, were first seen when Juan was only 5 months old. They were living together in a mother-and-baby foster placement. Cecilia had agreed to accompany Juan there when he was born rather than have him put, by himself, in a foster home. Cecilia's partner, Juan's father, was in prison for violence against a former partner. Now, with Juan just over 1 year of age, decisions must be made.

The history. Cecilia was one of several siblings, half-siblings, and step-siblings (see Figure 2.2). Her first-born brother died in infancy from shaken baby syndrome. Cecilia was hospitalized 7 times in her first year of life and 28 times before she was 18. Her mother was an alcoholic; sexual infidelity led to domestic violence that Cecilia both heard at night and sometimes witnessed. Her step-father and other father figures had criminal records, often including sexual offences against children. Her mother often abandoned her children to whichever man was in the house; she simply walked out and did not return for days or even weeks. After Cecilia's sister reported being sexually abused by one father substitute, she was placed in foster care and Cecilia moved to a relative's home. Cecilia denied having been abused, but her AAI (see Appendix 1, George et al. 1985–1996) had signs of childhood danger that she could not recall explicitly, specifically 'blocked trauma' from child sexual abuse. Overall, Cecilia appeared to have been cared for more tenderly by a series of father figures who were both temporary and abusive than by her neglectful mother. In her AAI, her feelings toward her mother were quite contained whereas her feelings about the father figures were strong and mixed.

To understand Cecilia as a mother, we offer insights from two DMM assessments and observations made by professionals working with her.

The Adult Attachment Interview discourse and Cecilia's self-protective strategy

Discourse evidence. Talking about parental fights, Cecilia used bitter irony to say it was 'normal or normal to me' and that she 'zoned out and just forgot it was happening'. Cecilia dismissed what she could not change. Although she delusionally idealized her

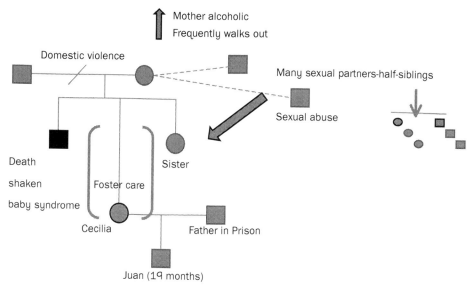

Figure 2.2 Genogram of Cecilia and her family.

step-father, she was unable to draw any semantic generalizations about herself, nor to reflect upon them; overall, she seemed unable to symbolize and, instead, used the interviewer as a mirror to inform herself about the feelings that she might have felt.

The most frequent form of memory used by Cecilia was displaced images. Auditory images, told in the present tense, suggested that she recalled most clearly in imaged memory and that images were experienced as continuing in the present, unlike other recall which was distanced and closed. For example, at the end of the AAI, Cecilia was asked if she wanted to add anything. She began speaking about her love of animals and said:

> If a baby is in pain, it screams –where if an animal is in pain, a lot of them go into shock and go silent – and can't move. My friend said – and she had – had somebody turn up on her door cause they had hit a deer, because it had stopped moving – she said – she thought, well, it's going to be fine sort of thing. She phoned the RSPCA and they had to put it down because it had so much trauma to it that it wouldn't survive. And she thought – because it wasn't screaming and that – it wasn't in pain so it couldn't have done that much damage. She said – whereas I would have known that that deer was probably in a lot of pain – I would have known to cover its eyes and I would have known it was in – like to move it from the road – but to move it so gently – that it didn't move anything – to have got on the phone to the police – because she phoned the RSPCA, I would have phoned the police, because it was a traffic hazard and, with Juan, I know if he's in – if he wants something because he screams – and I – I don't think I am doing a bad job of looking after him.

It was as if Cecilia could not close the AAI without clarifying how we should understand her communication: those who are most silent are in the most pain, need the most help, and, even with help, it may be futile. All this, of course, was displaced onto a deer. But Cecilia herself saw that it was relevant to her – and to Juan – and made sure it closed her interview.

Self-protective strategy. Cecilia protected herself from feeling vulnerable by denying that she was severely neglected and asserting her personal competence; this was probably necessary in childhood when her mother was not available to comfort and protect her. She relied on others for information, about herself, her perspective on herself, and facts about her experience. A particular effect was her lack of attention to her own pain, both physical and psychological. It is notable that observers sometimes process others' painful experience similarly to the person in pain (Avenanti et al. 2005); if observers, such as the interviewer and treatment staff reflected their response to her pain, it could inform Cecilia in early adulthood about the meaning of her childhood experience.

Unresolved trauma. Cecilia experienced psychological trauma from physical, medical, and emotional neglect, from bullying, and about her thoughts of suicide; all of these were denied, displaced, and dismissed, but they came up again and again in her AAI. To cope with trauma, she used both diminishing/dulling strategies and arousing strategies. With her mother, the strategies reduced her arousal. With father-figures, her strategies increased her arousal. Neither seemed to put her past experience to rest; instead her past seemed active in the present. The 'past-active-in-present' functioning is the critical danger for this dyad.

The CARE-Index and Cecilia's child-protective strategy

The observation. In her three-minute play interaction, Cecilia made musical sounds for the toy and Juan got excited. Juan watched the toy as his mother jiggled it, then his interest faded. He looked enquiringly at the camera and she looked up too, smiling happily. His eagerness began to take on a distressed sound and his face scrunched up in worry, as if he might cry. There was no apparent reason for this. He flailed an arm, lightly brushing his mother's lower cheek. She instantly grabbed her cheek as if she were hurt, her face froze in a blank expression, with eyes and mouth closed, and she cried out 'Opp!' She was still for an instant, then she smiled and kissed Juan on the head, vocalizing as if to emphasize the kiss. Juan appeared unaware of what had happened. As the interaction closed, something very similar happened again.

The evaluation. The overall dyadic synchrony was in the normative to mild risk range, but there were two concerns. First, Cecilia displayed a tendency to turn away or block out Juan's negative affect; noticing, understanding, and responding sensitively to it is necessary if his distress is to be comforted and prevented in the future.

Second, there were two moments of very great discrepancy in which Cecilia acted as if she had been attacked and injured. Juan appeared unaware of these, but he seemed bewildered at times and sometimes inexplicably worried or distressed. Cecilia seemed to expect attacks, to misinterpret random, but sudden movements as blows, and to react with pain even though there was none. She recovered quickly with a kiss.

The CARE-Index, a brief video-based assessment (see Appendix 1), offers a window into Cecilia's perception of Juan. She responded to him more than she initiated – as if he were in charge. Moreover, her initiations seemed artificial, as if she had been coached to stimulate him. Nevertheless both enjoyed these moments. In addition, she over-attributed intentionality to his behaviour and perceived it in ways that did not match observed reality. Because Juan did not hit or hurt her, her perception is a 'traumatic delusion'. It indicated that she perceived Juan as a man and, based on her past experience, she vigilantly guarded against his unpredictable moments of violence. When she perceived violence, she reacted instantly, without conscious thought. This, too, is a typical trauma response. Further, her kiss suggested the entwining of aggression and affection in Cecilia's mind; again, this is typical of trauma from family violence.

Cecilia's child-protective strategy. Cecilia was warm and interested in Juan, but she was excessively attuned to the possibility of painful violence. In a truly violent moment, she might choose self-protection over protecting her child. She might confuse affection with repairing interpersonal breaches, with the breach itself remaining unacknowledged. Finally, she might confuse her son with her father-figures.

Effects on Juan. Cecilia misattributed violence against her to Juan and rewarded his 'aggression' with affection. At the same time, his actual signals were overlooked, i.e., he experienced himself as invisible to his mother.

Later he may recognize that interpersonal violence is valued by his mother and begin to think of himself as being overlooked except when he is aggressive – and then he is loved. Is this the beginning of bullying in intimate relationships, both among school-age peers and later in adult relationships (Falb et al. 2011)?

Observations by professionals

Professionals reported that Cecilia described Juan as seeking to touch and expose her breasts – as if he were sexually mature – while, at the same time, she had exposed her breasts to professionals during interviews in inappropriate ways. The foster carer noted that Cecilia enjoyed bathing Juan and maintained a night-time breast-feeding schedule longer than necessary.

Given Cecilia's desire for but current lack of an adult male partner, her pleasure in intimacy with her son may be heightened. That is, Juan may provide some of the missing affection that a male partner would provide and, thus, be 'spousified'. In family systems terms, her attachment with her son is partially transformed into a spousal attachment – thus, filling the gap in the mother–father–baby triangle.

Functional formulation

As an adolescent in the transition to adulthood who was severely neglected in childhood, Cecilia did not expect much support from the world. Further, she understood that she must obey powerful people. In the past, men had provided both the majority of her care and protection and also the threats. She had learned to do what was necessary to elicit their caregiving and avoid threat. In addition, she had been exposed to domestic violence and may herself have been the object of violence. Finally, it is probable that she had experienced the sort of sexual abuse that her younger sister reported. It is also likely that this was mixed with affection and, thus, in her mind, was represented in the connection of safety, affection and sexualized aggression.

This is important because Cecilia appeared to have attracted the same sort of dangerous men that her mother had attracted. Her partner was both tenacious in holding his family together and also used violence to do that. Such patterns of attraction and aggression are not usually recognized consciously by those who use them and, thus, may be carried forward without intention to future relationships.

Cecilia seemed loving and was eager to raise her son, but she had confused his feelings and needs with her own. In addition, she associated Juan with the men in her life. That is, she may have mistakenly imbued him with characteristics and behaviours typical of the violent and loving men she had known. The confusion of past and present, hypothesized as the critical danger on the basis of Cecilia's AAI, is consistent with the CARE-Index observations and the history.

Recommendations

Three sorts of recommendations were made on the basis of the DMM assessments and functional formulation: for Cecilia, her foster mother, and the services. Change is a system-wide process.

Cecilia. Because she was a single adolescent mother in the transition to adulthood, the recommendations focused on her development as both a young woman and also as mother.

1   *Prioritizing needs*: Juan and Cecilia had too many needs to be addressed all at once, some were delayed so that Cecilia would not be overwhelmed and fail.
2   *Safety*: No baby is safe when his mother is not safe or feels unsafe. It was recommended that Cecilia stay in her foster placement as long as possible – until she learned to live in safety.
3   *Contraception*: Cecilia could probably not manage with two small children so contraception was recommended.
4   *Relationship with Juan*: Cecilia had mastered the basics of infant care and interaction. A crucial shift would be to move away from a strategy of behavioural 'stimulation' to supporting empathetic and emotionally attuned interaction. Work with a group of young mothers focusing on video-feedback and peer social skills was recommended.
5   *Relationships with men*: Cecilia needed to choose a safe and loving partner. To do this, she needed a group of suitable older adolescents and to have time for dating. Without this opportunity and an opportunity to understand her childhood trauma, she would likely select dangerous men or spousify Juan.
6   *Relationships with her family*: Although Cecilia's family had caused problems, understanding her family's way of functioning could help her to maximize their potential. Video-taped sessions of her interactions with Juan with an accompanying discussion could help her to understand connections between her own family history and how these shaped her interactions with Juan.
7   *Therapy for trauma and strategy*: Cecilia needed a short-term emphasis on defusing her unresolved trauma regarding sexual violence with men. This included enabling her to articulate in her own words the mixture of protection, love, and threat that men had had and how accepting violence had made love and protection possible. Cecilia needed to see how she carried fear to her relationship with Juan.
8   *Some outcomes*. Video-feedback helped. Once her trauma responses were calmed, she needed access to omitted and blocked information, to relate that information to her behaviour, and relate her behaviour to Juan's development.

Cecilia's AAI was used as a guide for gathering information. It took a long time before the attraction to violent men was replaced by attraction to less dramatically, but more reliably, loving and protective men.

The foster mother. The foster mother was a crucial mother-substitute for Cecilia. The recommendations were meant to assist her to discover and use her role to Cecilia's advantage.

1   *Consultation*: Because young adults generally refuse advice, but can benefit from hearing thoughtful reflections, the foster mother was advised to be less directive and to give Cecilia the space to ask questions and invite her involvement and self-directed, reflective participation.
2   *Support with professionals*: Because meetings with professionals are anxiety-provoking, the foster mother was advised to attend with Cecilia to take notes for her and to signal to the professionals when she thought Cecilia was becoming overwhelmed.
3   *Grandmothering*: The foster mother was asked to provide a safe back-up carer for Juan when Cecilia went out.
4   *Privacy*: Suggestions were offered to give Cecilia private space where Juan could sleep and she could still be awake and active.
5   *Moving to her own home.* If a genuine relationship developed between Cecilia and the foster mother, Cecilia's transition to an independent home would be made gradually with the foster carer remaining connected to Cecilia and Juan, supporting their young family (Crittenden and Farnfield 2007).

The professionals. The professionals identified that Cecilia was too compliant and too easily influenced. At the same time, they pointed out that she did not implement all the directions given to her and that some issues that concerned them were not important to her. There was an inherent conflict in this. It was as if Cecilia were being told: 'Think for yourself, but be sure to think like us!'

1   Cecilia needed fewer goals and directions.
2   Instead the professionals were advised to ask her to articulate her own plan, her reasons for the plan, how she expected to carry the plan out and what she expected as the outcome. This would guide her to reflect on her role as a mother.
3   After trying her plan, the professionals were advised to ask her to discuss, how and why she changed the plan, how it felt to her and Juan, and how it worked out. The goal was to elicit productive reflection.
4   The professionals were advised that it was more important that Cecilia generate the plan than that it be the best plan (as long as it was not harmful). It mattered that Cecilia thought about the plan both before and after implementing it. This would reduce her refusal and rebellion.
5   Finally, the professionals were reminded that Cecilia's authority to decide how to live her own life must always be respected. Nevertheless, (1) being shown alternative options; (2) being given guidance on how to carry out the alternatives; and (3) being helped to explore the possible consequences of different responses could be very useful.

Conclusion

This is a book about family therapy. Families come in many forms and Cecilia shows us three of them: (1) a dangerous family-of-origin with a revolving slot that various men filled serially, (2) an adolescent single mother/baby family that was not yet viable, and (3) an artificial foster family that could assist the adolescent mother to manage the transition from adolescence to adulthood, with her baby.

Therapy also comes in many forms. In this case, the assessment, formulation, and plan were systemic, but traditional family therapy was not the dominant change vehicle. Cecilia's family was too fractured and unavailable to meet for conjoint family therapy sessions. Nevertheless, family systems ideas and methods were crucial to understanding Cecilia's trauma-based parenting and constructing a plan of action that addressed that while building on her more adaptive behaviour.

A broad-framed, fully systemic approach was employed that involved facilitating change in all parts of Cecilia and Juan's world: the mother–infant dyad, Cecilia's two families, and the professionals in the child protection and legal systems. In particular it was recognized that the professionals had become involved in maintaining maladaptive systemic processes and effort was needed to encourage them to move from a judgemental stance of setting standards of performance and evaluating whether Cecilia met their standards. Instead they were encouraged to shift to a position of supportive, developmental guidance in Cecilia's ZPD (i.e. change from an authoritarian stance to an authoritative stance in Baumrind's terms, see Chapter 3). Of all the changes needed to give Cecilia a chance, this was the most difficult to accomplish – and everything hinged on it. The easiest, as it turned out, was enlarging the foster mother's understanding of her role to include being a transitional attachment figure to an adolescent mother as she made the transition to adulthood and learned herself how to be a mother. This included helping the foster carer to recognize her own attachment needs and to be validated as a 'good' mother by adopting the role of a 'grandmother' to facilitate the success of her transitional 'daughter' Cecilia.

The trauma of birth defects

Alexander (whose name means 'defending/helping others' (cf. Crittenden and Morrison 1988) was the first-born child of a nursing student. There were no problems with the pregnancy until 32 weeks when there was sudden toxaemia and an emergency birth. The amniotic fluid was green, Alexander had repeated seizures, and there was damage to his lungs, kidney, and liver. He was massively developmentally delayed; for example, he first achieved eye contact when he was 8 months old. It had never been clear, even during gestation, that he would live and it was not clear now. At 18 months of age, he had never been out of hospital, required both a breathing and feeding tube, and had a dysmorphic face. He could not speak and instead made hoarse whooshing sounds as he laboriously breathed. Alexander was every parent's fear during pregnancy.

Alexander's mother was unusually present and attentive to him while he was in the neonatal intensive care unit. In fact, she was so absorbed in her son that a psychiatric consultation had been scheduled. That and most other interchanges with the hospital staff were unpleasant, with the mother being almost accusing. In spite of guidance to the contrary, the mother maintained her preoccupation with Alexander to the point that her husband, Alexander's father, gave up and they divorced.

In the CARE-Index interaction with his mother, there was a striking difference in their presentation. She was beautifully made up and wearing a bright colour that highlighted her dark hair. He was in beige, from his skin tone to his clothing; his light brown hair stood up in unkempt tufts. He lay, with tubing, in his mother's arms. Her face was bright with love and happiness whereas Alexander's head was flopped away from her as if he could not hold it upward in a face-to-face position. Alexander's mother murmured softly, gently to Alexander, but at moments her face shifted, becoming deeply sad and distant. In just those moments, Alexander jerked his face toward her, looked directly at her, and trilled a high-pitched gurgling sound, with a smile-like open mouth. His mother 'came back' from wherever her thoughts had taken her and smiled beatifically at him. Then his head dropped back, as if he were exhausted by the effort of holding it up. This sequence was repeated four times in three minutes. Each time his mother turned away and let her sadness show, Alexander called her back with eye contact and trilling. Alexander, with all his massive limitations, was using a compulsive caregiving strategy and expressing it with the limited competencies he had available. Alexander would die six weeks later, but in this moment, with a body defined by life-threatening danger and as he approached death, Alexander was using everything he had strategically to keep his lifeline, his mother, engaged.

For Bonnie, it was a bit different. At 17 months, she and her mother participated in a CARE-Index video of play interaction. Bonnie was bright, cheerful, and competent. On first viewing, her interaction with her mother looked cooperative (Bonnie) and sensitive (mother); Bonnie looked securely attached to her mother. Viewed carefully, however, Bonnie seemed very concerned about her mother's state, checking her face again and again, but each time subtly slipping away from full eye contact. This suggested the need to look further at the videotaped interaction. As soon as she turned away from her mother, Bonnie's smile disappeared, leaving her face empty and sad – but only for a moment. She quickly looked back at her mother, with an over-bright smile and elusive eye contact, and all was well again. Careful viewing of her mother's face, when Bonnie was not looking toward her, showed worry combined with never taking her eyes off her daughter and mirroring her daughter's every move with subtle adjustments of her own body. It was striking also that Bonnie's mother only watched while Bonnie performed. The patterns were clear, compulsive caregiving and performance for the Bonnie ('Look mom! I'm healthy and competent! Don't worry!') and preoccupied over-involvement for the mother. But why?

Questions about Bonnie's brief history clarified the immediate problem. Bonnie was born with a heart murmur and her parents, naturally, feared for her life. But it cleared up quickly and her paediatrician declared her completely healthy and without further risk. Her father now felt confident of Bonnie's robustness; he played with her in the usual rough and tumble way that characterizes fathers. But his wife, while being adequately functional as a mother, was unduly worried, in ways that did not match the current context. An AAI clarified the basis of that in the past danger of her sister's early death from a sudden and unexpected heart attack.

We are struck by both the ability of very compromised children to organize adaptive self-protective strategies and by the long reach of danger in the past to shape behaviour in the present. When the present is different and calls for a different response, behaviour can become maladaptive. We think these cases demonstrate that the principles of FST have a proper place in early intervention, child protection, and fostering, where they can support the development of protective attachment relationships in emerging and vulnerable families. If we needed a term to refer to this, we might call it Developmental Systemic Treatment.

Summary of constructs and treatment principles

Constructs

1   *ZPD (the Zone of Proximal Development)*: The emergent abilities of the toddler can benefit from the parent's protective monitoring and assistance in learning: this area of functioning defines the ZPD. As development and learning progress, the ZPD changes. To keep functioning in it, parents need to observe their child's behaviour and construct their own behaviour carefully

2   *Goal-corrected partnership*: The construct specifies the processes of attachment of toddlers and preschoolers to their parents, featuring the verbal and non-verbal communication about danger, safety, exploration and the plans on how to manage them, and also the negotiation on how to accomplish interpersonally the goals that are agreed upon.

3   *Breaches and repair*: Mistakes in defining the limits of the ZPD or miscommunication within the goal-corrected partnership can create interpersonal breaches. Learning the interpersonal communicative and pragmatic skills to repair or by-pass these breaches allows the attachment relationship to continue functioning. If the breaches are repaired (as usual in Type B strategies), the relationship is stronger. If they are by-passed, either by minimizing them (as in Type A strategies) or by exaggerating them (as in Type C strategies), the breaches are more likely to recur, and repair skills are not learned.

4   *Coy behaviour*: This set of behaviours appear in toddlerhood first, serving the function of terminating aggression and eliciting nurturance. The behaviours include fearful displays of submission and displays of bids for comfort and nurturance. This is considered a distortion of the display of affect. The expected angry components of the anxious display are minimized, in order to clarify the fear/desire for comfort display.

5   *New strategies: A3–4, C3–4*: Compulsive caregiving (Type A3) and compulsive compliance (Type A4) are strategies that are first organized in toddlerhood and refined in the preschool years (see Chapter 3). They are based on the inhibition of negative affect (to prevent dangerous outcomes) and the display of compelled behaviours (false positive affect, to elicit parental caregiving and approval). They protect toddlers from parents' distance or unavailability (Type A3) or from parents' intrusivity and violence (Type A4). Coercive strategies (Types C1–2, C3–4), that are based on the alternation of split displays of negative affects of invulnerability (aggression) and vulnerability (fear and desire for comfort), simplify the unpredictability of complex environments; they regulate parents' attention by creating child-focused problems.

6   *Psychological trauma*: Is a psychological response to dangers from which the person was not protected and was not able to protect the self with a mature and appropriate strategy. If information about the dangerous event cannot be sorted by relevance to similar future dangers, the past danger is considered as unresolved trauma. The various types of lack of resolution of trauma have Type A, B, C or A/C forms that do not reach strategic functionality.

7   *Triangulation:* Refers to the inclusion of the child in the relationship between the parents. If the spousal boundaries are kept, and the role of the child in the triad is communicated about or otherwise visible and understandable to the child, the process leads to exploration of and learning about interpersonal complexity. If the spousal couple is affected by the child's functioning in ways that remain opaque or not clarified adequately by the parents, the triangulation contributes to anxiety and lack of clarity about the danger at hand. The term 'triangulation' used in description of cases usually refers to this latter form of the process.

8   *Spousification:* Is the process that balances some functional gap in the parental subsystem by having a child–adult attachment fill in the missing function. The child comes to partly function as a spouse to a parent.

9   *Transition from adolescence to adulthood:* Is the developmental phase in which the physically, intellectually and sexually mature individual can focus on the selection of a suitable partner and on practising symmetrical and reciprocal relationships that integrate attachment and sexuality. This promotes becoming a sensitive and protective attachment figure for children.

Treatment principles

1   Change is the norm, not stability.
2   Often problems that appear located in one (symptomatic) person may be better formulated as a family level problem.
3   Solutions to many problems require change in all parts of the individual, dyadic, family, and professional systems.
4   Ways to implement intervention should be developmentally attuned not only to children's development, but also to adults' readiness to learn.
5   Past experience with danger can make adults function in danger-related and danger-generating ways (due to their protective strategies or to unresolved trauma) that are inscrutable unless interpreted in the frame of their strategic attempts based on their learned experience.
6   Intervention involving toddlers must acknowledge the limited communicative skills of the children (greater non-verbally), their being focused on their family's strategies and not yet ready to learn easily about out-of-home strategies.
7   Parent education is usually counter-indicated in cases of triangulation of the child in the relationship between the parents because the problem is not about the child but rather is a function of the spousal relationship.

3   Preschool: Talking and negotiating

'It's time to go!' Johnny's mother calls him, saying, 'Hurry up, we've got to go to the store!' Johnny dawdles. He's engrossed in his building blocks and isn't a bit interested in shopping. If Johnny were a baby or even a toddler, his mother would just scoop him up and off they'd go – on her preferred schedule. But with the onset of language and self-awareness, it isn't so easy any more. Everything needs to be negotiated. How Johnny's mum and dad manage this will have implications for how Johnny manages with teachers in school, with his friends, with girlfriends and his wife, possibly even with his children. Something momentous is beginning in the third year of life and its development is very important.

Developmental change

Pre-operational intelligence

By about 2½ years of age, children have full access to 'pre-operational intelligence' (Piaget 1932). This means that they can understand and use language, but only in very direct and explicit ways. They can also draw conclusions about what follows what and, correspondingly, what causes what. They do not necessarily state these conclusions in words, but their behaviour makes clear that they have causal expectations. However, preschool-aged children perceive, but cannot understand inconsistency, subtlety, or deception. Consequently, when events or communications are complex or shaded by double or false meanings, preschool-aged children can draw inaccurate conclusions that distort the situation.

Communication, negotiation, and mutuality

Preschool children have ideas, plans, and desires, and they have many ways to communicate and insist on these. Where parents of infants protect and comfort their infant, using the infant's signals to inform them regarding the infant's needs, the parents of preschoolers need to negotiate with their child to find workable compromises. In other words, the systemic organization around the goals of children's protection and comfort is becoming more based on what children know about themselves. Children communicate about what they 'know' is best for them; parents, at least some of the time, know differently and must insist on their understanding taking precedence. Where possible, however, framing this in terms that children can understand brings child and parent DRs and priorities closer together. This process involves both direct content regarding safety and what we will each do and also a meta-message about the nature of the parent–child relationship (Watzlawick et al. 1967). This meta-message conveys both the parent's authority and his or her concern for the child, i.e., that the authority and power of the parent will be used on behalf of the child who can rely on the parent.

The parent–child relationship is important because, in the preschool years, it is undergoing a dramatic change from almost entirely protective and comforting of the infant toward the creation of a dominance hierarchy in which the parents yield some responsibility to preschoolers to protect and comfort themselves, while retaining ultimate authority about the children and family. For example, parents establish some safety rules that they expect their young children to respect: don't touch the stove, don't run into the street, stay on the sidewalk. The non-verbal aspects of such statements (e.g., voice tone and volume, eye contact, use of the child's full name) convey their importance; 'this is a command and it is important'. A process has begun that will change the boundary between child and adult authority until the child has become an adult.

Box 3.1   Attachments in the preschool years

* *Parents*: Disputes about symmetry and non-reciprocal.
* *Siblings*: Mediated by parents, without the preschooler having a fully independent relationship.

Parenting strategies and styles

There have been many attempts to describe effective parenting. Although they differ in the details, many coalesce around three types: too much, too little, and just right (Crittenden 2000). We suggest a basic typology that is consistent across theorists as well as having a DMM focus on threat. Ainsworth documented that the development of secure attachment in children is related to 'maternal sensitive responsiveness'. This connects with the emphasis on open communication in systems theory (Watzlawick et al. 1967). Satir (1972) described troubled interpersonal communication as distracting, computing, blaming, and placating; in the Ainsworth ABC model, the first two would reflect Type A strategies that avoid negative emotion and the last two would be seen as an alternating Type C strategy that employs alternating negative affect strategically. The advantage of Satir's work is the elucidation of non-verbal communicative processes. Likewise, Minuchin (1974) described families as balanced, disengaged and enmeshed. Olson et al. (1989) refined this as a two-dimensional model, with cohesion and adaptation defining four patterns that are analogous to Types A, B, C, and A/C. Moving to the spousal level, Gottman (1993) has described couples as conflict-avoiding, validating, and volatile, patterns that reflect Types A, B, and C quite closely. While each of these is a relevant perspective on the three basic patternings, Baumrind's focus on types of parental authority is particularly suited to the change from the comfort of infancy to the hierarchical structure of parent–child relations in the preschool years (Baumrind 1971).

Authoritative parenting: balanced families

In balanced family systems, parents adopt a clear decision-making position with regard to their child, but include the child's expressed preferences in their decision. An important feature of this process is that the parents consider safety and danger first; when there is danger, the parent's priorities prevail and discussion is secondary to respectful compliance. When there is no danger, children's preferences become more important. Under safe conditions, parents with a balanced parenting style actively listen to their child's ideas and elaborate his or her communication, making it verbal and clear (Bernstein 1971). They also describe the consequences of the various actions that could be taken, including punitive consequences if these are needed. Finally, all of this is managed in the child's ZPD (Vygotsky 1962) and with warmth and empathy for the child. That is, the explanations given to the child and the language used to negotiate are within the child's cognitive and linguistic reach and, bit by bit, expand the child's competencies, in the context of a supportive emotional relationship. So the parent isn't 'teaching', but the child is learning – about events, language, and relationships.

This description of authoritative parenting, with the addition of ideas about danger and ZPD, fits with Bowlby's idea of a 'goal-corrected partnership' (Bowlby 1969). With these added ideas, parenting style becomes less a behavioural description of what parents do and more an interactive process between parent and child occurring in a context that has specific safe and dangerous features. That is, authoritative parenting takes on a protective, systemic, and contextualized meaning; by its very nature, it will not typically occur when either parent or child feels pervasively threatened.

In our opening scenario, Mum is ready to go and Johnny isn't. He calls back, 'Just a minute' and promptly forgets her, concentrating on the garage he is building. She waits just a short minute and calls again. Johnny grunts. The dilemma of conflicting plans and priorities is upon them. Johnny's mum comes to him. She admires his construction and listens to his explanation of what he's doing. She repeats his plan (so that he knows she understands and he hears it in elaborated language), then she explains her plan: the groceries for dinner, being back home for his sister and having dinner ready for daddy. Everyone is accounted for and Johnny is losing the family vote; he will need to bend to the needs of the others. But how will mum facilitate that without having to impose her will? 'I wonder if you can finish the ramp you're working on, then we'll close the door so no one will touch it, and you can finish it after we get back. I think it will be ready to show Dad when he comes home. Okay? Shall I help you? It's really a fine garage!' Listen, elaborate, suggest, admire, and offer a reward (showing dad), but insist on going now. As long as mum remembers to mention the garage when they get home, this sort of parent-led negotiation should not only solve the immediate problem, but also shape how Johnny will learn to express and resolve problems in general.

Authoritarian parenting: disengaged families

How would it be different if Johnny's mum was using an authoritarian parenting style, combined with predictable consequences? 'John! Did you hear me? I said to come now and I meant now!' If Johnny responds, fine, but what if he continues playing? 'John! Come now or I will have to smack you.' Assuming that either Johnny comes or she smacks and hauls him away to the car, this is a short and efficient solution to the immediate problem, but it is a solution with unfortunate long-term consequences (Ainsworth and Wittig 1969; Thompson et al. 2003). Johnny doesn't learn to differentiate dangerous and safe conditions; all are treated as needing respect and compliance. Moreover, he learns nothing about the many perspectives and needs of family members and nothing about how to address this array of needs. His language doesn't improve; in fact, he learns that his ideas aren't really wanted.

Similarly, he doesn't experience having his feelings understood and is left to settle his frustration by himself. He'll probably learn to inhibit it. Finally, he's learning that relationships have fixed roles of power and submission. In the future, depending upon whom he is with, he is likely to take the dominant or submissive role. On the other hand, when outcomes are predictable, he will behave as adults would like and will do well in school. In some circumstances, especially threatening circumstances where time lost to discussion and negotiation could create problems, these outcomes are desirable.

Permissive parenting: enmeshed families

The parents in these family systems range from those who consciously wish to be non-punitive, accepting, and affirmative with their children to those who have other priorities that mean it is easier to go along with the child than to intervene. In both cases, the parents underestimate danger and fail to act authoritatively when safety is the issue. In the first case, they often respond to the child's negative feelings, but aren't especially effective in helping him to regulate them. Frequently these parents are trying to correct the over-control they experienced as children. In the second case, the parents are inattentive, leaving the child feeling both in charge and overlooked. In such cases, the child's mixed feelings are about the satisfaction of doing what he wants and the discomfort of feeling unprotected and unimportant. These parents often experience too many stressors themselves to attend predictably to the moment-to-moment details of parenting but, when they feel it necessary, override the child's preferences. Overall, permissive parents do not establish predictable external control and authority, leaving the rules that regulate the parent–child relationship unclear.

In our example, mum would call Johnny several times and receive no answer. Then she might go to Johnny and give a long explanation about the sister and dad and close by asking Johnny what he thinks they should do. If his truculent response was 'I wanna play here!', mum would be trapped. She asked, hoping he would be mature, but he wasn't and she had no back-up plan. She is left having to give in – and face the consequences with other family members. In this case, she might not get to the market because she must be home when Johnny's sister gets home. That means dinner won't be ready when Dad gets home: he may be irritated and may discover that he's competing with his son for his wife's attention. This sort of partial problem resolution leads to new problems, in which family members — who each have been given too much authority — come to feel in competition with each other and, ironically, that they receive too little support. Over the course of childhood, children who are raised permissively show poor emotion regulation, use more non-verbal communication than other children, are contrary and oppositional, give up easily when things don't work out, and, in cases of substantial threat to the child, may show antisocial behaviour (Crittenden 1999). On the other hand, they can be engagingly disarming, funny, and fierce; for sure, you want them on your side and not against you.

From dyads to culture

Although Baumrind did not use Ainsworth's patterns of attachment (which were published concurrently with Baumrind's), the two schemas fit together well (Ainsworth and Wittig 1969; Baumrind 1971). Missing from Baumrind's model, however, are the parenting correlates of parent–children dyads who show Type A/C combinations. Type A/C can be described as the outcome of parents who alternate between authoritarian and permissive patterns (Type A/C). It can range from mild alternations (that is, Types A1–2/C1–2) to more extreme alternations (Types A3–4/C3–4). Such combinations can co-occur at one time or reflect a change, for example, the permissive approach to Japanese infants followed by a more authoritarian approach when they go to school (Caudill and Schooler 1973).

One might ask why parents would select 'non-optimal' patterns. The DMM conceptualizes individuals in terms of family and cultural contexts that differ in the history of danger and current exposure to danger. When the context (both current and historic) is considered, the authoritarian and permissive styles become meaningful ways to solve real problems. For example, when the family – or culture – has faced extreme, life-threatening threat, obedience to rules that minimize the threat becomes more important than teaching children self-expression and negotiation. In these conditions, parents who use Type A attachment strategies may employ authoritarian parenting tactics which often elicit a compulsive compliant strategy in their children; this can make the child and sometimes the whole family safer. Examples of such contexts would be slavery, political repression, and economic subsistence living. In such cases, a false move could lead to serious consequences, even death. A parent's first responsibility is to keep their children alive and authoritarian parenting accomplishes this protective function. The disadvantage can be that children are not encouraged to think for themselves and are steered away from taking notice of their emotions. This means that important information may be excluded from awareness.

Families and cultures that enjoy relatively abundant resources in the context of variable and mild to moderate threat can afford to use permissive parenting, which is a quick way to implement a solution to a child-related issue. It reduces strife in the short term without incurring too much risk. The cost of this short-term advantage, however, can be children's long-term vigilance regarding unpredictable threats, anxiety when no threat is in sight, and a win – lose approach to social exchange.

On the other hand, when the family – and culture – face on-going changing and unpredictable conditions with a variety of mild to moderate threats, parents using Type C strategies can prepare children to adapt to complexity and uncertainty by being ever-vigilant. The disadvantages include the possibility that children can be overwhelmed by being drawn into their parents' anxiety without being able to see and evaluate the threat themselves, and that their constant vigilance to signals in the environment could prevent them from being able to focus their attention when this is required (see further discussion of attentional issues in Chapter 5).

When Mummy and Daddy don't agree

Children face a particularly difficult situation when their two parents respond differently to them. What's a child to do if mum is permissive and dad is authoritarian? This level of triadic complexity is faced by many children. Of course, no two parents are exactly alike and even babies quickly respond differentially to their two parents. The difficulties arise when:

The response suited to one parent is the opposite of that required by the other parent – and making a mistake could harm the child;

The child is used by one parent to undermine or coerce the other parent (triangulation).

The parents use the child to protect themselves.

The condition of needing two opposite strategies, each used at precisely the right time and not at other times, requires vigilance and flexibility. Children can manage opposite strategies, but doing so takes attention and effort away from other activities. Consequently, intelligence, i.e., the ability to process more information (both cognitive and affective information) more rapidly, interacts with other conditions to produce rapid adaptation in more intelligent children and less successful adaptation in those children who face complex family contexts with less intellectual capacity.

Children whose parents 'triangulate' them face a much more complex condition. Triangulation involves parents' motivations regarding each other being used to organize their behaviour with their child. Because motivations cannot be observed, because children could not understand adult concerns even if they could see them, and because all of us implicitly assume that behaviour directed to ourselves is about ourselves, triangulation can lead to a very distorted understanding of relationships for children who are pulled unknowingly into their parents' disputes.

The central problem is that triangulated children draw erroneous 'cognitive' conclusions about how their behaviour affects other people. They think, mistakenly, that their behaviour influences their parents' response. Because it does not (the parent's behaviour being tied instead to the other parent), the relation between child behaviour and parental response is quite erratic.

To try to improve the predictability, children heighten their behaviour. The outcome can be an array of extreme child behaviours, described by an assortment of diagnostic labels including feeding disorders (i.e., refusal to eat), acting out (i.e., the parents respond contingently to the child only if the situation becomes threatening or endangering), and serious psychosomatic symptoms (i.e., the parents respond more contingently to illness than to psychological or interpersonal distress).

Unfortunately, neither parent nor child is usually aware of the triangulated causal process and, therefore, no one can report properly on it. The risk is that intervention will be directed toward the child and changing the child's behaviour and that the family process will escape notice. It is important to differentiate between parents who simply employ different self-protective strategies acquired from their own childhood from parents whose own needs triangulate the child in processes that harm the child because these conditions have different clinical implications. When parents have their own needs, they need assistance articulating and resolving these.

Knowing in words

With pre-operational intelligence, children begin to use language to represent their meanings. Language is used in two new ways by two- to five-year-old children: semantic generalizations and episodes of daily events in their own lives.

Semantic generalizations

Children hear their parents use semantic generalizations to describe how things are: 'That's dangerous!', 'What a good girl you are!', 'Tut! Tut! Mummy said not to touch that.' Only later will children be able to draw their own conclusions, based on their own experience. Until then, they must 'borrow' their semantic DRs from their caregivers. This places quite a burden on parents. They must both articulate the child's perspective, giving him or her the language for the child's experience, and also keep an adult perspective in mind so as to guide the child's behaviour in safe ways. It helps children to be able to speak for themselves so it's good for children if the parent can articulate the child's perspective clearly. But it does not help children if they are permitted to do dangerous things. Authoritative parents articulate both the child's and their own perspective, while guiding children to accept safe behaviour. If parents emphasize their own perspective, their children's semantic knowledge will be 'borrowed'. Such children might substitute parental perspectives for self-generated information and fail to learn to make judgements of safety for themselves. If parents emphasize children's perspectives, they might both endanger the child and also convey that the child's perspective was sufficient. As always, balance is needed and balance is the contribution of mature adults.

Another aspect of semantic memory is its prescriptive use. Some semantic statements *describe* how things are, whereas others *prescribe* how they ought to be, should be or must be. Every child needs some prescriptive information, but when children hear too many prescriptive expectations, they may find themselves consistently not meeting expectation.

Episodic memory

Parents also help children learn to tell episodes and what information to include in episodes. Young preschoolers come running to mummy with three or four excited words about what they've done. What she says next matters. Maybe she elaborates what Mary said, 'Oh! You saw a big dog and his owner said you could pet him? Did you do that?' Mum and Mary are beginning to construct Mary's story. On the other hand, mum might have answered, 'What did I tell you about dogs? They might bite!' Mary's story is lost, replaced by mum's prescriptive prohibition. Other episodes meet a more permanent end: 'What were you and daddy fighting about?' And mum walks away. Or starts shouting at Johnny to clean up his room. Or pours herself another drink. In such cases, the child may experience intense feelings while not being able to understand the parents' behaviour and not being permitted to articulate and discuss the problem. This is poor preparation for future relationships.

Stories about the scariest things in life can easily become unspeakable stories. These events still have effects through non-verbal forms of communication; they just don't have clear representation in language. It will be very hard for Mary and John to think about marital conflict when it can't be talked about and, thus, has no representation in episodes.

Other information may not only be forbidden to say, but also forbidden to know. For example, often when we read AAIs of people who have been in and out of treatment over many years or who have lived especially troubled lives, we find the tell-tale markers of probable sexual infidelity or impropriety. Bedrooms and bathrooms. These fascinating places hold stories that excite, disrupt, and silence children – and the adults they become. Should Mary or John ever need help in dealing with the effects of their parents' conflicts, it might be difficult for them to tell this part of their history or for their therapist to find its remnants in the stories that they do tell. One purpose of good assessment is to reveal, connect, and give meaning to lost scraps of information.

This, we think, is what the AAI can do for adults; it can highlight the hidden bits of incomplete information that can lead back to frighteningly forbidden information. This can render bizarre behaviour meaningful and promote change in the family's current functioning.

Absolutist information

Information characteristic of the preschool years is 'absolutist'. This way of functioning is more complex than infants' 'realism': children know information can be inaccurate. Nonetheless, truth is treated as absolute.

Box 3.2   Absolutist mental processes

1   *Definition*: Recognition that (1) human minds produce information; and (2) therefore some information is false (mistakes and lies).
2   *Limitation*: Inability to accept alternative perspectives as valid.
3   *Information type*: Somatic, procedural, imaged preconscious information; personal body-talk, borrowed semantic information, and receptive connotative DRs; functioning is still primarily preconscious.
4   *Executive functioning*: Preschool-aged children do not regulate which DR disposes their behaviour.
5   *Individual differences*: Essentially all intact humans master absolutist processing.
6   *Treatment implications*: Treatment directed toward changing the child's interpersonal context is still preferred.

New self-protective strategies

The new abilities of preschool-aged children create the possibility for more sophisticated self-protective strategies. Within the self-effacing, other-embracing Type A strategy, compulsive caregiving (A3) (Bowlby 1980, Vol. 3) and compulsive compliance (Type A4) (Crittenden and DiLalla, 1989) refine the possibilities for coping with depressed/withdrawn and demanding/angry parents (respectively). Less intense forms of these strategies are compulsive attention and compulsive performance. Within Type C, aggression and its obverse, feigned helplessness, become new and more powerful forms of the Type C1–2 strategy.

Compulsive caregiving (Type A3)

The Types A3 and A4 strategies are used when children fear losing their parents' protective attention (Type A3) or eliciting dangerous punishment (Type A4). Children using a Type A3 strategy inhibit evidence of needing care and, instead, care for their parent.

They are solicitous of their parent, generous with toys, food, and comfort, and show bright positive affect when the parent is dejected. 'Look! I'm happy! You'll feel better if you pay attention to me. I won't make any demands!' Of course, these words are not spoken, but the child's behaviour functions to convey this message. The effect is to bring the parent closer psychologically to the child, which is good because children cannot be protected if parents are psychologically absent. In terms of Baumrind's parenting styles, parents of children who use a compulsive caregiving strategy have abdicated the parent role and the child has taken it on, in a role-reversing manner that leaves the child acting as an authoritarian parent. The psychological cost of the strategy is that such children may lose access to their own negative feelings, thereby not seeking protection from the threats that these feelings signal. Being too attuned to the parent, children may become dis-attuned to themselves.

Compulsive compliance (Type A4)

Children using a Type A4 strategy also attend closely to their parents' wishes, but, in this case, they seek information about what they should do (prescriptively). They fear that, if they do something wrong or don't do as the authoritarian parent wants, they will be punished in dangerous ways. So their first rule of self-regulation is 'Don't do the wrong thing!' They learn what their parents expect and, if possible, they do that even before the parent requests it. In addition, they stay vigilantly attentive so as to perceive unexpected parental preferences and comply with them as well. Such children are often fearful, which is understood by their parents as a sign of respect. On the other hand, they dare not show anger. Behaviourally, this leads to intense inhibition that can be observed as excessive stillness, frozen body parts, and unnatural or stiff movements. Compulsive compliance makes children safer in relationships where punishment could be dangerous; the strategy occurs most often in families in which external danger is – or has been – very great, such that keeping children safe means keeping them under tight control. The costs of the strategy are loss of awareness of the child's anger (by both the child and adults) and reduced spontaneity on the child's part.

Type A strategies prioritize adults' perspectives. It is no surprise that parents, teachers, youth group leaders are pleased with the behaviour of children using Type A strategies. Good grades and good marks for conduct follow. The concomitant intense anxiety and inhibition are often overlooked, but fear of doing the wrong thing or making mistakes can hamper children's learning. Children using compulsive Type A strategies are unlikely to be picked out for referral because, in adult terms, they seem so mature. Nevertheless, if they and their families receive no assistance, problems can develop. Both depression and explosions of forbidden negative affect can occur. Explosions of negative feelings that are forbidden to be displayed occur when feelings that have been inhibited become disinhibited; this most frequently occurs when the inhibitory strategy has failed to protect the child and the child's arousal drops in a manner that reflects feelings of failure or depression. Without active inhibition, formerly 'suppressed' feelings may become disinhibited; when displayed, they can show a 'rebound effect' of extreme intensity without conscious awareness (see Hakim case study, below) (Sayers and Sayette 2013). Prevention is needed; this requires early recognition that the child's anxiety reflects a family-level problem and implementation of procedures to resolve the problem, including the prohibition against displaying negative feelings. This, of course, is a complex process involving the parents becoming aware of the situation, then learning to make more positive attributions around children's negative feelings, and ultimately assisting children to regulate the expression of negative feelings.

Coercive aggression (Type C3)

When communication is ambiguous or outcomes unpredictable, children try to bring clarity and predictability to their relationships. To retain parental attention, many children become unpredictable themselves. Some exaggerate the display of anger, while inhibiting the display of desire for comfort and fear, in order to increase the probability that adults will try to placate them. They become aggressive (i.e., dangerous to others), provocative (i.e., doing what the parent forbids), or risk-taking (i.e., dangerous to themselves). This engages the parent, but if no resolution is found and the struggle continues, the parents may become angry. To be effectively – and safely – coercive, children must be able to disarm parental anger.

This is where the other side of the strategy becomes important. Instead of displaying and emphasizing the anger, the coercive child whose parent is angry inhibits the display of anger and displays exaggerated fearful desire for comfort. The thumb goes in the mouth; the head drops and the shoulders rise; a pre-cry looks trembles on the lips . . . and the once angry parent crumples. 'Oh! I didn't mean to scare you! Mummy loves you!' And the struggle continues. The child has 'won', but really no one has won because the child is as trapped in the struggle as is the parent. The struggle, however, functions protectively because it keeps the parent's attention on the child. Thus the cost of safety is anxiety and strife. If parent and child cannot find a better way to solve disagreements, the family will need help.

Coercive feigned helplessness (Type C4)

Alternatively, children can emphasize fearfulness – and hide the evidence of anger. Instead of pretending to have power, they pretend to have none. They simper, they hesitate, they start and restart and accomplish nothing. They need help! Without asking – in words – for help, their ever-so-evident incompetence forces adults to rescue them. Their charmingly coy demeanour (Marvin and Mossler 1976) endears them to others and makes giving help feel good. At least for a while. Eventually, parents get tired of attending to their hothouse flower. They want performance; they want their own freedom from the children's yoke of incompetence. The sympathy turns to anger. But, of course, children with a good coercive strategy are ready for the unexpected. The children inhibit the fearful desire for comfort and flash a burst of anger! Oh, dear! The parent didn't want this! The parent backtracks, cuddling and soothing and helping! They rescue themselves and the child from the child's anger – and the struggle goes on.

The problem with coercive behaviour is its reliance on non-verbal communication. Sure, the child got attention, but what was the message to the parent? Usually, parents don't know. Instead they just cope with the child one crisis at a time, never seeing the 'big picture' – that is, the function of the child's behaviour to make their own attention and behaviour more predictable and protective to the child. Without words, this is hard to discover.

This is a central issue with nice, but permissive, parents who are unable to tolerate their child's distress and, therefore, comply with children's demands, without understanding their needs. In addition, the child's intense behaviour makes it very easy to see the child as presenting a problem (rather than the child trying intuitively to solve the problem of unpredictably protective parents). This can lead to diagnostic labels being applied to the child. Finally, children's development can be restricted because they must devote so much effort to the struggle for attention. Exploration is crimped when children are always getting into trouble. Speech is hampered when acting takes priority over talking and negotiating.

Although it has been assumed that children's Type C strategies emerge when parents also use Type C strategies, research has shown that Type C strategies can develop in response to parents who use Type A strategies (Crittenden et al. 1991; Hautamäki et al. 2010; Shah et al. 2010). A combination of Type A and guilt-motivated permissiveness can lead to mixed and confusing messages to children, who drift progressively towards intensifying their communication by demanding more, threatening more, becoming provocative, and even taking actual risks.

When there are problems

Learning to negotiate verbally, including especially putting non-verbal information into words so that it can be addressed explicitly, is a central age-salient process in the pre-school years. Problems occur when a struggle replaces decision-making (yielding a coercive strategy for the children), when no negotiation is permitted by excessively authoritarian parents (who fear the consequences to their child of excessive leniency), or when the connection between parent and child fails (such that communication itself fails). We have discussed the coercive strategy above. In the following section, we focus on the second and third of these situations.

Intervening with compulsive compliance (Type A4)

Early intervention. Hakim was 3 months old when his mother was offered an early intervention programme for families at risk for abuse and neglect. In her case, she hadn't completed school, had emigrated from a dangerous country that tended to use harsh punishment, and lived in a high crime area. The parenting classes emphasized child development and positive behaviour: talking to children, highlighting toys, and putting feelings into words. The mothers were encouraged to use non-physical disciplinary techniques such as time out.

Assessment of outcomes. When Hakim was 2 years old, he and his mother participated in a 'Strange Situation' as part of the evaluation of the intervention. The Preschool Assessment of Attachment (Crittenden 1992a) was used to interpret Hakim's pattern of attachment. With the advantage of early intervention, it was hoped that Hakim would be securely attached (Type B) to his mother.

During the Strange Situation, Hakim's arousal was extremely high (his voice squeaked, he stumbled, etc.), especially in his mother's presence. This was unusual because most children are calm when their mothers are nearby; instead, Hakim seemed very anxious. His mother sat very still without smiling; when she spoke, to highlight or name toys, her voice seemed forced. When she spoke *nicely* to him, Hakim had sudden peaks of arousal, throwing toys and laughing screechingly. This suggested that her being nice distressed him more than her being still. She departed without speaking to or looking at Hakim. His arousal dropped sharply: he looked dejected and lay face down on the floor, very quiet and still. Sometimes he calmed himself by touching his crotch; genital self-soothing usually indicates intense distress. Extreme swings in arousal, occurring very rapidly, usually signal extreme distress in the context of a failing strategy. Nevertheless, Hakim didn't protest when his mother left. Instead, when she was present, *he* tried to get out of the room, but he didn't protest when she brought him back. On reunion, his mother could see Hakim's distress, but she offered no comfort. After the second reunion, when she asked him if he was angry, he ran behind her, then waved his arms with jittery agitation and made grimaces that she couldn't see.

Clearly, Hakim was not securely attached to his mother. But his behaviour also didn't fit the usual ABC strategies. Instead it raised questions. Why was Hakim's mother's arousal so constrained and his so extreme? Why did discussion of anger distress him and why did he hide this from her? Why did his positive affect feel brittle (like laughter that could crack to tears)? All of this pointed to a compulsive compliant Type A4 strategy in which anger was the most forbidden affect.

But some things didn't fit Type A4. Although Hakim's anger looked like Type C, his outbursts occurred when his mother wasn't present. Neither did he struggle when she called him back to her. Instead, he complied when she took control. Type C was eliminated as a possibility. Hakim's angry outbursts were directed away from his mother (displaced onto toys). Moreover, when she put his anger in words (as she had been taught to do), he ran away and had a 'fit' (that is, a sudden disinhibition of intense negative affect) behind her.

Inhibited children of very strict and harshly punitive mothers sometimes have 'intrusions of forbidden negative affect' that seem like explosions of pent-up anger, fear, or desire for comfort. Hakim also had *positive* outbursts of 'manic', 'hysterical' behaviour. Both followed mum being 'teachy-talky', something that seemed uncharacteristic for her. Hakim's effort to escape from the room and his mother suggested he wanted to be alone, an A6-like strategy of compulsive self-reliance. Of course, 2-year-olds cannot be self-reliant; the strategy must fail and this shows as depression. Hakim seemed forced to choose between intolerable closeness to his mother and the impossible condition of being on his own.

Understanding the outcomes at the familial level. In trying to understand Hakim and his mother, we thought about the possible unintended effects of the early intervention programme. Guiding Hakim's mother to use less physical punishment seemed to have reduced Hakim's inhibition, but not his anger. Possibly his mother's newly learned behaviour was reserved for calm moments or moments when the intervention staff were present? Hakim seemed to know about other times and to feel more confident of what he should do when she was strict. Why didn't these very common techniques for encouraging development and supporting secure attachment work for Hakim and his mother?

Taking a systemic perspective, it seemed possible that the intervention had focused too narrowly on what (all) mothers *should* (prescriptively) do with their young children without considering the context of family, neighbourhood, and culture. What did Hakim's father think about this approach to raising his son? Not infrequently staff say that it is not possible to reach fathers because they are unavailable during work hours. However, in father-headed households, failure to include the fathers may sabotage the entire intervention, leaving the mother in an impossible bind: please the professionals while obeying her husband. Asking questions, for example, using a family tree, might provide information about the parents' behaviour even without seeing the father. This need not require sophisticated training in systemic family therapy and might point to the essential need for greater family inclusiveness.

Understanding the outcomes at the cultural level. Moving beyond the family, were there dangers in Hakim's neighbourhood that made Hakim's emerging independence unsafe? What had Hakim's cultural group learned, over generations, about danger and the best way to keep children safe? Most programmes on cultural diversity discuss cultural values, but they neglect to describe the history of threat and loss in the culture. Neither do they describe the culture's evolved strategies for preventing harm. People do not readily set aside old and trusted strategies for new notions. Asking community leaders to assist in designing interventions might make cultural differences explicit and foster discussion of how a cultural minority can best adapt in the context of the majority culture.

In this case, a manualized intervention was delivered to groups of culturally diverse mothers and had unexpected negative effects in some cases. Possibly the mothers' strategies were adaptive in specific contexts. Cultures tend to use adaptive strategies, not self-defeating ones. Understanding this requires an on-going dialogue with many representatives of the culture. Finally, processing evidence gathered during the intervention could have revealed unexpected outcomes before they became fixed. With such information, a change in the intervention plan could have been made before Hakim's relationship with his mother deteriorated.

Overall, this intervention didn't consider what the critical danger was for this family, and what would be protective for this family about the intervention.

Autism

Randy can't move into social settings

Recently, one of us was startled when a shopkeeper announced that he had an autistic son, Randy, but 'We love him dearly. We think of him as having special gifts that will be an advantage later.' This statement was striking, coming as it did in an exchange tied to antique furniture. Several things stood out. First, Randy's father seemed to carry thoughts about his autistic son into every activity with everyone. Second, autism was offered as if it were something special.

Aetiology and epidemiology of autism

Autism is a major clinical concern that raises very basic questions regarding the biological and experiential processes underlying psychopathology. It also highlights the processes through which decisions about research are made and disorders are defined, the access of working clinicians to current scientific knowledge, and the application of this knowledge to treatment. Because clinicians are the connection between scientific information and its application as treatment, their understanding is crucial.

Rates of diagnosis of autism have risen sharply recently with autism now affecting approximately 1.13 per cent of all children and 1.84 per cent of male children (Centers for Disease Control and Prevention 2012). In the section below, we summarize the scientific literature on the aetiology of autism. We use the word 'autism' to include the milder forms of Asperger's syndrome and autistic spectrum disorders. Three features of autism will be treated as defining: social withdrawal, limited communication, and repetitive behaviour.

Our goal is to derive a more comprehensive model of its aetiology, particularly as it suggests approaches to treatment. To do this, we explore many causal factors, embedded in developmental processes, and potentially reflecting more than one developmental pathway. In systemic terms, we explore the many developmental pathways to autism (von Bertalanffy 1968). We organize our discussion systemically from micro to macro systems, beginning with genes and ending with culture.

Genomics

Genes contain information about how to structure the brain and body. Genomics encompasses the study of structural variations in DNA (genetics) and regulatory processes (including the impact of parental experiences) that control the expression of genes (epigenetics). Although early studies suggested that autism was genetically determined (Folstein and Rutter 1977), an 'autism gene' was never found and recent studies suggest that environmental factors account for approximately 55 per cent of variance (Hallmayer et al. 2011). Genetic researchers have changed their focus from inherited genes to examining: (1) the role of de novo mutations and their potential impact on genes that regulate synaptic and axonal development; (2) how variations in the DNA combine with other variations in DNA sequencing (loci-to-loci interactions) to increase the risk of autism and other psychiatric disorders; (3) epigenetic mechanisms that control gene expression; and (4) gene by environment interactions.

Neurological differences

The data supporting differences in brain structure of children with autism as compared to those without are clear and without controversy (Ecker et al. 2012). Functionally, children with autism have too many neurons, resulting from too little pruning of unused neurons and insufficient priming of frequently used synaptic pathways. Pruning normally occurs during the first 2 years of life, and functions to prioritize neural pathways, such as those involved in extracting meaning from human faces (Glaser 2000). Pruning is context-dependent and adapts each infant's brain to his or her unique developmental context, making behaviour more efficient and effective. Because individuals with autism lack precisely this efficient adaptive quality, consideration should be given to whether they might lack particular sorts of experience that the human genome 'expects'. Both contingencies in interpersonal behaviour and specific facial stimuli warrant investigation. If infants on a pathway toward autism experienced fewer perceived contingencies (for example, from parents who behaved at too simplistic or too advanced a level for the infant or with less clear facial cues), then the child's brain might fail to organize properly. Contingency, however, is relative, based on child development; near perfect contingency is necessary in the neonatal period (Gergely 2001), with increasingly attenuated contingency as infants' brains mature.

Psychological information processing

Children with autism also process information, especially social and linguistic information, differently than other children. These differences become apparent between 2–4 years of age, when language and social engagement develop rapidly.

- *Behavioural evidence.* Children and adults with autism look less at faces, especially the eye region, than do typically developing individuals (Spezio et al. 2007) and are less responsive to faces than to objects (McCleery et al. 2009). Neuro-imaging studies show that the subset of younger siblings of children with autism who later develop autism display less neural activity in response to faces than do other children (Elsabbagh et al. 2012). These differences suggest that individuals with autism do not experience faces as providing useful information.
- *Theory of mind.* Studies of emotion recognition and theory of mind (the capacity to comprehend other people's emotions, thoughts, beliefs, and intentions) show that children with autism have difficulties recognizing their own and other people's feelings (Samson et al. 2012). Similarly, they have less differentiated, more negative, and less positive emotional responses than those of controls, and find it difficult to assess and label their own feelings (see Samson et al, 2012, for review). The conditions leading to these deficits have not been explored in longitudinal studies.

Relational factors

Two of the defining characteristics of autism, social withdrawal and lack of communication, are interpersonal. This suggests that family members' behaviour may be important.

Child-based differences

In play interactions, infant siblings who were subsequently diagnosed with autism looked at faces less, sought physical contact less, and smiled to people less than siblings who did not develop autism (Cassel et al. 2007). After 6 months of age, they responded less to their names and by the age of 2, they engaged in less interpersonal play, used gaze and pointing less, attended to language less and used repetitive behaviour more (Palomo et al. 2006). Both groups of siblings were less 'lively' than normally developing children (Wan et al. 2012), suggesting slower responses. Studies that focus on child differences do not typically report parental behaviour.

Parent-based differences

Although mothers of children with autism were not less sensitive to infant signals than other mothers (cf. van Ijzendoorn et al. 2007), their responses were less mutual, elicited more child negative affect and less positive parental affect, contained fewer supportive scaffolds, highlighted symbols less, and were more directive and less contingent than the responses of other parents (Adamson et al. 2012; Wan et al. 2012). The mothers called their child's name and spoke about themselves more often (Venuti et al. 2012). Low dyadic synchrony in infancy predicted reduced joint attention and limited language at 16 years of age (Siller and Sigman 2008). The difficulty with these studies is that they do not untangle the direction of effects, whether parental differences are in response to child behaviour, are causal to child behaviour, or if the differences develop in a recursive and expanding manner from very subtle initial miscuing. Nevertheless, these findings suggest that parents of children who will be diagnosed with autism might be sensitive without being contingently responsive.

Families with a child with autism

There are only a handful of papers about family functioning and the role of fathers. The responsibility for raising children with autism still falls primarily to mothers and this pattern of role function shapes the quality of parental experiences (Gray 2003). Parents of children with autism, especially mothers, experience higher levels of stress than that experienced by parents of typically developing children and of parents of children with other disabilities (cf. Baker-Ericzn et al. 2005).

Families also report lower family functioning (adaptability and cohesion), lower marital satisfaction, and higher rates of divorce (Higgins et al. 2005). Importantly, parental stress levels are, at least in part, predicted by psychological coping strategies, locus of control, social support resources, and beliefs about the efficacy of the intervention rather than demographic variables (Hastings and Johnson 2001; Jones and Passey 2004). This highlights the importance of looking at parental factors as they impact on the developmental outcomes of the child.

It is important to note that: (1) most aspects of infant and preschool interaction were not significantly different from normative dyads; and (2) fewer differences were found in infancy before diagnosis than among older diagnosed children. The pattern of findings suggests that autism may result from either impoverished (e.g., neglect, institutionalization) or enriched and unusually complex adult input (e.g., over-performing parents). In both cases, there is a lack of perceived contingency and affective attunement for the child.

Attachment relationships

Attachment is the cumulative outcome of repeated interactions. Children with autism are attached to their mothers, but usually in atypical ways (Sigman and Ungerer 1984; Naber et al. 2007, 2008; Marcu et al. 2009). Severity of autism was associated with greater insecurity, higher heart rate when stressed, and lower cortisol response (Naber et al. 2007), suggesting that children with autism may be both highly stressed and also unable to produce an interpersonal protective response. Parents of autistic children have been found to have had stressed attachments to their own parents (Oppenheim et al. 2009; Seskin et al. 2010) with some of the mothers having experienced childhood abuse (Roberts et al. 2013).

Treatment studies

Treatment studies can identify the conditions that cause therapeutic change. Behavioural interventions show that increasing adults' predictability and consistency of response reduces autistic symptoms and improves language development (Green et al. 2010). One study found that imitation, which is very contingent, was the 'active ingredient' as compared to parent education, joint attention, and affect sharing (Landa et al. 2011). More parent participation predicted better long-term outcomes (Nix et al. 2009). Technological interventions seek to reduce symptoms by giving absolute predictability as compared to the less perfect predictability of parents (Baron-Cohen et al. 2009; Golan et al. 2010) but recent research suggests that such interventions do not bring about lasting change (Williams et al. 2012). A study by Rutter et al. (2007) found that children who were highly deprived of social stimulation lacked contingent responding and showed autistic features but some of the symptoms reversed when their environment changed.

An interesting recent development is the therapeutic use of oxytocin, a neuropeptide which is necessary for emotional bonding in mammals (Feldman et al. 2013; Gordon et al. 2013). The positive results from preliminary studies suggest that disruption of the oxytocin system – in children or parents of children with autism – is an important area of future research. Other medications have been used primarily to reduce comorbid difficulties (e.g., sleep difficulties or aggression) (Politte et al. 2014). By affecting neural networks globally and without feedback, medication may fail to promote attunement of the child to the context.

It should be noted that adults with autism vary greatly, with some unable to live independently while others live normally (Mottron 2011). This suggests that autism may reflect dimensional variation among humans, as opposed to a categorical disorder (Robinson et al. 2011).

Contextual factors

Cultural shifts in the diagnosis of autism

The clinical literature in the 1950s and 1960s postulated an aetiology of inappropriate maternal behaviour (e.g., 'refrigerator' mothers; Kanner 1949). Not only were empirical data to support that hypothesis lacking, but the hypothesis was framed so strongly and with so much blame of mothers that the ideas elicited a strong backlash. Powerful parent advocacy groups (cf. Rimland, 1964, himself the father of a child with autism) reacted strongly against 'mother-blaming theories' and re-directed funding from family issues to genetic and extra-familial factors. When twin studies reported that autism was genetically determined (Folstein and Rutter 1977), research into other explanations for autism was largely suspended. Subsequent research regarding environmental insults suggests that severe deprivation (Rutter et al. 2007), prematurity (Lampi et al. 2012), use of antidepressants early in pregnancy (Croen et al. 2011) and inflammatory processes (Braunschweig and Van de Water 2012) may account for a subset of cases.

Broadened diagnostic criteria

Since then, the meaning of the term autism has broadened and the number of children diagnosed with autism has increased dramatically (Rutter 2009). The increased attention to autism shown in availability of services has resulted in a cultural shift: some parents now seek, rather than shun, diagnoses of autism, so as to acquire help for their child. Physicians may contribute to this process, particularly in response to parental concerns and when there are services available (Lord et al. 2012).

Conclusions regarding the aetiology of autism

The results of our review indicate that no one factor or set of factors can account for all cases of autism; instead interactions among child, parent, and cultural factors appear to coalesce to yield autism. The child factors include the interaction of variations in those genes that regulate neural development with relational and environmental factors, and structural and functional brain differences that result in more diffuse and less efficient processing, especially in brain regions associated with social and language processing. Behaviourally, individuals with autism avoid face-to-face contact as if it contained no meaning or held aversive meanings and males process facial information more slowly than females. Maternal factors include mothers of children having had troubled attachment with their parents, abuse in their childhood, depression around childbirth or increased exposure to inflammation. Culturally, an increased readiness to diagnose autism may be a factor. This list is not exhaustive and has gaps, e.g., father and family contributions, but it also clarifies that anomalous genes and toxins do not contribute to autism. Notably, when treatment programmes focus on increasing adult contingency, children's behaviour improved.

Based on this review, we offer a hypothesis regarding the aetiology of autism that is multi-causal, strengths-based, and developmentally dynamic (meaning the system could be changed even after it is in motion). We propose that autism may be a symptom cluster that reflects a misconnection between the intra-personal neuro/psychological levels and the interpersonal relational level; the term 'interpersonal neurobiology' (Siegel 2012) captures this transactional state. In autism, it refers to a parent–infant mismatch with at least two distinct developmental pathways: impoverished and enriched input. Either way, the adults' input is outside the infant's zone of proximal development. When infants' readiness to signal, perceive and respond or adults' ability to attend, interpret, and respond, or both are outside the other's ZPD, then infants may not experience the temporal contingency and affective attunement necessary to facilitate some neural networks while pruning others through disuse. This will produce interpersonal ruptures which yield either repair (i.e., dyadic learning and a developmental pathway away from autism) or continuing mismatch and the mutual discomfort (i.e., a dyadic pathway toward autism).

This hypothesis focuses attention on the moments of mismatch, when dyadic synchrony is ruptured. The issues are the relative frequency of these moments and the probability of dyadic repair. When the moments come too frequently and repair is infrequent, the development of the infant's brain is affected, both mothers and children feel uncomfortable in interaction, and a cycle of infants avoiding and mothers trying ineffectively to correct the problem may ensue. Given enough repetitions over many months of development, this dyadic process may result in the symptoms defined as autism.

Crucial to understanding this hypothesis is that not every case will have all or the same contributing factors. For some, infant risk (from de novo mutations, epigenetic stress factors, low birth weight, etc.) would limit infant's capacity to signal to the mother or to process and respond to maternal signals. For others, maternal risk, including the impact of past stressful experiences on maternal neurophysiology and behaviour, would lead to misattuned maternal behaviour. In many cases, child and maternal factors would interact. Nevertheless, all would contain the crucial element of the infant not being able to experience temporal contingency and affective attunement in interaction with the parent. Once this process is in place and with repeated lack of successful repair, the cycle of infant avoidance and parent 'chase' may take on a life of its own, being discerned by parents early on and becoming visible to professional as the symptoms of autism by the second year of life. Inherent in this hypothesis is that there are multiple points at which the cycle could be changed by addressing critical dangers affecting families.

This conceptualization moves toward a nosology defined by both aetiology (as called for by Insel and Wang, 2010) and functional psychological processes (that can be addressed by treatment), but leaves some important questions unanswered. Why are boys affected more than girls? If older fathers' de novo genetic changes on the Y chromosome were a factor, they would affect boys, not girls. If mothers' stress or depression were related to prior negative experiences with males, that might affect sons more than daughters. If boys were preferred, that might result in more concern about slight variation in boys' development. The point is that anything that singled boys out might, under the scrutiny of a highly attentive parent, yield a cycle of disappointment. What about fathers and families? Too little is known. What about the 80 per cent of siblings who will not be diagnosed with autism? Are they really okay or are some caregivers for their mothers or autistic siblings? Finally, what about affect? Affect, particularly parent–infant attunement (Stern 2000), has received little attention in studies of autism. Finally, if combinations of these factors contribute to diagnoses of autism, is it necessary to blame anyone for the unintended consequences?

We hope this hypothesis and the unanswered questions can generate a new wave of research that combines many levels of causation (from genetic to biological, psychological, relational, and contextual/cultural) to form a fuller understanding of a complex condition. Even before then, we hope our ideas can enable clinicians to rethink their approach to families with a child with a diagnosis of autism.

A case of autism prior to diagnosis

Daniele and his mother

This long discussion leads us back to Randy and his father. We never met Randy himself, but his father chatted with us about his son for almost an hour. As we talked, we recalled viewing videotaped interactions of mothers with infants who would later be diagnosed as autistic. The striking features of this description of these recorded interactions are the normality of both infant and mother behaviour, the frequency of lack of connection, and the lack of repair of the ruptures. Indeed the lack of connection is so pervasive that connection is almost entirely absent. What is present, however, is hope on both the baby's and mother's part. Daniele and his mother are both eager to find and please each other.

This three-minute CARE-Index interaction was taken a year before there were concerns about autism. It opened with 8-month-old Daniele on his back in a playpen and his mother reaching down to shake a stuffed rabbit over him. She bounced it on his chest and up to his chin. Then she paused and pulled the toy back a bit. Daniele looked up, past the rabbit, at his mother as she leaned down and he smiled. She smiled back and, almost immediately, jiggled the rabbit between them. Daniele's smile faded and he looked at the toy with displeasure. His mother continued to smile; her smile was big, bright, and unchanging, and at such a distance that it was not personal to Daniele. Instead, it seemed vaguely inclusive of the camera person.

Daniele's mother touched him softly from time to time, but not in response to any signal from Daniele. By the time Daniele had oriented to the unexpected touch, it was finished and his mother had straightened up. Daniele hadn't caught her brief moment of availability and, in the aftermath, they both looked empty. Daniele's mother vocalized frequently, but her voice seemed loud compared to the silences between vocalizations; she didn't seem to expect Daniele to respond and she herself didn't respond when he made sounds. At times it was very quiet and his mother filled the quiet with the sounds of wind-up toys. Daniele tried to find a focus. At one point, his mother wound up a music toy behind and above his head; he tried to look up to see the source of the sound, but could not move his head back far enough.

Over the three minutes, Daniele's mother became increasingly agitated, shaking more toys in front of her son and winding up toys that hung on the sides of the playpen. She found a toy camera and mimed adjusting the camera so she could take Daniele's picture. She smiled at the camera person as she did this, as if she were showing off her son, but Daniele was oblivious to what was happening.

As the three minutes drew to a close, Daniele's mother picked her son up, but turned him away from her body. She kissed his head several times, from behind and without any signal to him. Daniele did not respond.

Careful observation indicated that Daniele was responding to specific stimuli and that his one smile was elicited by and directed to his mother's face. His mother continued to try to reach him, but her pace was too fast and she missed his signals. If we counted behaviours, both were normal, but they did not connect temporally, in turn-taking sequences, nor affectively in mutual attunement. Instead, Daniele turned away and his mother 'evaporated' as if she felt uncomfortable being viewed by her son. Instead, she pushed her baby forward as the person to be viewed. This case is similar to the longitudinal case reported by Dawson et al. (2000) in showing the early social alertness and responsivity of the baby; our case is unique for giving information about the mother's interactive behaviour.

A hypothesis. Taking these observations and the review of the literature into account, we wonder if these caring parents needed care themselves, but did not know how to invite or accept attention. Possibly, they were uncomfortable with sustained and reciprocal social interaction. Their apparent availability, combined with unpredictable stimulation, may have demanded high attention from their babies while yielding few contingent patterns and little affective attunement. We think that a family-centred perspective, embedded in a hierarchy of biological through cultural systems and focusing on interpersonal behaviour, may offer opportunities for understanding and treatment that our current focus on the biological aspects of children's pathology alone cannot. Before recommending any specific approach to treatment (other than improved contingency), we suggest family-focused research. Such research would address interpersonal processes, parents' past experiences and the meanings they have drawn from it, the impact of past experiences on biological systems, and the role of fathers and siblings in family functioning. We especially would like to see research on facial expression, touch, and other aspects of affect attunement. The gaps in what we know are so great – and therefore so open to misunderstanding – that a new research initiative is needed.

Summary of constructs and treatment principles

Constructs

1   *Knowledge, communication, and organization*: Preschool-aged children's new competencies in terms of knowledge, communication (verbal and especially non-verbal) and organization of behaviour force their relationship with

their families to acquire a hierarchical organization (authoritative, authoritarian, permissive, or alternately authoritarian and permissive).

2   *Adaptation*: New self-protective strategies are organized by children with depressed, strict, and permissive parents. Strategic functioning reflects the most adaptive choice in terms of how to deal with the dangers in the environment, based on maturation, direct experience, and cultural knowledge.

3   *Family processes*: Triadic complexity in the family organization can lead to differentiated strategic responses. However, when complex conditions are not visible to the child, triangulating processes can lead children to erroneous cognitive predictions (and disorders). Usually, in such cases, no single family member has a clear knowledge of the full process.

4   *Personal or borrowed language*: Preschool children's use of language reflects their parents' greater competence and hierarchical dominance: if the parent doesn't acknowledge the child's perspective, the shared language will reflect the parent's perspective and their rules about what is speakable and not speakable.

5   *Compulsive strategies*: Compulsive caregiving (Type A3) and compulsive compliance (Type A4) are strategies based on: (1) the inhibition of negative affect to prevent its dangerous interactive outcomes and (2) the display of compelled behaviours (false positive affect, behaviours that are positive from the parents' perspective) to elicit parents' positive attention or avoid punishment. The strategies reduce parents' distance or unavailability (A3) and punishment and violence (Type A4).

6   *Coercive strategies*: Coercive strategies (Types C1–2, C3–4) are based on the alternation of split displays of invulnerability (aggression) and vulnerability (fear and desire for comfort). Children use the strategy to increase parents' predictability.

Treatment principles

1   *Assessment*: Attachment patterns are self-protective strategies organized on context-specific experience. Assessing strategies enables professionals to look at how family members make sense of their experience of danger and seeking safety.

2   *Intervention and harm*: Interventions that are not developmentally, ecologically or culturally informed, or do not acknowledge the critical danger a family is facing may decrease adaptation and increase suffering and symptomatic behaviour.

3   *Overlooked children*: Children using compulsive Type A strategies successfully may be exposed to danger within their family, but are often overlooked by professionals. Type A strategies function by hiding evidence of problems.

4   *Overlooked families*: Children using obsessively coercive Type C strategies successfully are likely to be viewed by professionals as individually problematic while the complex family issues that underlie the strategy are likely to be overlooked. This is consistent with Type C strategies aiming to focus the parents' attention on the child.

5   *Family concerns*: Focusing treatment on either biological or interpersonal factors leaves families alone to cope with the interaction of all factors.

4 Four- to five-year-olds: Confidence, competence, and other kids

Cousins Gianni and Maria are turning 4 and 5 years old. What a joy they are! They know so much already. They can hold conversations, they dress and feed and bathroom themselves, they play games and know what is safe and what isn't. They sleep through the night! Not only that, but their parents are beginning to feel competent, like old hands at raising children.

What a perfect moment to have a new baby! In many families, the second baby comes along about three years after the first, that is, a year or so after the first baby stops breast-feeding. The timing is as good as it can get because the older child is now much more independent and needs less direct attention than does a baby. Moreover, the parents really are more competent. They will be able to manage the second infant with much more ease than they did with the first.

Of course, their new-born sibling is the most important change of all; he or she will turn their cosy, single-child world upside down. But there are other new relationships as well. There's grandma and grandpa and Aunt Margherita and Uncle Lorenzo and ever so many cousins . . . Yes, they've been there all along, but now they are coming into focus for Gianni and Maria and their influence on the children's development is felt directly. Plus mamma and papa have friends – and now their children are becoming playmates for Gianni and Maria. These new friendships will carry the children from house to house and yard to yard. Keeping Gianni and Maria safe and keeping their playtimes happy and peaceful will require new social skills for the children and management skills for their parents.

Siblings

Becoming a big brother or big sister: a child's perspective

Pregnancy and birth

Change in the family begins when mama becomes pregnant; once her husband knows, the family begins to change. A mental place is being made for a new baby and this diverts attention and feelings away from the first-born toward something invisible. As parents try to prepare their child for the new baby, they talk about 'a baby in mama's tummy'. They hope to make the coming child real and precious to their first-born by having him or her feel the baby move and helping to select new toys, etc. But nothing can prepare a first-born preschool child for a sibling, especially not for mama going to hospital and the flurry of attention she and the new baby will receive. The central discovery of first-born children when a sibling is born is that the world does not revolve around them.

Caregiving or jealousy

The first challenge for parents is to define a role for their preschooler with regard to the new baby. With enough parental understanding, bad feelings can be named and responded to with empathy. 'Are you feeling a bit jealous? I can understand. Let's find a toy just for you ...' The child's desire to help can be accepted with both praise and reasonable limits while the parent still maintains a caregiving role to the older child. 'Thank you! Bringing me the towel is a big help! Do you want to get your tea set ready and I'll come play with you after the baby falls asleep? That will be our time.'

As the baby grows up, the relationship with older siblings changes. Toddlers are both more irksome and also more interesting for an older sibling than a baby. Children quarrel endlessly about siblings messing with their things and toddlers are superb at messing with things. Such disputes invite the intervention of parents. Older siblings will be expected to show more emotional control and be less demanding emotionally than toddlers. They may be expected to be able to defer their attention-seeking to appropriate times and not be as reactive as the toddler. How these expectations are managed by the parents will have important consequences, for example, in setting the siblings against each other or helping them to forge warm bonds that will last a lifetime.

A major function of parents with two or more children is to shape the functioning of the 'sibling subsystem'. Too much involvement, with moment-to-moment micromanagement, and the boundary between children and adults will be blurred. Too little and the children might not find their way into a shared relationship and, instead, fight among themselves for the attention of their parents. As always, balance between the extremes is needed and parents are crucial in promoting this.

Adapting to a more complex context

Parents who focused excessively on the baby's expressed attachment needs (see Chapter 3, permissive parenting) often have problems when the second baby arrives. When parents cannot be so attentive because there are two children, excessive focus on satisfying all expressed needs can lead to very demanding (C3) or very helplessly appealing (C4) children. When parents try to meet every whim of their children, they are likely to become both more unpredictable and also exhausted and frustrated. If their frustration flips into angry outbursts and commands, the effect can confuse the child. The child's demanding or helpless strategy does not seem to be working so they, in turn, flip to the opposite half of the coercive strategy; they suddenly become charmingly coy and helplessly needy (if they had been demanding) or angry (if they had been disarming). Some of these children will show up in doctor's offices with behaviour or somatic problems; others might elicit sexual advances from men who confuse the meaning of coy invitations (signalling desire for comfort) with flirtatious sexual invitations (Abrahams 1994).

Other parents give excessive weight to respect, discipline, and approved behaviour; these more authoritarian parents use strict rules and punishments. Their preschoolers quickly find the role the parents prefer: independence with few demands (Type A1), independence, but with a bit of resentment showing – and redirected to the self (Type A2); caregiving to her mother (Type A3), being mother's helper to the baby (Type A3 parental), high achieving (Type A4⁻), or compliant (Type A4). Very few children with stricter than usual parents will be referred to professionals because they satisfy – and do not irritate – adults. Nevertheless, some of these children will be on a pathway to problems of excessive inhibition of negative feelings and personal desires; their strategies can have repercussions in adolescence and adulthood when self-generated plans and intimacy become important.

Maybe father will use the arrival of a new baby as an opportunity to begin a more direct relationship with the older child, one that is not mediated so much by his wife. This can be really good, giving a boy a masculine role model or guiding a girl to appreciate her femininity. In both cases, something new and special with the father is gained, just as something with mother is slipping away. On the other hand, dad might come too close, offer too much comfort or even want too much intimacy. This can be the worrisome side of a change that could have been so desirable.

These seem like big changes in the organization of the family – and they are. But they are shaped, often without anyone's awareness, in the accumulation of moment-to-moment daily exchanges between parents and children.

Sibling attachment

Older siblings often take a protective role toward the baby in a one-sided relationship in which the baby does not yet take a conscious role. Over time, this special relationship between two related peers living in the same family deepens and becomes mutual. When one is upset, the other can understand. When other children attack one sibling, the other siblings defend him or her. In addition, watching their siblings with the parents gives children a different perspective on their parents. Is my mother really an angry woman – or is it me who makes her angry? If I disobeyed her, what would she do? Will Dad carry out his threats? How bad could it get? This can provide a window through which a child can gain a more balanced and less self-influenced understanding of the parents. Of course, it will take a lifetime to sort out what your sibling is really like, what you are really like, and how your parents, separately and together, contributed to this. Nevertheless, this process begins with intuitive observations of parents when they are interacting with your sibling.

Sibling attachment is quite different from child–parent attachment because it is symmetrical with regard to power. Although it will be a long time before it becomes reciprocal with regard to protection and comfort, that essential process has begun. However, when families are seriously distressed and especially if there is danger in the family, siblings may be in competition for what little parental protection and comfort there is. Life-long struggles can ensue or silence can create gaps that cannot be bridged. Over and over in the AAIs of troubled adults seeking treatment or facing problems with the law or child protection, we hear of brothers and sisters who no longer see or even speak to each other.

Usually, however, sibling relationships begin forming at 4–5 years old and endure for a lifetime. Walter was 3 years old when his sister Wendy was born; he was excited, but in much the same way as when the family got a new dog – except his sister wasn't much fun to play with. Three years later, when he was 5½, his baby brother Will was born. This time Walter had waited for six months with increasing anticipation, watching his mothe's belly grow and grow. He had shown a burst of personal pride when Will finally appeared. It was as if he had accomplished this miracle and he wanted all the world to know that he was a Big Brother. He was a tender and protective big brother, listening for Will's cry, advising his parents on Will's needs, and dashing off to get a toy, a clean diaper, or a fresh shirt for his baby brother.

Even at 5½, his relationship with his sister (who was now 3) was still cool; they were usually like differently aged friends doing the same things, sometimes in parallel and sometimes in competition. They ran to the swings at the same time, they squabbled over the plate of cookies. Wendy looked up to and followed her brother, but being older, faster, and better able to anticipate what would happen next, Walter usually got there first, got the best, and led the way. He was focused on what he was doing while Wendy was focused on him. She became tough and demanding, trying to keep up with her big brother.

With Will, Walter was very different. He took Will 'under his wing' and became protective of him. He held Will tenderly and played with him gently, doing things that pleased Will, even though they weren't really interesting to 5-year-olds. Already, Walter was managing four major attachment relationships (with his two parents and two siblings) and each was different. Add his four grandparents, and three aunts (with husbands) and his adolescent cousin, who all lived nearby and shared in his upbringing, and Walter was developing the array of attachment relationships within his family that would prepare him for the complexity of family life and for life outside his family.

For Will, everything was simple. As he was passed from one set of arms to another, he felt how the bodies held him. He looked up and found eyes. At that point, the dyadic process of creating contingencies and experiencing affective attunement began (see Chapter 1). With each family member, the experience was a bit different. Although Will wasn't yet attached to anyone, he experienced vividly the different styles of the bonds family members were forming with him. He relaxed with Walter, but felt Wendy's more fleeting and less attuned touch. Already, he too was sorting out his different experiences with the members of his family.

Box 4.1   Attachments in 4- to 5-year-old children

- *Parents*: Less non-symmetrical and non-reciprocal.
- *Non-parental adult figures (including grandparents)*: Less non-symmetrical and non-reciprocal.
- *Siblings*: Symmetrical and non-reciprocal.

Learning to manage two at a time: the parents' perspective

Differentiating needs from desires and managing different developmental needs at one time

Children cannot differentiate what they want from what they need so they ask for both with the same intensity. It is the parents' responsibility to decide who needs their attention at which moment. The task is more complex with children at different ages because their needs and ability to understand rules will be different. Younger infants will require more physical (procedural and sensory) input, whereas older ones can be reassured and guided by words and integrative advice.

Parents who try to be continually responsive to children's signals are unlikely to be able to stand back and think about the children's real needs. Some parents find that children's distress makes them too uncomfortable; they must act immediately. Others try to implement a 'corrective script' (Byng-Hall 1995); these parents find negative aspects in their own parents' behaviour that they don't want their children to experience. They form a semantic DR (the corrective script) that their own parenting should 'correct' these aspects of parenting for their children. Sometimes, parents using corrective scripts overshoot the mark, that is, they swing to the opposite style of parenting, 'pendulum parenting' (Crittenden, 2008). For example, a parent who regards her parents as having been authoritarian and distant seeks the diametric opposite and becomes excessively permissive and emotionally connected with her children, being unaware that the opposite of something bad can present an equally great, but different, problem for children. Either way, when needs and desires get confused, some children learn to heighten their demands, and others become quiet, unable to compete with their more insistent siblings. Ironically, the children who seem most effective at getting parental attention often seem least satisfied with what they get. Maybe this is because they know that their parents' attention must be maintained and that their real need, that of knowing that their parents are in control and able to evaluate and meet their children's needs, is unfulfilled?

Even when parents evaluate well, it can be difficult to meet the needs of several children, each in a different ZPD. The eldest, most cautious, child might need to be encouraged to take risks while the second-born might need to slow down and think ahead, and the youngest, the baby of the family, might need to become more competent and independent. Parents must not only adapt their behaviour to each child, but also be sure that each child knows that they all are being treated fairly.

This is a tall order that can be difficult to fill, but some conditions make it even more difficult. When there is only one parent, when one child has exceptional needs, and when both parents work and come home tired, it can be difficult to meet family members' needs. The point is that family life involves compromises between what is wanted and what can be managed. When parents are both predictable and empathic, they promote independence and patience in their children.

The best outcomes involve parents standing back from time to time to consider everyone's needs and developmental readiness. This is where parents' greater mental maturity becomes essential. Young children cannot reflect on their own experience, far less on that of others, but adults can. Nevertheless, in Parents Interviews and AAIs that we have read, it appears than many parents – and essentially all parents of troubled children – do not have even a tentative idea of how they want to raise their children. Without calm moments of thoughtful reflection, parents are forced to react on a moment's notice. This is not the best way to meet children's long-term needs, or to balance the needs of different family members.

Sharing the job/spousification of children

Even more than when the first baby was born, parents in families with two or more children need to share the jobs of raising the children, earning an income, and caring for the house, car, garden, etc. Again, well-functioning two-parent families have an advantage. More hands, more skills, and greater confidence in the durability of relationships promote family harmony.

When parents must function without the advantage of a helpful partner, or where one or both adults have intense needs (for example, illnesses, addictions or depression), adaptations must be made. Sometimes the family can expand to include a grandparent, unmarried aunt or uncle, or other parental adult. Sometimes one child, often the oldest, is put in charge of the younger children. When inadequate support is given or when the child must give up developmentally appropriate activities of their own (for example, friendships, finishing school), then the child is considered 'parentified' (Jurkovic 1998;

Byng-Hall 2002). Parental children resolve the parent's problem, but do so at the expense of their own development and their younger siblings' safety. Of course, helping with younger children is an advantage to everyone when the older child is supervised, when the tasks required are in the older child's ZPD, and when the older child's own developmental progress is not constrained. Finally, some parents need the emotional support of an adult partner and, lacking that, look for it in a child. Single mothers are especially likely to 'spousify' a son; fathers left with too much responsibility may spousify a daughter (Minuchin 1974).

Strategic choices for the second child/attachment in a family context

The oldest child has become a master at regulating the parents with one or another of the DMM self-protective strategies. If that strategy is Type B, there's plenty of opportunity for all the children to organize Type B strategies. The Type B strategy is about expressing oneself clearly and engaging with others about one's desires and needs; everybody in a family can be equally competent at that when their development and personality are treated sensitively. But if it's Type A or C, then the second-born child has a problem. He or she cannot be a better caregiver, more obedient, more effectively coercive, etc. than the older sibling. Often the second-born goes for the opposite strategy. My big brother is the family good boy? I'll be the bad boy! Some of this, of course, is tied to temperament and birth order doesn't explain everything, but it remains the case that first- and second-born children are born into very different families (Dunn 1991) and often organize very different strategies (see Rupert and Rob Ruggles, Chapter 5).

We think that is to be expected. When one moves from a dyadic notion of the mother's strategy being transmitted directly to her children (Main et al. 1985), it becomes obvious that each child grows up in a different family constellation. Often this produces reversals in non-B strategies from mother to first-born (Hautamäki et al. 2010; Shah et al. 2010). That is, mothers using a Type A strategy usually had a first-born child using a Type C strategy – and the reverse. In clinical contexts, this becomes possibly even more complex with the child displaying problems frequently developing complex A/C combinations because there is no clear effective alternative to the strategy employed by an older sibling. Also, as we have emphasized earlier, some of the most complex problems may be associated with family systems where the parents elicit different insecure patterns from their children (for example, Rupert and Rob Ruggles, Chapter 5).

In a family constellation, both child characteristics and those of other family members affect how self-protective strategies are organized initially and modified over time. Parents routinely deal with these differences among their several children, knowing that no two are alike. There is, however, one special case that deserves mention. When one child is physically disabled, diagnosed with a psychological disorder, or maltreated, there is often the expectation that this is an isolated, child-specific event. We think that the absence of obvious and similar disorder should not be considered evidence that the siblings are okay. To the contrary, they often display opposite, compensatory strategies, but these may carry risk of different sorts (Jean-Gilles and Crittenden 1990). Often this risk is tied to an inhibitory strategy: compulsive caregiving, compulsive compliance, compulsive performance, with or without unresolved trauma and depression.

Getting to know grandma and grandpa

Someone special for me

Grandparents often have special relationships with their grandchildren. The combination of childrearing experience and lack of responsibility often gives grandparents greater freedom with their grandchildren than they felt with their own children. Especially if they are no longer working, grandparents have the time to listen to children's chatter and a readiness to take it seriously. Having extended family nearby – when all get along reasonably well – can be a boon for young children.

Staying overnight/alternate attachment figures

Very often a child's first night away from home is to stay overnight with grandparents. Sometimes, however, a child cannot leave the parents without very great distress. When this happens to a 4- or 5-year-old, many people explain it by saying that the child is shy or anxious. Instead, one should wonder whether something at home needs guarding.

Ana's first night away

Ana, aged 5 years, for example, was going to stay overnight with her granny. It was to be her first time away from her parents and the trip had been planned and talked about for weeks. Ana's best friend, the little girl who lived next door, was coming too. Although it wasn't her granny, she knew Ana's granny very well from her many visits to play at Ana's house. When the day came, Ana's friend came running out of her house, overnight bag in her hand, and hopped into the granny's car. Ana stood in front of her house, her bag on the ground beside her. Her mother encouraged her and put the bag in the car. But Ana stood still. She looked longingly at the car, her friend, and her granny. But she didn't budge! A thousand explanations and encouragements were given, but she didn't budge. Her longing expression changed to sadness and eventually the car pulled away with her friend and without her. She entered her house sad and confused. She didn't know why she couldn't go.

Was she really that fearful? Surely the description that Ana was fearful fit what everyone knew about her, but no one had an explanation for either this event or for her overall shyness. Years later, when she entered therapy as a depressed and angry adult, this memory came back. At that future time, however, her recall had a familial context. Her mother had been chronically depressed. Her parents' marriage had always been near divorce. She had been her mother's caregiver – and her father's as well.

Was that true as early as the preschool years? Ana couldn't know for sure, her memory didn't have the needed details, but she knew she could not recall any time when it hadn't been true.

Possibly Ana was not afraid of what would happen to herself if she went with her granny, but she had no such recall. Possibly, instead, she was afraid of what would happen to or between her parents if she were not there to oversee the family. Her parents' inability to reassure Ana and assist her to cope with her feelings was striking. By allowing Ana to fail, the parents were both maintaining Ana's role as their carer and also allowing her to feel ashamed of herself for letting everyone down. The appearance was of a feature of Ana as a child (fearfulness) that was maladaptive to an absence of danger; the reality was that indeed the family (and Ana) faced a critical danger: the possible break-down of her mother or divorce of her parents.

The burdens of being a caregiving child can be both heavy and invisible. In Ana's case, they came to be attributed to her character, her personality, and it would be many, many years later before anyone would question that obvious, but vacuous, explanation. Until that time, family history, relabelled as 'Ana's personality', would trap her in a developmental pathway filled with sadness and isolation.

Some babies don't live – and that changes the whole family

Death is the ultimate danger; it is the event that everything else is meant to prevent. Of all the deaths we wish to avoid, the death of a child is possibly the most painful to bear. Even with recent reductions in infant mortality, some babies die within the first year of life (4.91/1000 in the UK and 6.81/1000 in the USA; Wikipedia: List of countries by infant mortality rate). Even more painful are stillbirths (1 in 100 births in developed countries and higher in undeveloped countries) or miscarriages (cumulative risk of 11–22 per cent between 5–20 weeks of gestation) (Say et al. 2006; Ammon Avalos et al. 2012). Another cluster of babies is born with a serious, life-changing handicapping condition (Lobo and Zhaurova 2008). When the baby dies or is seriously disabled, the parent experiences a loss that will affect all the other children. The effect is especially troubling when the living, healthy children do not understand the situation.

There is often a special effect when a first-born baby dies. Many parents are so heartbroken that, when the next pregnancy comes, they dare not believe in it. They might hold their emotions in check and this affects their psychological preparation for the baby. Depending upon when the first baby was lost, this might last for the entire pregnancy, well into the next infant's early childhood, or for all of that child's life. Sometimes, when the early death cannot be spoken about, an invisible shadow is cast over the family. Too often the first living child bears an unannounced burden; he or she must become all that the parents imagine that they lost. Alternatively, the child may learn not to get close to people – because the parents, after losing one child, were adverse to touching and attaching to another. Or the child may become the comforter and consoler of the parent – and this may occur without the child even knowing the source of the parent's sorrow.

Learning to care for your parents

Maija was born a year after her twin sisters. One twin lived, but with extreme brain damage; the other was stillborn. Maija and her family came to attention through the educational service for Maija's disabled older sibling. She was videotaped playing with her father as an example of a normative dyad. (Her mother had declined to be video-taped and watched from just out of sight.) Maija sat in a chair; her father knelt on the floor in front of her; they were playing ball. Dad tossed the ball gently to Maija and Maija caught it and laughed. This went on for a few minutes with slight variations. Was there a problem?

There was. A major problem, really. Maija was afraid to let her father approach her! She slipped away from every moment of possible closeness, especially when he leaned in close to her. Slow-motion viewing of the video showed that Maija's ball catching was pieced together in jerky segments: ball lands near Maija, then she reaches, then she smiles, then she laughs. But these things did not happen together; they happened in sequence, as if Maija had to remember, one act at a time, how to fake happiness. Her smile was tense, limited to her mouth (and not including her eyes), and fleeting; as soon as she had smiled, she looked away and sadness filled her face. Her laugh was shrill, sudden, and suddenly silent; it felt choked. Her father was totally centred on her; his eyes never left her; he seemed to hang on her slightest move; his body movements mirrored hers. He seemed to adore her. Close viewing of him showed that they mutually agreed not to look, not to touch, and to appear close without being close. His face, however, never lost its look of adoring hope.

If one only noticed Maija's physical well-being and her sister's disability, one would misunderstand this family. Maija's mother was deeply depressed: a dead child and a profoundly disabled child to remind her daily of what was lost. Maija's father placed his hope in her, but dared not touch her – as if he feared that she might disintegrate and disappear. Maija didn't know about the death and took her disabled sister as she was. She had no understanding of grief, nor could she name depression. But she felt the invisible barriers that separated her from her parents and wasn't yet old enough to wonder how she could be treasured and abandoned in the same moment. Without the concept of compulsive caregiving and an understanding of the effects of parents' unresolved loss on children, we might have thought all was well with Maija. With an understanding of family systems, including families with deceased members, we could see that the some of the intense professional effort being expended on Maija's sister needed to be redirected to her parents and herself.

This family needed a family-level intervention and the only entry to service was the disabled child. A frequent dynamic in families with losses is that the parents drift away from each other emotionally. It sometimes looks as if they are frightened to be alone together because there would be no distraction from their shared grief. When a parent, such as Maija's father, turns to a child for emotional support, a systemic process can begin in which the distance between him and his wife increases and possibly also between daughter and mother. Why did his wife not want to be videotaped? The predictable answer is because she 'was depressed'. But the depression may not be solely about the twins; it might be aggravated by resentment at seeing her husband so preoccupied with their daughter. Of course she wants him to be close to their daughter, but she may also feel inexpressible anger at why he seems not to care about her, his wife and their daughter's mother. Such mixed feelings can be very difficult to articulate.

Although the disabled baby has needs, so do Maija and her parents. Too much attention to one person can blind us to other problems. If the parents fracture as a couple, they may not be able to help any of their children. If one turns to their child for support, new problems may develop. A helpful intervention can be to suggest to them that they need time for themselves as a couple. Although they would resist this suggestion, they might agree to it for Maija's sake. Treatment of the disabled child should encompass assisting the parents to avoid chronic depression, spousification of the living child, and possibly even family break-up. Had such attention been given to Mrs Freeman's needs (see Chapter 1) when her daughter was young, she might have been less intensely reactive when her grandson was born.

Change, families, and culture

All families and cultures change, but usually the process is too gradual to notice. When change comes rapidly, it can be disruptive, pitting old and new values and ways of being against one another.

Across the world, non-technological cultures are racing at breakneck speed into modern life. In the process, hunting and agrarian families are moving to cities, the knowledge base is moving from the old to the young and old ways are being replaced by new ways that challenge tradition. Africa and Asia are changing rapidly; the Middle East is erupting with the tension between old and new. Basic family functions adapt. Fathers who used to hunt often work far away from their families. Mothers who stayed home now have jobs. Technology is replacing people.

Even something as simple as the naming of children can express this jolting forward of culture (cf. Crittenden and Morrison, 1988). Three years ago, when she was born in a tiny bush village in Botswana, Boitumelo was named in honour of her father's mother. In Setswana, her name and her grandmother's name mean 'happiness'; three generations were tied together in joy and love. When her sister Tracy was born in Maun, a young and bustling city in Botswana, she was given a 'modern' name, one without a specified meaning, but filled nevertheless with the ideas of cultural change and embracing the future. Three thin years separated two sisters and a traditional family from a family reaching for a new kind of future. Such families, living all over the world, face greater threats than families in more stable cultures, both traditional and modern.

Immigration from one country to another pits hope for change against the often unexpected conditions of change. Often the emigrating family expected to be released from experienced constraints or even dangers, but thought relatively little about the culture to which they were fleeing. When familiar and safe ways of raising children are brought to a foreign culture, they may be applied out of their context of adaptation. This can bring immigrant families in contact with mental health and child protection systems. In many cases, the parents are offended and feel justified in what they do. Moreover, the more threatened they feel, the more they will use their traditional child-protective strategies. Making the mismatch of traditional practices to those suited to the new context explicit can help to ease the accusations from the receiving country's authorities. Recognizing that many emigrants flee danger and arrive with unresolved trauma can further reduce misunderstandings.

In less threatening circumstances, children often provide a bridge between their parents and the new culture. Children acquire the new language quickly and often use this skill to negotiate the cultural shift for their parents. This form of caregiving is common among immigrant children, especially the older ones. Ironically, as the children, and later their children, adapt to the new culture, they often become distant from the old culture. Grandchildren may not be able to talk with their grandparents – and their behaviour may make them seem foreign. Easing this transition, when professional systems become involved, requires someone with a sensitive understanding of culture (in general) and an eagerness to learn about the new culture (in particular) and to re-view one's own culture, as seen through foreign eyes. Family and systemic therapists are well prepared to take on this task of separating the universal functions of families from the strategies they learned implicitly in one context, but applied in another.

When there are problems

The changes discussed above, both in children's competences and in families' cultural and economic circumstances, often mean that children aged 4–5 are required to attend preschools or other forms of out-of-home day care. This gives them opportunities to practise relationships with peers, but it also pressures them towards some developmental tasks (discussed in Chapter 5) usually more easily accomplished during the 5–7-year developmental transition. In these circumstances, families face many problems because children protest the separations or because the family as a whole is not ready to have the child out of home.

For many parents, this is an opportunity to return to work or engage in activities for themselves. Others become aware that time is moving on and that that their 'baby' is going out already into the big world. Feelings about the child growing up and the changes that this brings may become confused with the parent's own feelings of loss and loneliness. If a child has become very central to one parent's emotional well-being, the child starting preschool can indicate a loss for the parent. A child may feel the mother's distress and develop 'symptoms' to avoid the separation and thus, in a caregiving way, protect them both from anxiety (Bowlby 1973). Children whose parents have been in conflict may also be anxiously preoccupied that their parents are safe.

If a child uses a Type C strategy, separation nullifies the strategy and is therefore difficult and anxiety-provoking. As helplessness is more acceptable in girls, boys who have relied on the feigned helpless strategy at home may do less well in out-of-home settings. Boys who display coy and helpless behaviour at school may be labelled a 'mummy's boy' by peers and may be ridiculed or teased. The use of the aggressive component of the coercive strategy also has risks: it is unlikely to be tolerated by the teacher, may lead to punishment, and if the angry behaviour persists, to exclusion from non-familial social groups. Not infrequently such a scenario can be accompanied with formulations and diagnosis that the child is displaying ADHD or 'conduct disorder' (see Chapter 5). Children who had been developing a compulsive performing or compliant, or even caregiving strategy will face different challenges. Although these children will be liked by non-familial adults since they adhere to rules and try to please, they may find it difficult to ask for help, to articulate emotional distress, and when help is needed, they may suffer in silence.

Mummy's boy

Presenting problem

Majella met with the school counsellor to discuss whether her 5-year-old son Billy needed referral to a psychologist for treatment of his extreme shyness. Billy's mother was worried that Billy was fragile and that he might not cope well with starting school. She was considering holding him back a year. At the current preschool, Billy wasn't mixing with the other children and at the end of each day he resisted staying in the playground to play and wanted to go home with his mother. The preschool teacher said Billy hadn't mastered the task of following rules and instructions and needed a lot of her attention. Even at home, Billy was struggling. When family friends dropped in, he wouldn't talk to them and told them to go away when they tried to join in the games that

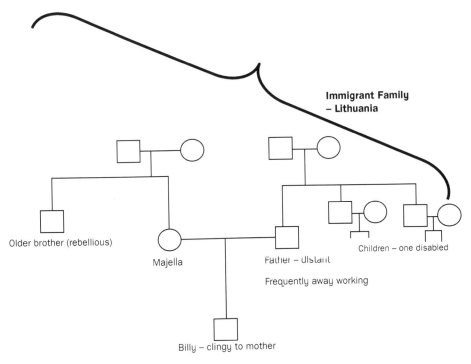

Figure 4.1 Billy's family genogram.

he played with his mother. Billy looked very frail; he cried easily, seemed anxious and fearful, and needed coaxing to participate in age-appropriate activities.

Family history. As he usually did, the counsellor first talked with Billy's mother. After hearing about Billy's problems, he probed Majella's history. Majella had immigrated with her family from Lithuania when she was an adolescent, but she couldn't remember why her parents had chosen to leave (Figure 4.1). Even now she relied on their advice and tried to meet their expectations. When recounting her early experiences, Majella repeatedly commented that her parents were the best possible parents a child could have. Nevertheless, she had found it hard to find her own direction in adulthood. After completing a number of academic degrees, she still didn't know what she really wanted to do, and she had married late, finding a husband who fit her notion of what her parents wanted. He ran a business to support the family, worked long hours, and was often away.

Although Majella said nothing about being fearful, she had seen what could happen if her parents' expectations were not met. Her older brother's marriage to an atheist had caused a rift within the family. Her parents had not acknowledged her brother's wife and his children did not know their grandparents. Her brother lived his life separate from the rest of the family, and conversations between him and Majella were usually strained. To the counsellor, Majella's semantic descriptions of her childhood family seemed idealized; her spare episodic recall suggested a learned pattern of inhibition of negative recall, except the clear warning of the cost of her brother's non-compliance. He wondered whether inhibition of her feelings and recall plus generalized respect for her parents, combined with the example of her brother, functioned to enable Majella to stay within the safe limits of parental approval.

Assessment. Billy's preschool teacher reported that Majella treated Billy like a much younger child and that she was excessively attentive, responding to his every whim. Billy used displays of helplessness to elicit his mother's attention. For example, though he was perfectly capable of climbing onto the play gym, when his mother was present he would suddenly become wobbly and need her help. Likewise, even though Billy needed practice playing and sharing with other children after preschool, his mother would take him home as soon as he began to cling and to whine that he wanted to go home. The teacher had witnessed a number of occasions when Majella had tried not to allow Billy to get his own way; for example, she had taken away a broken toy because it was dangerous. Billy had thrown a tantrum. His mother had given in and then held him tenderly until he quieted. Strikingly Majella's conversations with the school counsellor were all about freedom and creativity: what choices she should make for her children to maximize their free expression and independence from rigid rules.

Formulation. Billy used coy and helpless behaviour (Type C4 strategy) to regulate his relationship with his mother. Intermittently, he also resorted to throwing tantrums, reflecting the aggressive half of his coercive strategy (Type C3). The counsellor thought that Majella's permissiveness with her son reflected a reversal (that is, 'pendulum parenting') with regards to her own childhood experience where she had had to comply with parental expectations or risk rejection. Although she pushed away her childhood feelings of being constrained and emotionally limited, she enacted her desire for emotional freedom through her son. She was excessively attuned and responsive to his signalled needs and found it difficult to provide predicate external controls and authority, saying that she feared oppressing him.

The critical danger for this family was the confusion between Majella's and Billy's childhood conditions, which was not understood and corrected by either of his parents. Majella had been born into a Catholic family who had continued to practise their faith in the context of a political oppression where religious behaviour was punishable and advancement was not possible without Communist Party membership. Like many people in Soviet-dominated countries, her parent had valued closeness with dependency and without aggressiveness while also harbouring an unspoken resentment of authority and a secret desire to undercut it. Billy's current cultural context, in a safe Western democracy, was very different. People there valued independence and open expression of feelings, even strong disagreement. Majella's confusion about these cultural value systems showed even in Billy's name. 'Billy' was a doubly foreign name, being both an Anglo name and a nickname. This suggested that semantically she wanted Billy to embrace his future in a safer country than Lithuania, while nevertheless, procedurally, she continued to raise him in preparation for her childhood context.

Treatment. The school counsellor reminded Majella that she had the two months of holidays to prepare Billy for school. He suggested that Billy was fragile because he had not been practising a range of skills: letting his mother take charge, respecting the limits that adults set (especially those around safety), accepting appropriate consequences for inappropriate behaviour, and cooperating with the predictability of a daily routine. He provided Majella with a copy of a parenting programme that focused on predictability; parents were advised to be in control and offered strategies for setting limits. He suggested that Majella set up a daily routine for the holidays and use it as a means to practise for the routines of school. Finally, he suggested that Majella share all of this with her husband and include him in instituting the changes in their family.

Outcome. The counsellor's statement of what Majella could do to augment her own predictability for Billy spontaneously produced support from the father, which Majella used to pursue appropriate developmental goals for her son. Billy's father, who was not an immigrant, had been aware that Billy needed to learn to manage rules and expectations like other children his age. He actively supported his wife to try the counsellor's suggestions so that they could send Billy to school, rather than holding him back for a year. With her husband's support, Majella implemented the behavioural strategies suggested by the counsellor and, over the holiday period, Billy became more robust and, as an unexpected benefit, his parents became closer and his mother became less dependent on Billy to meet her emotional needs from her past and with her husband away working. Billy's functioning further improved when he started school and was exposed to the repeating routine of the classroom and where he was expected to behave with the same politeness and respect as the other children. These changes, implementing the temporal order that had been lacking in Billy's life and Majella's willingness to work with the school, allowed sufficient reorganization of Billy's attachment strategies that he became somewhat more independent and less helplessly and aggressively coercive. Billy was able to go to school.

Intervening in a triangulated family following family separation

The presenting problem

Five-year-old Denise came with her father (Doug), older sister (Tina), and step-mother (Louise) for family therapy. They had been referred by the family doctor because Denise was displaying behavioural problems. It was reported that she shouted angrily at her step-mother (Louise) and sometimes at her sister as well. In addition, she was suffering with diabetes and her father complained about her refusal to take her insulin. The girls were living with their father and step-mother and the referral also mentioned conflict between the girls' mother (Helen) and their father (Doug) which might be related to Denise's problems.

Family history. Denise and her sister Tina had lived with their mother (Helen) and father (Doug) until one year previously (see Figure 4.2). Doug had frequently worked away, but the girls said that he had always spent time with them when he was home. The times when he was around had not been very easy because Helen had been drinking quite heavily when Doug was away and he had criticized her for not looking after the girls properly. The arguments had escalated and had reached a point where they decided to separate. Since Helen did not have somewhere suitable for her and the girls to live, it was decided that, as a 'temporary' measure, she would move out until she found a suitable living space. A half year later, both parents had new partners: Louise was married to Doug and raising Denise and Tina as her children.

Family therapy. The request for family therapy had come from Doug and Louise, hence this part of the family system was convened first, with the possibility of Helen joining at a later stage. The therapy was conducted with a team of three clinicians, a lead clinician and two colleagues who observed from behind a one-way screen. The therapy employed a reflecting team process (Andersen 1987) whereby, near the end of each session, the observing team engaged in a conversation to reflect back to the family their thoughts about family difficulties and their ideas for change. These ideas were subsequently discussed between the lead therapist and the family to summarize and consolidate the ideas from the session.

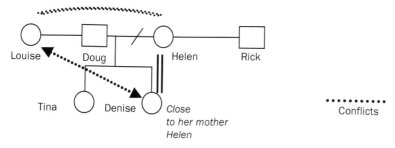

Figure 4.2 Denise's family genogram.

One of the significant contributions of observing teams is that their members are better able than the therapist to notice interactional patterns between family members and to formulate how these might be related to the individual and shared procedural, imaged, semantic, and connotative representations of family members. Their observations can be fed back to the family and the therapist in reflective conversations and this can allow discrepancies among DRs to be noted and discussed. Observing and acknowledging discrepancies among DRs form a crucial pre-condition for reflective integration and intentional change in what one does.

An important part of the early sessions in any course of therapy is to promote a sense of safety for all the members of the family. In this case, the process included a consideration of their expectations, including a discussion regarding whether they wanted to start by focusing on changing the problems (behaviours/procedures) or on gaining understanding (semantic/integrative), or a mixture of the two.

Denise's father and step-mother expressed concern about Denise's angry outbursts and hoped for some immediate change in these. The therapist noticed that Denise had come into this session holding two soft toys: One was a soft, cool blue seahorse, the other a vibrant, red and orange tiger. As the interview progressed, Denise started to describe her experience in ways that fit the imaged aspects of the two toys – sadness that could turn into anger. The therapist made a light-hearted reference to this towards the end of the session, suggesting that perhaps, like her toys, sometimes her sadness turned into anger. Denise replied, 'Yes, it is a bit like that.'

Formulation process and initial formulations. The approach to formulation drew on Palazzoli et al.'s (1978) idea of 'progressive hypothesising'. In their approach, formulation about a family is regarded as a dynamic process that is altered as new information emerges from the clinical work (feedback). This may include both further information about their individual DRs as well as information about the family dynamics that shape and maintain the DRs. An important part of the process is to describe how family dynamics contribute to the lack of integration, distortions and exclusions of information held in their individual and shared memories. By shared, we mean that family members may come to hold convergent ways of viewing the problem, most commonly a shared view that one of them 'is' or 'has' the problem. When this occurs, discrepancies in representation may be overlooked. For example, despite Denise's sister also getting angry or her father and step-mother also arguing, the shared family view was that angry Denise 'was' the family problem.

In the first session, an interactional pattern among the four members of the family became apparent: Louise did most of the talking and the girls eagerly took up the

Figure 4.3 Drawings of dragon and hands.

therapist's offer to draw, while listening and contributing when they wanted to add something. Denise drew a fiercely self-satisfied lime-coloured dragon with bright spikes down his back; Tina drew jointed multi-coloured 'love hands' that floated, without any body, in a sea of bright red hearts and yellow stars (Figure 4.3). As an assessment of imaged DRs, the drawings expressed dramatically what the girls could not say verbally. Denise and Tina didn't fight while they drew, but neither did they pay much attention to one another.

> **Louise**: She [Helen] has her own problems, she has a problem with alcohol . . .
> **Denise**: No, she doesn't, she never used to . . .
> **Doug**: When she drinks . . . her personality changes . . . that's all, Denise.
> **Tina**: When she looks after us, she'll often make us stay up late and she drinks quite a lot. It's quite scary.
> **Denise**: Yeah, it's scary, but you can't (inaudible quiet talk).
> **Therapist** (to Denise): What does that feel like? When other people say she lets you down?
> **Denise**: It makes me feel quite sad sometimes . . . cos people say things like . . . it's hard to explain.
> **Therapist**: What happens to that sadness? Does it turn into something else, does it turn into other feelings?
> **Denise**: It turns into anger . . . Sometimes, if I get angry, it turns into . . . like last few times I have been in my room and I get a bit . . .

The lead therapist remembered feeling pleased at this point in the session that a 'core repetitive pattern of interaction' (that is, a 'circularity') in the family had been drawn to the attention of the family. Denise's anger could be seen as related to her attempt to be a caregiver for her mother and this placed her in a complex triangulated position between her mother and her father/step-mother (who were angry at her mother for being 'irresponsible'). The two sisters did not join in an alliance; instead Tina appeared to side with her father and step-mother (she appeared to have adopted Louise as her mother). Possibly this was her way of avoiding the dilemma of split loyalties to her parents, but it also cost her some closeness to her sister.

An exploration of Denise's anger revealed that she tended to become angry with her step-mother and sister after having spent the weekend with her mother or talking on the phone to her. The initial systemic formulation was that Denise was entangled in the conflicts between her father/step-mother and her mother and that this split of loyalties presented a dilemma which Denise found impossible to resolve with her compulsive caregiving (Type A3) strategy. Although she tried to be a very good girl and to please everyone, the conflict between adults made this impossible: pleasing one meant disloyalty to the other. Not surprisingly, when Denise found herself in this predicament, she was overwhelmed by feelings of sadness and anger and these mixed feelings emerged in unregulated outbursts of distressed anger.

The therapist described this to Doug and Louise and suggested that it was possible that when they criticized Denise's mother, Denise experienced feelings of loyalty to her mother and became confused and unsettled by conflicting feelings. Despite this suggestion, Doug and Louise returned repeatedly to complaining about Helen, apparently ignoring this 'insight' into the 'split loyalty' underlying Denise's distressed and angry behaviour. Given that a straightforward verbalization of the formulation did not allow Doug and Louise to respond differently, i.e., their unchanged representations disposed them to the usual behaviours, another approach was needed.

Subsequent formulations. At about this time, the team members became curious as to why the girls lived with a father who was frequently away from home and who had limited time to spend with his daughters. Questions inspired by the AAI regarding the father's own childhood produced an interesting response:

Therapist (to Doug and Louise): Can you say a little bit about your family backgrounds?

Doug: Nasty . . . with my own children, I've always wanted to be a full-on parent because I never got it . . . My parents were never interested in anything I did . . . my mum and dad just fell out . . . I went to live with my dad.

Therapist: So it's a bit similar to what happened to your own children?

Doug: Yeah, but then my dad just dropped me at my grandparents and my grandparents brought me up . . .

Denise: That's not very nice (walking over to her daddy and gently touching his knee and then walking away to get on with her drawing).

This conversation brought to mind the idea of 'corrective scripts'. In DMM terms, however, Doug appeared to be drawing on semantic representations from his childhood featuring an explicit wish to 'correct' his own childhood experience, yet, procedurally, he appeared to be repeating important aspects of the paternal absence that he had experienced. However, Doug hadn't noticed this discrepancy and this omission may have been compounded by his wish to reassure Louise that she was an excellent and superior mother, as compared to his ex-wife. Again he appeared to be doing this procedurally without explicit semantic awareness that he felt she needed reassurance and also possibly that he feared losing her if Denise's anger drove her away from the family.

This progressive formulation dovetailed with the idea that Denise's A3 strategy was a response to her father. Denise seemed to be very aware of her dad's emotional state and responded by offering him comfort despite his joining with Louise to criticize both her mother (Helen) and also her own 'naughty' behaviour. The team hypothesized that Denise was attempting to employ a compulsive caregiving strategy (Type A3) with both her father and her mother; moreover, both behaved in ways that elicited caregiving from Denise. When Helen drank, Denise tried to look after her mother and, later with her father, to protect her mother from criticism. When her father experienced pain for his unresolved family of origin separations, she tried to comfort him. The recent family history suggested, however, that Denise was finding it hard to sustain a functional A3 strategy, given the conflict between her parents. It appeared Denise was not always able to inhibit her negative feelings, and that when she became overwhelmed by distress and anger (triggered by the 'no win' triangulated situation in which she found herself for trying to defend her mother while protecting her father), the unregulated anger spilled out and was directed towards Louise or her sister Tina. Louise, who was unable to understand Denise's behaviour, experienced the explosions as personal attacks.

Developing the treatment strategy. The family were seen for a further two sessions (four in total) and the therapy built on the story of Doug's difficult childhood. The therapist's goal was to find ways to let Doug and Louise take Denise's perspective; in other words, to assist them to represent Denise's 'problematic behaviour' differently. Working with Doug's history was intended to clarify for the therapist whether Doug's own experiences could help him represent Denise's failing strategy or whether he was so traumatized that he could not represent her perspective plausibly. Doug's wish to be a 'good' father was validated, but the lead therapist (and the reflecting team in their feedback to the family) also articulated how hard Doug must find it to achieve this goal: despite wanting to be a 'hands-on' father, he was often required to be away from home and his daughters in order to earn a living and support them.

The same logic was used with Louise: was her need of validation from Denise related to her lack of understanding of Denise's complex behaviour? If Louise had had no bias in her thinking or feelings tied to her childhood history, validating her as a parent might have allowed her to represent Denise differently. Because that hadn't happened, the team tried to take her perspective as perceiving herself to be rejected. It was noted that Tina had solved the problem by shifting her support from her mother to Louise. So Louise's central role– taking on most of the parenting of the girls – needed to be validated in an empathic manner. The team both highlighted how much responsibility she had taken on and also sympathized about how frustrating it must be for Louise, as a responsible parent, to see the girls' mother not trying 'hard enough'.

It was also suggested to Louise that she had become such an important point of security for Denise that Denise could 'trust' her enough to show her some of her distress and frustration. In actual fact, it was evident to the therapists that Denise's anger was unregulated (intrusions of forbidden negative affect) and that Denise did not actually have her anger under control. Nevertheless, this 'reframe' (which is a distorting transformation of information for the purpose of increasing both Louise's and Denise's comfort) was used to provide an explanation that could help Louise to feel better about herself as a step-parent and less angry with Denise. Interestingly, the more accurate explanation suggested earlier (that Denise's anger was triggered by the frustration of split loyalties) had not been accepted by Louise who thought that Denise 'should' be able to control her temper better and 'should' be able to appreciate how much Louise was trying to do for her.

Following the reframe, Louise was more able to consider the earlier idea that Denise's explosions were fuelled by Denise's mixed feelings following contact with her mother. She was also able to reflect on the possibility that it was difficult for Denise to get angry with Helen because she feared losing her mother completely. Across the next two sessions, Louise's empathy for Denise and her predicament – wanting to maintain a connection with all her parents – increased. This happened only after the therapists showed Louise an appreciation of what she was trying to do and of the problems involved. In a sense, the therapists modelled for Louise the active compassion that they hoped she could offer Denise.

In the final session, the parents reported that the problems with Denise had improved and that they had noticed her caring and thoughtful side. Louise talked about some of the good times she had had with Denise, and said that she felt they were connecting in new ways. When a conversation regarding Helen's failure to make a financial contribution for the girls' forthcoming holiday crept into the discussion, the parents halted midstream, noted this was a conversation that was not appropriate with Denise in the room, decided they would discuss the issue with Helen, and went on to discuss other concerns. As they demonstrated behaviour that was compatible with releasing Denise from her Type A3 strategy, the adults took charge and made protective decisions. This change was important because they were now acting in a caring and parental role towards Denise rather that placing their desire to complain about Helen ahead of Denise's needs. Complaining had elicited Denise's compulsive caring for her mother as well as triggering angry intrusions of affect when this became incompatible with her caregiving of Doug and Louise.

Doug re-introduced their concern about Denise's diabetes. He described how he had noticed Denise becoming anxious– tearful, fidgety and sweaty – around injection times, and that her distress seemed more intense when Denise was worried about her mother Helen. At this point, the meaning of these behaviours appeared clearer to the therapists: Denise was using the medical issue (without awareness or intent) to communicate how important it was that her parents attend to her needs. The combination of intrusions of forbidden negative affects and issues of physical integrity made Denise's signals appear quite desperate. There was also the beginning of a shift in Doug's perception of Denise's difficulties with the insulin; this was indicated by the softer manner in which he (and Louise) discussed Denise's distress about her mother and her needing support with her medication. In the reflection at the end of the session, the team commented on Doug's new capacity to read Denise's somatic signals of distress. The team also told Doug and Louise that they would be interested to know whether Denise's body signals of distress settled, once Denise felt more able to talk explicitly about her worries about Helen. This, they hoped, would encourage the parents to stay attentive to somatic communication.

After voicing how difficult it must be for a young girl to suffer the regime of medication and normalizing her protest at it, Doug and Louise said they would visit the paediatrician to seek advice. The normalization didn't fully acknowledge the interpersonal meaning of Denise's protests about the insulin, but did acknowledge the importance of her safety.

Phone contact three months later (checking whether a follow-up session was required) confirmed that things were still going well and that the family did not need further assistance. They were now an 'independent and adequate' family, able to identify and manage their own problems (Crittenden 1992b).

Summary

The therapist's attempt to bring a core circularity to awareness (that, as Doug and Louise criticized her mother, Denise's loyalties to her mother were triggered, and Denise became distressed, angry, and defended her mother) was not initially effective with this family. It is not unusual for such integrative interpretations to be difficult for parents to accept early in family work; often the parents' own feelings about their failures (procedural and imaged/somatic representations) cloud their capacity to sort through complex information. Specifically, it seemed that Doug and Louise's ability to semantically accept Denise's wish to defend her mother was blocked by their arousing affective representations of anger and resentment about Helen; these led to procedural complaining that, in turn, distressed Denise in irresolvable ways, leading to her intrusions of forbidden negative affect. We note that aroused negative affective states are associated with extreme semantic dichotomization that interferes with both negotiation and moderate solutions that require complex judgements of causality; the underlying process was based on early misattribution of the cause of arousal (Brown and Curhan 2013). The combination of their aroused states that misattributed causality to Denise with Denise's now intensely aroused state blocked their ability to stand back, reflect and ultimately understand Denise's attachment dilemma: how to be loyal and connected to both her parents (her primary attachment figures) while also managing her emerging attachment relationship with her step-mother.

By offering Doug aspects of an AAI, the therapist helped Doug to connect his adult behaviour with his childhood experience, thus facilitating his discovery of the repetitive pattern with his father. More broadly, assisting families to understand multi-person attachment relationships might be semantically accepted by families, but if their own self- and partner-protective strategies conflict with the new formulation, their behaviour might still be motivated by older and implicit representations. When implicit negative DRs (for example, of anger, frustration, and resentment) are in conflict with 'good' semantic DRs, verbal acceptance of therapeutic reframes might not produce change. This is frequently seen when families repeatedly say they 'do not understand' their child's behaviour and wish to do so, but then appear to block formulations that are suggested. In DMM terms, this suggests that the 'unacceptable' negative affect activated by procedural memories and exacerbated by current family dynamics interferes with reflective integration. Some family therapists argue that what is needed is a new or better story for the family. Instead DMM suggests this may be fruitless unless the underlying procedural and affective DRs have been identified, explored, and accepted as relevant. Once the negative affect is accepted verbally, its enactment procedurally becomes less necessary and reflective integration and genuine 're-storying' (around the former child's competence in the face of threat) can proceed.

Work with Denise's family illustrates the relevance of these DMM ideas: Turning to the father's family of origin history provided a highly relevant and influential difference to the formulation. It revealed the father's own vulnerabilities and corrective scripts from childhood which appeared to have been 'invisibly' maintaining the key circularity. The unprocessed discrepancy between what Doug sought semantically (his desire to be a more hands-on parent) and the contradiction created by his absences from the family (procedural knowledge) made it difficult for him accept his own contribution to Denise's behaviour. Articulating his negative affect and this bind in his fathering role (travelling and caring for his children) enabled him to accept his limitations and support his new wife's role.

Recall of memories from childhood helped Doug access procedural and sensory memories of what it felt like to have an absent father. It is possible that sensory memories of his own distress in childhood allowed Doug to become more aware of Denise's somatic signals of distress: her tears and her fidgety sweating body. Importantly, for the therapists, the recurring presence of such intense somatic signals highlighted the intensity of Denise's distress and her inability to communicate her distress using verbal representations (Hoffmeyer 2008; Kozlowska 2013). The vital importance of Doug accessing these early procedural representations from his childhood was poignantly marked by his daughter's procedural and sensory response – her gentle loving touch on his knee that signified recognition of what her daddy had missed in his childhood. But it could not be left to his 5-year-old daughter to help him resolve this.

Interestingly, the two girls were possibly also communicating these previously unacknowledged representations in their drawing of the dragons and embracing hands – danger/threat versus connection/love. Being split in their strategies for managing the adults' conflict left them without each other as resources; that is, their sibling attachment was affected by their attempts to retain parental protections. Exploring Denise's situation from this point of view revealed, in turn, the caregiving function of Denise's position in the family and also the cost to Denise of taking on this role for both parents. When the parents are in conflict, the caregiving child is almost certainly going to face an impasse; for Denise, these led to intrusions of negative forbidden affect and estrangement from her sister.

The therapeutic relationship and context

Families typically come for family therapy knowing that something is amiss and that they may be 'doing something wrong'. This can be translated in DMM as having some awareness of discrepancies in their representations, together with failed reflective representations or meta-cognitions about what is going wrong and what to do about it. Frequently, parents skip from one attempt at understanding and integration to another as their uncertainty and anxiety mount. For example, Louise did not want to feel angry (semantic representation) with Denise for her outburst, but found herself feeling angry, rejected and upset (imaged and somatic representations).

This mixture of confusion, anger, upset and failure is a strong feature of many families who come for family therapy. In fact, we want to give them credit for being courageous enough to come, knowing they might have to face criticism and exposure of their failings. The role of the therapist and the team is to offer to function as a secure transitional attachment figure for all the members of the family. This is a hard task but is necessary to help contain and reduce family members' negative affect and arousal such that reflective integration becomes possible. How this occurs is different for children and for parents. Usually both children and parents need to experience changes first implicitly (in procedures, images, and somatic states) before they can apply semantic or integrative ideas to their behaviour. How sophisticated these semantic representations are will differ for children at different ages and for adults as their awareness develops. However, it should be noted that from its outset family therapy emphasizes that, if procedural representations are not activated and revised, change will be superficial and transitory. This is consistent with a DMM emphasis.

For this family, access to procedural and affective (both imaged and somatic) information enabled Doug to become more aware that his own absences were repeating his own father's pattern, that they had had an impact on his children and partners, and that his semantic expectations of what a parent should be like functioned to fuel his impatience with Helen for her 'irresponsible' parenting of the girls. Connecting with his own vulnerabilities allowed Doug to acknowledge his daughter's position: he became more able to recognize her feelings of hurt and was able to respond with gentleness such that their relationship improved. Louise, on the other hand, needed her position and competence as a parent validated. Once this occurred, she was able to consider Denise's predicaments from a more emotionally calm, balanced and, hence, emphatic position; she came to understand that Denise's angry outbursts reflected severe distress and anger, with Denise feeling torn by conflicting loyalties to her parents.

Returning to the therapeutic relationship, we suggest that becoming aware of discrepancies in our representational systems is in itself potentially highly confusing and anxiety-provoking. So for Doug to mention his childhood distress also runs the risk that he may feel ashamed of what he could perceive as his failure as a man and father. The risk of this needs to be foreseen and reduced by the therapist and team communicating acceptance of him at all representational levels; that is, the therapists offer a secure transitional attachment relationship to each of the family members. So the therapists' manner (procedural and affective DRs) communicated acceptance and caring and this then allowed some reflection on semantic DRs to enable more integrative reflective DRs.

The importance of forming positive attachment relationships with each family member is also illustrated by how Louise 'allowed' Doug's revelations about himself to be connected to Denise's symptoms. Arguably if she had not trusted the therapist and the team, she might have drawn Doug away at this point and returned to angry accusations. This happens frequently in systemic family therapy when a member of the family feels disrespected or ignored. Had she done so, Doug's integration of his procedural, affective, and semantic DRs might have been aborted, with a risk of a return to the former process. We note here that Louise was also invited to discuss her own childhood and, in subsequent sessions, further attention would have been paid to her needs. But her choice not to speak at this point allowed uninterrupted space for Doug and hence for his integrative processing to occur. Importantly, integration is occurring not just for Doug but vicariously for each of the family members. This fosters the development of similar – or less discrepant – DRs among family members.

In the end, it was decided not to involve Helen in this treatment. The judgement was made by the therapists that the critical danger was Doug and Louise feeling rejected by Denise, which could in turn lead to their rejection of her. This threat and each parent's distortion of information and consequent DRs and behaviour with the girls had not only affected Denise's and Tina's self-protective strategy, it had also affected Denise's mental and physical health, the sisters' attachment, and the attachment between Doug and Louise. Until a means of undoing one or the other (or both) adult's distorting processes could be found, the family was stuck and Denise was in danger. Therefore, addressing the critical danger as a priority was both the safest option and a crucial step forward; everything hung on it. At the conclusion of treatment, Denise's Type A3 strategy might still imply some long-term developmental risk for her, but the short-term risks of intrusions and of insulin deprivation were resolved. Further, Doug and Louise's ability to seek help for their family problems, and their quick change in representations about Denise and her behaviour, suggested that this family might create a sufficiently different developmental context so as to allow Denise to reorganize her strategy towards more open communication of her needs and desires.

Summary of constructs and treatment principles

Constructs

1   *Sibling subsystem*: As new children are born in a family, the roles of each family member change. The relationships between siblings are shaped by the parents' expectations and behaviour. The parents can deal with shaping the sibling subsystem in various ways:
    (a) If the parents are over-involved, the boundaries between adults and children are blurred.
    (b) If they are under-involved, competition between siblings for scarce resources is likely.
    (c) If the parents can function in the various, different ZPDs, comfortable attachments between siblings are promoted.
2   *Needs versus desires*: Parents need to function reflectively to differentiate accurately the needs and desires of the various family members. This will enable them to give appropriate priority to children's signals for attention. Observing the parents deal with siblings' requests can give children the opportunity to practise intuitive reflection on their own relationship with the parents.
3   *Corrective and replicative scripts*: On the basis of their childhood experiences, parents form intentions about their own parenting. They can develop 'corrective scripts', that is, plans about parenting that are intended to correct negative aspects of their childhood experience. They can also develop 'replicative scripts', that is the intention to repeat with their children aspects of their childhood experience which they view favourably. These intentions can be conscious or unconscious. In DMM terms, corrective and replicative scripts can be seen as semantic DRs about parenting.
4   *Pendulum parenting*: Parents who use absolute semantic corrective scripts can show an extreme style of parenting that 'corrects' what they found negative in their childhood, but 'swings' to the opposite extreme. Their parenting is as unbalanced (in the opposite direction) as what they experienced and sought to redress. These pendulum swings often occur when parents are unresolved regarding their childhood experiences of danger, or use strategies that forbid reflection and integration of multiple DRs; the intense attempts to correct are therefore fuelled by powerful implicit DRs.
5   *Siblings' attachment*: In the context of balanced parental protection and comfort, siblings can avoid competing for parental resources, and form a relationship which is symmetrical regarding power, and which, in time, will approach reciprocity regarding protection and comfort.
6   *Parentification of children*: When circumstances do not allow sharing the family workload between the parents, and other adult support is not available, children can be given responsibility for the protection and comfort of

the siblings beyond their developmental abilities. Inadequate support is given to the child who takes care of the siblings, so all children are unsafe and the 'parentified' child is limited in her/his development.

7   *Effects of birth order on strategic development of children*: First-borns generally organize more closely around parents' expectations or needs, while later-born children have less attention from parents, but are also under less stress. If the first-born uses a Type B strategy, it is likely that other children will also use Type B. If the first-born uses a Type A or a Type C strategy, often the second-born child reverses strategy. If the family is particularly troubled, it might be that there is no effective alternative to the Type A or Type C strategy used by the older sibling, so later-born children might structure complex Type A/C strategies or strategies of isolation.

8   *Unresolved loss*: The death of an attached person or of an attachment figure is the ultimate danger. When a child dies before the parent, it reflects a failure of the basic goal of parenting: keep the baby alive. Consequently, a child death holds great potential for eliciting trauma from parents. Information about loss can be sorted regarding future deaths of attachment or attached figures so that the experience can be considered resolved or unresolved. Alternatively, lack of resolution of loss of an attachment or an attached figure can interfere with daily functioning, including the care of living children.

9   *Intrusions of forbidden negative affect (INA)*: When a compulsive Type A strategy is used in the context of conflicts that are impossible to manage by inhibition of negative affect and that involve substantial danger, the Type A strategy might fail, the inhibition might yield to intense negative arousal, and the negative feelings (that are usually forbidden by the strategy) might be displayed in intense and unregulated ways. Such blatantly negative behaviour can be so discrepant with family rules that other family members cannot accept any personal role in eliciting it and, therefore, the disruptive person is held solely responsible. In addition, it can be so disruptive that the parents sometimes decide to involve external resources or authorities to support them or even take charge. The lack of self-regulation of behaviour in these episodes differentiates INAs from disruptive behaviours used in the context of a coercive strategy, where the individual carefully monitors others' responses to his/her own behaviour in order to maintain maximum attention with minimum risk of punishment.

10 *Somatization*: Somatic symptoms function as signs that signal the presence of internal or external events that threaten the physical or psychological well-being or integrity of the individual (Kozlowska 2013). Representations of body state hold information about the individual's well-being at a very basic somatic level, and the body may signal distress (somatic DRs) even when this information is omitted from semantic or episodic representations. Somatic DRs should be considered very important because physical well-being is compromised. At the same time, they are very imprecise about the basis for the distress.

Treatment principles

1   If the presenting problem is 'obvious' (for example, a handicapping condition of a child), care should be given to determine its effect on other family mem-

bers. When a problem stresses the family too greatly, family members may accommodate by chronic depression of some family members, by spousification of 'non-affected' children, or isolation of family members. Family break-up might be the central danger hiding behind the 'obvious' problem.

2   Intrusions and somatic symptoms are intense signals that should be understood as indicating extreme and 'unspeakable' distress for the individual with the behaviour.

3   Family behaviour occurs within cultural contexts. When cultural contexts change rapidly or when families move to a different cultural contexts, the adaptiveness of behaviour can depend on how the adults' DRs are updated to reflect the new context and its specific dangers. When intervening with families showing maladaptive behaviour in a new culture, professionals might make sense of behaviours by investigating the cultural change and the set of dangers the family faced before and after the change.

4   Verbalized interpretations about current circular processes that maintain family problems are usually difficult for family members to accept early in treatment, before exploration of individual and shared DRs. In fact, early acceptance of therapists' interpretations might rather reflect superficial compliance with therapists as authority figures; this is unlikely to produce effective change in daily behaviour. Early interpretations are better used as therapist's private working hypotheses to guide the family's exploration.

5   Alternate positive narrations about the family problem are unlikely to produce adaptive change without prior identification, exploration, and recognition of the relevance of the underlying procedural and affective DRs. Once the content of the implicit DRs is accepted verbally, their enactment becomes less necessary and reflective integration can proceed, yielding productive 're-storying'.

6   Family of origin work with parents is frequently a fruitful way to gain understanding of current family circularities. This can be done either in the presence of the whole family, or in a collateral individual setting. The presence of the whole family allows for the observation of how other family members react to the discussion of relevant representations. The individual setting is more likely to be emotionally cooler and foster reflective functioning more efficiently.

5   Going to school

It's the first day of school! John's house is abuzz. He and his parents have been preparing for weeks for this day. He has his new notebook and his pens and his lunch money. In his pocket, he has his special plastic spider that he will show everyone. He's going to ride the bus like the big boys and girls.

John and his mum walk to the corner where the bus will pick him up. She's holding his hand, like always. Then he sees the older kids, clustered in a group. They don't even see him when he drops his mother's hand and steps a bit ahead of her, almost as if he was unaware of her. He waits, neither with her, nor with the big kids. As the bus pulls up and the doors open, the other children scramble on. Without even a glance back, John stretches up to reach the first step and pulls himself onto the bus and disappears down the centre aisle. His mother strains to find his face in a window, but he's gone. Today he entered a new world. He needs her waiting behind him to support him, but he has to go alone. The future beckons.

Developmental advances

Compared to earlier development, the maturational changes underlying development in the school years are slight. But the interpersonal consequences are massive. Life changes dramatically, beginning at 6–7 years of age.

Concrete logic

Cortical maturation takes off in the school years, giving children the ability to think logically in ways that adults understand. No longer do they pester 'Why? Why? Why?' in ways that produce no understanding or satisfaction, no matter how many times a logical answer is given. Suddenly, logic reigns supreme. Children ask why and expect comprehensible explanations. 'Because I said so' won't do any more. But neither will abstract and philosophical explanations. School-age children want facts, concrete facts that they can see and feel and hear. Given concrete information, especially personal concrete information, children can think. That is, they can both comprehend the logic connecting events and also stand back to reflect upon the events, considering both their own and other perspectives. They can use the ability to reflect to consider alternative solutions. But they do this for specific, concrete issues, not in general, abstractly.

Drawing one's own semantic conclusions

The linguistic skills of school-aged children, coupled with their new cortical maturity, allow them to develop their own semantic conclusions. The more precise their description of cognitive contingencies, the more these generalized semantic DRs can be used as self-prescriptions to shape their behaviour. Knowing what is likely to happen if one acts one way or another can keep one safe on the basis of personal experiences, thus complementing and extending familial and cultural prescriptions.

Using language to focus affect's motivating potential

Language can also represent feelings. Verbalized images and connotative language are language-based DRs that permit children to express their feelings verbally. This makes the children more aware of how they might act and permits listeners to empathize with them.

Constructing one's own episodes

Narrations of autobiographical episodes were possible for preschool-aged children only with assistance from parents. By the school years, children have learned, through parents' questions, what belongs in an episode and how to put it together. Their intellectual maturity now allows them to sequence events and images, constructing an integrated DR of a past experience. This episodic DR contains both cognitive and affective information, in variable proportions according to the self-protective strategy used by each child. It is crucial that children recall (or rather, reconstruct) episodes in strategically sound ways, because an episodic DR is a powerful way to represent protective behaviour that has worked in the past. Strategic distortion of episodic DRs ensures that protective behaviour is repeated in circumstances that can be associated with past danger. Of course, the drawback is that perception that is distorted by episodic DRs can re-shape current experience in maladaptive ways that create danger.

Learning to think about what to do

A major task of middle childhood is to learn to regulate one's own behaviour. School-aged children use verbal representations (that is, body-talk, semantic descriptions and prescriptions, and connotative language) to represent the relation of self to context. These representations dispose their behaviour, that is, they are DRs. Because each DR is derived differently, using different processing networks through the brain, they do not always dispose the same response. Non-verbal DRs can be quickly and preconsciously processed (somatic states, procedures, and sensory images), yielding a rapid and automatic self-protective response which cannot be evaluated before being implemented. Non-verbal DRs can be processed further and transformed into verbal DRs. What's a kid to do when his mouth salivates (somatic state) at the smell (sensory image) of something sweet, but his mind reminds him that his mother said not to eat before dinner (semantic prescription) and he can almost feel the swat on his rear if he gets caught (procedural consequence)?

Resolving these sorts of inner conflicts is everyday business for all of us – and we handle the job in different ways. Because the non-verbal representations operate most rapidly, endangered people use them preferentially. That means that endangered children and adults will not be able to describe their behaviour with language as accurately as children and adults growing up in safety. When parents guide children through this process of transforming implicit DRs into verbal DRs, children will learn to reflect upon their multiple DRs so as to generate an integrative, context-specific best choice. This is easiest to do when the context is safe.

Returning to the example of forbidden sweets, a neglected and hungry child might act on somatic states and sensory images. An abused child (with harshly authoritarian parents) might inhibit taking the sweets with a somatic representation of painful punishment. A child raised in a permissive manner might think 'No matter; I'll talk my way out of trouble if I'm caught'; this child has moved to the verbal level and chooses to disobey. A child with authoritative parents might carry out an inner dialogue, like the ones he has with his parents from time to time, about his options: 'I'd really like that biscuit and I sure am hungry. But I know mum has made a good dinner and it will be ready in an hour. I don't want to disappoint her – even if she'd understand. Hmmmm. Maybe I can take just one biscuit to tide me over?' This is the amazing process of integration: access all the DRs, generate a DR about the other person (Fonagy calls this 'mentalisation'), and then, holding all of this in mind, choose a course of action for this precise situation. That final integrative DR could be one of the simpler DRs or, as in our example, it could combine something from several DRs (Fonagy et al. 2002).

Who me?

Usually, we experience ourselves as whole and coherent. It is only when we are confronted with our own unexpected – and often unacceptable – behaviour that we consider who we really are. I did that? I couldn't have! I'm nice, I'm good, I'm strong. I . . . I wouldn't do that!!! This happens because the 'self' is not a unified whole, but rather a host of different probabilities of acting (that is, competing DRs) that result from the parallel attribution of meaning to different aspects of sensory stimulation (Damasio 1994; Hoffmeyer 2008; Eagleman 2011). Among the DRs are incompatible motivations, most of which are not conscious; even the DR that is ultimately acted upon may not be conscious. To regulate our behaviour, we need to discover these hidden DRs, consider them carefully, and learn to regulate the process that yields behaviour. Being calm and comfortable supports the extended processing that allows us to acknowledge and accept some of our less desirable motivations and can yield more coherent and context-adapted behaviour.

Language is the means for reflective thought, but language comes late in development and late in the processing of information. Preconscious DRs have sometimes been acted upon before a verbal DR is generated. Therefore, to know oneself and to regulate one's behaviour, pre-linguistic DRs must be recognized quickly. This means both becoming aware of non-verbal meanings and also transforming them to language. Once that can be managed with empathic parents, children can transfer what was learned about interpersonal dialogue to an inner dialogue among the various selves of their own minds. Sometimes this happens quite concretely, by talking to the family dog, a teddy bear, or generating an imaginary friend. As long as these are known to be imaginary, they can ease the transition from interpersonal dialogue to an inner, private decision-making process.

One function of this dialogue is to explain why one did what one was not supposed to do. Ironically, the same maturation that makes concrete reflective integration possible also makes deceptive processes possible: 'I didn't clean my room [parental semantic prescription] because I was doing my homework instead [alternate parental semantic prescription that nullifies the first prescription]'. The crucial aspect of such explanations is that they make the self both internally coherent and also congruent with parental DRs. The problem is that they use omission of information and self-deception about the omission to do so.

Box 5.1 *'Absolutist'* **thinking**

1   *Definition*: Recognition that differences in knowledge can result from differences in the source of knowledge. Hence the need to identify sources to resolve differences in truth.
2   *Limitation*: No awareness of different, but equally valid, perspectives.
3   *Information type*: Somatic, procedural, imaged, body talk, semantic, connotative, episodic, and 'concrete' integrative DRs.
4   *Executive functioning*: Adults require school-aged children to consider which DR disposed their behaviour (in specific 'concrete' situations). This is the beginning of the executive function of the maturing brain.
5   *Individual differences*: Integrative cortical processing is not developing in some children (despite brain maturation); they are not able to explain their multiple dispositions, nor to know which regulated their behaviour. Experience of danger may lead to by-passing this potential in favour of rapid, self-protective responding.
6   *Treatment implications*: Both guidance to parents to change the interpersonal context and also support of children's conscious awareness of themselves and emerging reflecting skills are recommended.

Exposure to new strategies

In the preschool years, children became specialists in their own families' ways of functioning. In a sense, this has narrowed their range of adaptiveness to only their own family. Going to school reverses that process. Children are exposed to teachers' strategies and expectations – and these might be quite different from those of their parents. In addition, children coming from other homes use strategies that might be incompatible with their own. This is unlike siblings' strategies that are developed in the context of other family members and, though they are not identical, they usually fit together in ways that the child can predict.

In school, children must adapt to unfamiliar strategies and this expands their own range of adaptiveness. They discover that they need to think about what the teacher expects and will do – and to adapt accordingly. They need to think about what other children will do. Indeed, a major topic of children's conversation is what other children are like. This can seem gossipy or catty, but in concrete ways, children are exploring the world of perspective-taking, personality, and personal adaptation to a range of different people.

Interpersonal relationships

In the school years, children broaden their range of attachment relationships while changing their relationships with each of their parents. Siblings take on new roles with each other, best friends develop out of earlier playmate relationships, and sometimes an adult forms an alternate or ancillary relationship with a child.

> **Box 5.2   Attachment relationships in the school years**
> - *Parents*: Non-symmetrical and non-reciprocal.
> - *Siblings*: Symmetrical and non-reciprocal.
> - *Best friend*: Symmetrical and non-reciprocal.
> - *Alternate figures*: Non-symmetrical and non-reciprocal.

Alternate attachment figures: teachers, club leaders, friends' parents, etc.

Like parents, teachers make demands, guide, educate, discipline and encourage a child. However, teachers don't dote on a child just because he exists. Children must earn their approval in school and, in a whole group of children, teachers typically prefer children who fit in, are helpful, and perform well on learning tasks. Teachers are not expected to meet the full range of children's needs, but they should keep children safe and guide them to regulate their behaviour, that is, teachers function as alternate attachment figures. Dangerous events, such as accidents, emotional upsets, bullying, failure, can and do occur at school. Teachers are likely to be first on the scene at these events and can enact responses which may be more adaptive than those of parents, for example, calm concern rather than anxious distress at an injury. They may show more compassionate care and attention than a distracted and unavailable mother. That is, for some children, school can be a 'haven of safety' (Ainsworth's term for a secure base) from physical dangers or emotionally disturbed family interaction. The coping strategies that children learn from teachers can augment what they learned at home. This is especially important when parents' own upbringing under threatening conditions has restricted their range of adaptability.

Managing the differences between teachers and parents can be difficult. When the differences are great, maintaining the balance can be a delicate issue. If children talk too warmly about their teacher, an insecure parent may feel incompetent or unimportant. That can produce self- and child-protective behaviour from the parent. Complaining about the teacher can generate a conflict between the school and family. Parents who pursue complaints can be seen by the school as difficult and interfering and this might affect the child. Moreover schools have a powerful role in surveillance of families and parenting. Signs of neglect, physical violence, sexual abuse may be reported if a child shows signs of distraction, intrusive emotions, lack of concentration/dissociation, excessive anger, and so on. Conversely, widely reported examples of abuse at school by teachers can make parents suspicious. Especially when both parents and teachers use distorted strategies for processing information, communication between parents and school personnel can break down. Sometimes children become triangulated in this conflict. The focus on the child's needs can be lost when a school and family become mistrusting and critical of each other. When children cannot adapt to school, problems are likely to follow.

When there are problems

Between the ages of 5–7, in every culture, the ritual of leaving the family to join the community is enacted. From an evolutionary perspective, joining the community adds a new selective pressure on children's strategies, both increasing children's range of adaptation and also highlighting problems brought from home. In the past, this meant joining non-familial adults in their daily activities. In technological countries, children go to school. Because school requires sitting still and focusing on verbally communicated information, it might not fit our evolved developmental expectancies. That is, a misfit between a recent cultural adaption to the post-industrial demands of adult life and children's maturation might explain some of the problems children face in going to school. To address this, we look at ADHD. We first summarize the literature on the ontology of ADHD, then present two clinical cases that show the range of difference within this single diagnosis.

Attention deficit hyperactivity disorder (ADHD)

ADHD has become a major clinical problem, being diagnosed in 5 per cent of all children, most of them boys (Faraone et al. 2003) (from five to nine times more often than girls; Faraone et al., 2003). During the recent decade, rates of diagnosis of ADHD have increased dramatically (Akinbami et al. 2011). A crisis in the development of boys is upon us.

ADHD is defined by two symptom dimensions: inattention and hyperactivity/impulsivity (by the APA in DSM 5, and the World Health Organization in ICD 10). This heterogeneity of symptoms may reflect causal and functional differences among ADHD cases. Further, it is unclear whether these symptoms are categorically different or only quantitatively different from normative children. In addition, ADHD is almost always co-morbid with other diagnoses, e.g., oppositional defiant disorder in 40 per cent of ADHD cases, anxiety disorders in 34 per cent, conduct disorder in 14 per cent, tics in 11 per cent and mood disorder in 6 per cent (Simonff et al. 2008). This makes it unclear whether ADHD is a discrete disorder or a collection of different conditions.

Crucial to diagnosis is functional impairment such that there is harm to the child in terms of increased mortality, morbidity, or impairment in major life activities. Although ADHD is often diagnosed in the preschool years, its major impact is on functioning in the school years and adolescence e.g., 40–50 per cent engage in antisocial activities, 40 per cent experience teen pregnancy, 32–40 per cent drop out of school, and 50–70 per cent have few or no friends (Barkley 2002). Further, ADHD may persist into adulthood (Doshi et al. 2012) with possibly a spontaneous remission rate as high as 60 per cent (Hill and Schoener 1996), though more recent work suggests that the rate depends on the definition of remission (not full syndrome: 60 per cent; sub-threshold symptomatology: 30 per cent; full recovery of functions: 10 per cent) with higher remission for symptoms of hyperactivity/impulsivity than for inattention (Biederman et al. 2000).

We review the literature on the aetiology of ADHD for the purpose of clarifying possible approaches to treatment. As we did with autism, we divide the studies into genetic, neurological, psychological, relational, and cultural.

Genomics

Studies of genes

The search for single genes or gene clusters associated with ADHD has not yielded evidence of anomalous or ADHD-specific genes. Because the medication drug methylphenidate (i.e., Ritalin, that reduces ADHD symptoms) inhibits the dopamine transporter, many studies have focused on the dopamine system (Kent 2004), as well as genes involved in neural development and growth, and in synaptic transmission (Kent et al. 2005). The associations between ADHD and specific genes tend to be: (1) with one specific symptom dimension of ADHD (not the same across studies); (2) equally strong with other psychiatric disorders; (3) of limited power (i.e., 1–2 per cent of the variance); and (4) unreplicated (Bidwell et al. 2011). They leave the majority of variance to be explained by other factors.

Inferential studies of heritability

Despite these results, the hypothesis that ADHD is mostly determined by genetic factors is the current working hypothesis for many investigators and clinicians. This is possibly based on studies of behavioural genetics (Plomin et al. 2001) that have estimated a mean value of 76 per cent for heritability of ADHD (Barkley 2002). Reviews of inferential studies find that, though the hypothesis of a genetic contribution to ADHD is supported, environmental factors have a strong role as well (Hechtman 1996). Further, many of the studies are methodologically and theoretically compromised in ways that challenge their validity (Nikolas and Burt 2010). The discrepancy between the variance explained by genes (approximately 1 per cent) and that inferred from heritability studies (approximately 70–75 per cent) is dramatic.

A meta-analysis aimed at differentiating genetic and environmental aetiologies of the symptom dimensions of inattention and hyperactivity found a high heritability of both inattention (71 per cent) and hyperactivity (73 per cent), but with dominant genetic effects larger for inattention (especially before age 5) (Nikolas and Burt 2010). Inattention had more non-shared environmental influences whereas additive genetic effects were greater for hyperactivity. Environmental factors appeared to be more important for hyperactivity in adolescence than childhood. The results, however, differed depending upon mothers and teachers as the source of information. Children themselves were not assessed directly by the investigators and no study included direct assessment of genes; such studies are needed before conclusions can be drawn.

Epigenetic factors

Recent studies explored the possibility of gene by environment (G × E) effects with epigenetic mechanisms explaining some of the heritability of ADHD. Studies of primates demonstrate that: (1) the maternal genotype had a moderating effect on the association between a specific variant of the DRD4 gene and higher rates of social impulsivity; (2) highly protective mothers produce juvenile offspring who are less impulsive and more inhibited in their approach toward novel objects and spaces; and (3) variant mothers with variant offspring had the lowest level of maternal protectiveness whereas variant mothers with non-variant offspring had the highest level (Fairbanks et al. 2006; Fairbanks, et al. 2012). In humans, children with a specific variant of the same gene are more likely than other children to have parents with adult ADHD (Lynn et al. 2005) and fathers' ADHD symptoms add to genetic risk for child hyperactivity/impulsivity (Auerbach et al. 2010). Other parents with the same variant were more likely to be impulsive, have sexual/spousal instability, and misuse drugs and alcohol, suggesting a common environmental contribution (McGeary 2009; Garcia et al. 2010; Reiner and Spangler 2011). In sum, the behavioural genetic approach indicates that ADHD is more heritable in a risk environment (Pennington et al .2009) with epigenetic mechanisms having a substantial role in transforming genetic risk for ADHD into phenotypic symptoms.

Conclusions

Genetic studies demonstrate the heterogeneity of ADHD and of its modulating factors. Effects of single genes seem to be strongly modulated by epigenetic and environmental factors in ways that suggest ADHD symptoms (especially hyperactivity) are adaptations to stressful environments. Inferential studies confirm the familial quality of ADHD symptoms, but fall short of demonstrating the genetic basis of this. Stressful environments appear to be a crucial component of gene expression as attentional problems and hyperactivity (Slavich and Cole 2013).

Biological and neurological factors

Gender-based differences

The greater prevalence of ADHD in males, as well as greater mean levels and variability of symptoms in males (Gaub and Carlson 1997), suggest that gender-based differences may be important. Two findings stand out: (1) the prenatal, organizational effects of gonadal hormones on ADHD were found to be different in boys and girls (Martel et al. 2008); and (2) girls with ADHD showed predominantly inattentive symptoms, were less likely to manifest problems in school or in their spare time, and to have co-morbid diagnoses (Biederman 2002). These findings suggest that the boys' ADHD may be structurally different from girls' ADHD.

Toxins

Chemical toxins and inflammatory processes could provide a direct risk or could activate a genetic susceptibility to ADHD. Maternal gestational diabetes mellitus, low socioeconomic status (SES), perinatal health problems, maternal smoking during pregnancy, and atopic eczema in infancy raise the risk for ADHD; full breast-feeding appears to protect against ADHD (Nomura et al. 2012; Schmitt and Romanos 2012). Exposure to lead, which affects development of the striatum and prefrontal cortex, increases the frequency of ADHD symptoms in children, especially hyperactivity (Lanphear 2012). Animal studies indicate that lead exposure early in life causes problems in reinforcement response and response inhibition (Nigg 2010).

Neurological differences

Electroencephalogram (EEG)-based (Clarke et al. 2001) and functional magnetic resonance imaging (fMRI)-based (Tamm et al. 2006; Li et al. 2012) studies suggest that ADHD is associated with unchanging neural deficits. The specific deficits include less brain matter, less metabolic activity in this brain matter, less brain electrical activity, and less reactivity to stimulation in the frontal lobe, its connections to the basal ganglia, and/or their relationship to the central aspects of the cerebellum as compared to normative comparison groups (Barkley 2002). The overall decrease in brain volume, especially basal ganglia, cerebellum, and prefrontal cortex was also found in unaffected first-degree relatives (Castellanos et al. 2002; Nakao et al. 2011). This suggests that ADHD involves a disruption of specific neurodevelopmental trajectories, rather than a simple deficit.

Neuroimaging studies showed that in ADHD maturational changes in cortical thickness are delayed, but follow the same sequence of normal development with mid-range effects for individuals with below-threshold hyperactive/impulsive symptoms (Shaw et al. 2011; Ducharme et al. 2012). Further, cerebellum changes correlate with changes in ADHD symptoms for adolescents (Mackie et al. 2007). These results support a view of ADHD as a delay of normative development rather than a different type of development (Rubia et al. 2001; El-Sayed et al. 2003).

Conclusions

The biological picture of ADHD is multiple and complex, with strong gender differences, and differences in brain morphology both substantial and durable but also changeable (in synchrony with changes in symptoms). For both gender effects and brain development, maturation seems to be a relevant factor.

Psychological information processing

Psychological theories and test data

ADHD patients' various patterns of performance in cognitive tests associated with executive brain functions led Barkley (Barkley 1997) to discard the idea of ADHD as an attentional deficit and propose a neuropsychological model of ADHD based on problems in executive functions (located in the frontal lobes). The executive functions generate and maintain goal-directed and experience-based behaviour. Several neuropsychological studies (reviewed by Nigg, 2010) found that most kinds of attention were intact in ADHD, with only differences in vigilance being atypical. This suggests ADHD's attentional components are only secondary.

Nigg (2010) proposed that executive control of one's behaviour, especially in terms of interrupting, regulating or changing the course of complex, goal-oriented behaviours, could be of two types. One was 'bottom-up' regulation, driven by activation in subcortical or posterior brain regions, reflecting the potential relevance of information not related to the current situation, but potentially threatening, promising or novel. The other was 'top-down', informed by prefrontal brain activation, driven by new information that is goal-relevant such that it could modulate previous plans. ADHD was proposed to result from problems in both kinds of control system. At present, evidence on this theory is inconclusive.

Response inhibition is often impaired in ADHD (Willcutt et al. 2008). This function has been considered as a possible marker for causal risk, because it can be seen to be impaired in non-symptomatic relatives of ADHD-affected children. This, however, was found valid only for a subset of families of children with ADHD (Nigg et al. 2004).

Recent studies have found that the neuropsychological features of ADHD are neither homogeneous, nor specific to ADHD (Nigg 2010) and do not always reflect deficient functioning. To the contrary, increased activity levels in children with hyperactivity may improve performance in short-term memory tasks (Rapport et al. 2009). Further, children with ADHD do not show a consistent pattern of strengths and weaknesses (Fair et al. 2012) and their performance distributions overlap considerably with those of children without ADHD (Nigg 2010). In other words, neuropsychological functioning is not diagnostic for ADHD.

Behavioural evidence

Naturalistic observation in ecologically valid contexts has generally not been used to describe ADHD; the sources are usually parents or teachers who each have biases (see Chapter 3) that result in low correlations between their reports (Achenbach et al. 1987). Professional observation with reliability measures has not been used.

Conclusions

Information processing in ADHD individuals is not homogeneous, nor unequivocally deficient. In fact, some evidence would be compatible with a theory of ADHD as specific adaptation: decreased reactivity to 'cognitive' information (in DMM terms of contingency and cerebellar brain pathways) might be more adaptive for processing information from specific environments. This is consistent with an evolutionary biology perspective that reframed ADHD as a 'response-ready' pattern of personal characteristics, including having high levels of motor activity, acting without delay, being hypervigilant, and scanning widely (Jensen et al. 1997). This pattern would be adaptive for environments that are unsafe, resource-impoverished and requiring quick 'time-critical' responses.

Relational factors

The fact that approximately 20 per cent of parents of children with ADHD have ADHD themselves (Faraone et al. 2000) has been held as evidence of the heritability of ADHD, but Carlson and her colleagues (Carlson et al. 1995) recognized that the parent information was indirect, based on parents' self-reports, obtained after the child's diagnosis, and could reflect environmental input. We summarize that information below; in all cases the comparative findings are in contrast to normative comparison groups without ADHD.

Parent and family differences

Children diagnosed with ADHD differ on interaction with both parents and peers (Hinshaw and McHale 1991; Buhrmester et al. 1992). Their parents have higher rates of single parenthood and marital discord (e.g., Cunningham et al. 1988), whereas their siblings (particularly brothers) have higher rates of hyperactivity and more depression-anxiety symptoms (Hechtman 1996). In addition, biological parents of children with ADHD have higher rates of many forms of psychiatric disorder, including ADHD, antisocial disorders, mood disorders, and alcoholism (Biederman et al. 1987; Biederman et al. 1992; Lahey et al. 1988).

Mothers of inattentive/overactive children (based on teacher reports from ages 6 to 11) were often single, divorced or separated and had poor quality of perceived emotional support from partners and social networks (Carlson et al. 1995). The other predictor of ADHD-type behaviour was the poor quality of the early interaction between mother and child. Specifically mothers were: (1) more intrusive at 6 months during feeding and play situations, that is, disruptive of the child's on-going activity; and (2) over-stimulating caregiving at 3.5 years, that is, 'non-responsive physical intimacy' (not signalled by the child) and 'dissolution of generational boundaries' (provoking and teasing when the child was already aroused, and might have benefited from mother's reassurance).

Hyperactive children, on the other hand, were more often first-born and had parents with a punitive-authoritarian parenting strategy, had stressed marital relationships with a negative and tense family climate, and had more mental health problems (often undiagnosed), but not more physical illness (Hechtman 1996). Both mental health and emotional climate improved at the ten-year follow-up when children with hyperactivity had left home, suggesting that the family context was relevant to symptoms.

Researchers suggested both commonalities among disorders (e.g., ADHD and major depressive disorder, Biederman et al. 1987; Lahey et al. 1988) and also the possibility of subtypes within ADHD (e.g., without or with conduct disorder, with the latter having significantly higher parental antisocial, oppositional, depressive and anxious disorders than in normal controls, Hechtman 1996).

Interaction

Mothers of highly active males were found to be critical, disapproving, unaffectionate and punishing severely, especially in the middle-childhood years (Battle and Lacey 1972). On the other hand, mothers of hyperactive children used both more encouragement and suggestions and also more disapproval during difficult tasks (Campbell 1975); though the authors considered this evidence that mothers were responding to children's characteristics, the data do not indicate the direction of effects. Similarly, mothers of children with ADHD interacted less with their children during free play (less initiation, response and encouragement) and used more control; their children complied less and the mothers' reward of compliance and desired behaviours was less and inconsistent. Similar effects were observed when children were given experimental tasks (Cunningham and Barkley 1979).

Effects of medication

Psychostimulants are prescribed to children with ADHD, with their effect being considered 'paradoxical' in that psychostimulants reduce (rather than augment) motor activity (Rubia et al. 2009).

Early studies reported that, when on medication, hyperactive children complied more and mothers reduced commands and increased responsiveness, but without reaching normative levels (Barkley 1980; Mash and Johnston 1983; Hinshaw and McHale 1991). Older hyperactive children (both treated and non-treated) were more compliant, but again did not reach normative levels (Campbell and Ewing 1990; Barkley et al. 1991). Especially in cases where adolescents had both ADHD and oppositional defiant disorder (ODD), the patterns of interaction remained aggressive and negative, as in childhood. It has been argued that the interactive style of mothers of hyperactive children is a consequence and not a cause of the child's hyperactivity, but again causal hypotheses could not be tested in the data. On the other hand, because medicating children does not fully alter the interactive patterns (Hechtman 1996), circular causality involving parent features might be a more accurate explicative model.

More recently, a meta-analysis found only a mild short-term reduction of ADHD symptoms in medicated preschool-aged boys. Primary school-age children, mostly boys with ADHD combined type, showed improvements in symptomatic behaviour for 12 to 14 months using methylphenidate or atomoxetine. Long-term outcomes were inconclusive, as was evidence at other ages (Charach et al. 2011).

Effects of psychosocial treatment

The same meta-analysis found that the only intervention for preschoolers with diagnosed ADHD or at risk for ADHD that showed strong evidence of positive effects was parent behaviour training (PBT) that guides parents to use rewards and non-punitive consequences more predictably (Charach et al. 2011).

Conclusions

Children with ADHD often live in highly stressed families. Older studies focus on how such children learn to cope through interpersonal strategies including 'hyperactivity' and 'inattention'; more recent studies focus on the interpersonal effects of interventions, especially medication. The efficacy of psychosocial interventions challenges the view of ADHD as a static, child-based deficit.

Context and culture

Environmental factors

A strong relation between the solar intensity on geographical territory and the prevalence of ADHD has recently been reported: high solar intensity prevents ADHD, explaining 34–57 per cent of the variance in three international datasets (Arns et al. 2013). Although this effect might be explained through a connection of ADHD with circadian rhythm regulation problems, cultural effects have not been ruled out as additional factors.

Diet, in westernized countries, has a role in modulating ADHD symptomatology (Millichap and Yee 2012). Apart from iron and zinc supplementations for known deficiencies, and a possible role of long-chain polyunsaturated fatty acids in moderating ADHD symptomatology, negative effects have been shown for fast foods, red meat, processed meat, potato chips, high-fat dairy food and soft drinks; no association to ADHD has been shown with fish, vegetables, fruit, legumes and whole-grain foods (Howard et al. 2011). No negative role of sugar or aspartame has been documented (despite many parents' reports).

Cultural factors

Since the 1990s, rates of diagnosis have varied greatly by country, with Australia and the USA having more than double the rate of the UK (Singh 2002). Further, there is wide variation across nations in recommended treatments for ADHD (Hinshaw et al. 2011). Americans used dramatically more methylphenidate than other countries (Singh 2002), with a substantial proportion of visit time in outpatient treatment being used for prescription and monitoring of drug treatment (Garfield et al. 2012). Further, within countries, there are ethnicity-based variations, for example, medication use is lower among Mexican – American children compared with non-Hispanic white, non-Hispanic black, and Puerto Rican children (Akinbami et al. 2011). Such differences point to cultural factors as possibly implicated in the cause and maintenance of ADHD.

ADHD might be tied to culturally based values regarding appropriate behaviour, especially in boys. The gender bias in ADHD diagnoses suggests that 'normal', even if at times extreme, boys' behaviour may be pathologized (Nylund 2000), with methylphenidate seen as a way to improve boys' performance (Kindlon and Thompson 1999). This process of 'correcting' boys may reflect a trend in modern societies to use medication to correct imperfections (e.g., depression, lack of drive, lethargy) that may be part of normal diversity among children (cf. Kramer 1993). Instead, the mean for children and families may be confused with the ideal, that is, a perfect family with children who conform to adult wishes (Little 1998). In this way, methylphenidate can be seen as a technology that sits on the border between treatment of disorder and correction of normal imperfections (Parens 1998). Supporting this dour view, children prescribed methylphenidate have reported feeling that their personality has been taken away, such that they are no longer free to be themselves (Cole-Turner 1998).

Taken together, these findings raise questions about whether medication is unintentionally being employed by professionals as a form of imposing middle-class, white values, especially regarding masculinity, on children. Black and Hispanic children in the UK and the USA are far more likely to have diagnoses of conduct disorders, but less likely to be diagnosed with ADHD, possibly because inattentive, restless, excitable behaviours are more likely to be construed as part of a 'natural black temperament' (Pastor and Reuben 2008). Importantly, such cultural and racial stereotypes serve not only to shape diagnosis and delivery of treatments, but also the self-concepts of minority groups, such that, for example, black boys may come to accept this as an accurate part of their biological make-up.

Conclusions

The meaning of ADHD-related behaviours appears to be determined by the cultural context. When adults believe that the behaviour does not serve a beneficial function in their culture, medication is often used to reduce it, thus reframing its meaning as pathological.

Toward a DMM/systemic formulation of ADHD

ADHD as a diagnosis appears to reflect several genotypes, each modulated during maturation by stressful features of the environment (Webb 2013) and each having high levels of distractibility, that is, scanning widely and being 'response-ready' (Jensen et al. 1997). Although the meaning of 'distracted' behaviours can be construed negatively (i.e., children's performance is discrepant according to adult expectations), nevertheless they can be adaptive, preventing the child from becoming too focused to maintain the scanning for unexpected threat. ADHD symptoms seem to change most when the children's context changes (e.g. family structure, school, residence).

One adaptive function of the symptom of distracted/distracting behaviour might be for the child to be able to avoid attending to inescapable and threatening parental problems. Examples of such problems might be days of silence at home, repeated severe injuries to a parent, parents' suicide attempts, or temporary abandonment by a parent. Parental problems might be too threatening for children to attend to while concurrently being too important to fully ignore; short attention spans would permit children to monitor the situation without becoming fully aware of it. Moreover, if parents' explanations denied the problem, children might doubt their own sensory information. By flitting from one thing to another, they could escape both knowing about unchangeable frightening events and also experiencing discrepancy between what they observed and what they were told. Such regulation of attention would require high arousal. When the problem could not be avoided, alcohol, marijuana, and precocious sexuality might all function to calm and comfort such children without, of course, making them safer. In sum, given children's limited ability to protect themselves or their parents, early developing ADHD behaviours might function self-protectively in unclear, inescapable, and dangerous contexts.

This framing opens two DMM hypotheses for ADHD. The first fits unpredictable contexts that vary in their dangerousness (including, for example, some stressed parents and parents with spousal discord and drug or alcohol addiction); the hypothesis is that children will develop and use a Type C^+ (Types C3–8) self-protective strategy, with higher numbered strategies associated with greater danger and greater deception regarding the danger. The odd number forms, i.e., Type C3 aggressive, Type C5 punitive, and Type C7 menacing are possibly more compatible with traditional male roles. In these situations, the child's behaviour would function to defuse the parental problem (for example, through distracting parents' attention from their own problems or through forcing changes in their behaviour). The other hypothesis fits inescapable, predictable, and potentially irresolvable problems (including particularly critical and punitive parents who are never satisfied); the hypothesis is that children will develop and use a Type A⁺ strategy (especially Type A4 compulsive compliance or Type A7 delusional idealization), sometimes with intrusions of forbidden negative affect. In these cases, the children would be forced to accommodate the stressful situation because their behaviour was ineffective at modifying or reducing the threat. It should be noted that it is not the stressor itself that determines which strategy the child will adopt but rather the effectiveness of the Type C⁺ strategy at changing the threat. When coercion did not reduce the danger (or even increased it), the children would be predicted to employ a Type A⁺ strategy.

The two following cases show the different processes of working with ADHD in an enmeshed family with permissive parents and a disengaged family with authoritarian parents, respectively.

ADHD Type C strategy

The presenting problem

Rupert Ruggles' parents sought an evaluation of Rupert because his first grade teacher was concerned about his behaviour at school. Previous diagnostic work pointed toward ADHD. Consistent with this diagnosis-based formulation, manualized cognitive behavioural therapy (CBT) with Rupert had been tried at school, but his behaviour had not improved. A family evaluation was scheduled.

The family. The Ruggles family consisted of Joe and Jenni and their sons Rupert (aged 6 years) and Rob (aged 5 years) (see Figure 5.1). Although Rupert was the focus, in fact,

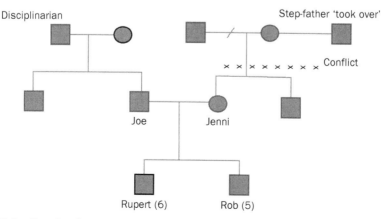

Figure 5.1 Ruggles family's genogram.

the family was strife-ridden, with fighting between Rupert and his brother, struggles around every family decision, and hours of battling around homework each night.

Rupert was easily frustrated, with many 'meltdowns' each day, and interpersonal problems at school (but his grades were okay). His parents were distressed and overwhelmed by trying to keep Rupert happy and reasonably calm. Unlike Hakim's 'intrusions of forbidden negative affect' (see Chapter 3), Rupert's apparent loss of control began with mild negative affect that quickly escalated to intense negative affect, but then temporarily subsided when his immediate demands were satisfied. Negative affect was not inhibited: to the contrary, it characterized Rupert and generated interpersonal contingencies.

The many diagnoses that Rupert had received (ADHD, conduct disorder, learning disability, and depression) confused the parents. Medication had been recommended, but the Ruggles wanted a coherent explanation before agreeing to it.

A multi-modal assessment

The assessment had three components: neuropsychological, family-of-origin for the parents, and structural. The neuropsychological component was begun first, but its results were the last to become available. Consequently, assessment and treatment overlapped in time. This commonly occurs and permits therapists and family members to slowly develop and refine their understanding of the family issues.

Family-of-origin work. Each parent was separately given an interview about their childhood, focusing on their own experience of being parented, sibling relationships and how these connected to choice of each other as marital partners.

Joe was the youngest child in his childhood family and was used to others knowing more and making the decisions; he just wanted to please them and be accepted. His father had been away from home quite a bit and, when he was around, he dispensed the discipline. Joe remembered admiring his father, but not feeling close to him. His mother had been available, but she had deferred to his father when it came to discipline, 'Wait till your father gets home.' However, he remembered playing with her and he thought that Jenni was in some ways like his mother with their children. He explained that he had wanted to be a different kind of father, one who was not frightening to his children. On the other hand, Jenni was assertive and involved more in managing the children's behaviour than his mother had been and he welcomed that.

Jenni was the oldest girl in her childhood family and was used to being in charge; she was the family achiever. Her parents had separated when she was 3 and she had seen little of her father thereafter. Her mother had raised her and her brother until her step-father entered the family when she was 8. At first, she had liked him, but later she began to resent his taking over; she remembered wanting to get back to how it had been before he arrived. Asked to think how this had influenced her ideas about being a good mother, Jenni said that women should be assertive, taking firm control of their lives and those of their children.

A meeting was devoted to describing these patterns as they might relate to their relationship as a couple. Jenni's semantic statements seemed to match Joe's: fathers should stand back from discipline and mothers should be in the driver's seat.

The children's self-protective strategies. Rupert was administered a School-aged Assessment of Attachment (SAA) (see Appendix 1). Rupert appeared to be using a coercive

Type C3–4 (aggressive and feigned helpless) strategy with his parents. Every time they let his mood or disruptions determine what the family did, they reinforced positively his negative behaviour. This happened intermittently and unpredictably; Rupert had to attend to subtle shifts in their non-verbal signals to guess what they would do next. Learning to do this likely increased his perceptual skill while his parents' unpredictability lowered his concentration on other things, like school. The unpredictability and reversals of family plans (often occurring to placate him) made him prone to emotional outbursts. Also, Rupert was not using deception. This highlighted the importance of change now, before the situation could deteriorate, possibly resulting in his feeling he needed to deceive or bully to get what he wanted. What did he want? In the fantasy stories of the SAA, the parents were always predictable and the boy was comforted. If these were Rupert's desires as well, could a way to communicate this to his parents be found and would they respond?

Rob's Preschool Assessment of Attachment (PAA) indicated that he used a compulsive performing strategy ('good boy' Type A4) – and showed no ADHD symptoms. He too was highly vigilant, but entirely without obstreperous behaviour. Instead, he tried to please his parents.

Neuropsychological evaluation. At this point the results of the neuropsychological assessment became available. Rupert had a mixed profile: above-average perceptual skills and reasoning, but deficits in focused attention, language, cognition, and working memory. He was diagnosed with ADHD, writing disability, and marginal obsessive – compulsive disorder. The neuropsychologist recommended stimulant medication. Both parents were unsure, but agreed to a six-week trial. At the end, they felt the medication had made no difference and it was discontinued.

Functional family developmental formulation of the problem

Many people assume that siblings share the same environment so differences between them can be attributed to their different genes. But in fact the family context differs for each child (Dunn 1991). As the second-born child, Rob was born into a family with a very demanding child. It was unlikely that he would be able to use Rupert's emotionally coercive strategy more effectively than Rupert. Moreover, doing so might so overwhelm their parents that Rob would get almost no attention. Instead, his mother's relief and reward of Rob's good behaviour, together with the increased predictability of his home environment when he was 'good', might have led Rob to organize the compulsive Type A strategy shown in the PAA at age 5.

Once this happened, Rupert's aroused behaviour might have been highlighted, leading to both greater parental dissatisfaction with Rupert and also Rupert's resentment of 'wonderful' Rob. A downward spiral of Rupert's attention-seeking and negative affect with both his parents and his brother might have ensued. What is certain is that, when Rupert was 6 and Rob 5, there was intense sibling disruption and parental distress. Moreover, the brothers used opposite Type A and Type C strategies whereas their parents used opposite sides of the Type C strategy (with mum dominating angrily and dad submitting placatingly). In this context, Rupert was singled out. The critical danger for the Ruggles could be conceptualized as lack of clarity in the family authority structure, due to the parents' current DRs reflecting more of their experience as children than as parents in a new family.

Family treatment of ADHD

Family structure. The family was assessed informally during family sessions. It was notable that Jenni answered all the questions, Joe agreed with or deferred to her (even changing his stated opinions), and Rupert created numerous disruptions. Both in the sessions and in the parents' report of home life, it appeared that Rupert's mood and needs dominated the household. The subsystem boundaries appeared weak, with the children often given executive functions, and with a substantial imbalance between the parents in which Joe seemed barely present in the family.

The family sessions moved between explorations of past events and the relation of these to current processes in the family. In order to give both family members and the therapist a clearer picture of current processes in the family, a brief enactment combined with a structural task was employed (Minuchin 1974).

The therapist asked adults and children to reverse roles and arrange a family dinner. The children were to decide who would be father and mother. They disputed, decided, reversed their decision, and got nowhere – mirroring their parents' inability to act as an executive parental system. The therapist intervened saying that their most recent decision would be final. Rob, as father, was asked to sit at the head of the (imaginary) table. As he did, Jenni reached out affectionately and straightened his clothing. Rupert was signalled by the therapist to take 'mother's seat' and he started to move forward, but began to fuss and pull back as he passed his mother. A mild sibling-like battle ensued between Rupert and his mother, with Jenni trying, in a whisper, to bribe Rupert with an ice cream cone. As the session ended, the therapist commented on the parents' responses and encouraged them to consider how they might offer a clearer structure to enable the boys to interact more constructively, for example, without attempts at using bribes. In addition, he decided to address the parents as 'Mr and Mrs Ruggles' when the children were present to clarify their executive role; he explained this to them privately.

Two sessions were focused on feeding back inconsistencies between the parents' words and actions. In the end, the subsystems were separated by ends and sides of the dinner table – and the parents were more authoritative and less indecisive.

Based on parents' complaints, a second enactment was tried. The stated problem was that, when deciding where to go out for dinner, Rupert rejected all possibilities (as a good Type C child would) and sometimes the family didn't even go out. In the enactment, Rupert complained, his choice was accepted, then he refused it too – as always.

The therapist took the role of commenting on discrepancies and inconsistencies, but didn't suggest solutions. 'Mr. Ruggles, you said you wanted to be more involved and in charge, but it seems like Rupert is in charge and doesn't know what to do.' 'Mrs Ruggles, you said you wanted your husband more involved, but you are accepting Rupert's complaints.' These comments encouraged the parents to take charge to change and resulted in immediate changes in their behaviour. Mr Ruggles became firmer and Mrs Ruggles found a solution: 'We're going to the barbecue place and, if Rupert doesn't like it, he can eat something when we get home.' In the final session, the parents were asked if they had noted any changes. They thought the family had greater structure and that there was less fighting. But they said it was because the therapist was present.

A trans-generational approach: re-writing family scripts. Consistent with the notion of corrective family scripts (Byng-Hall 1995), Mr and Mrs Ruggles were encouraged to discuss their wishes for their relationship and their marriage. Mr Ruggles said he wanted to be a more involved father, but did not want to become the disciplinarian that his own father had been. When he tried, however, Mrs Ruggles tended to negate what he said. On reflection, Mrs Ruggles volunteered that perhaps Joe's taking over reminded her of her step-father moving in and taking over. With a bit of sadness in her voice, she recounted that his arrival had cost her intimacy with her mother and comfort when she was distressed. A discussion ensued of how some of these early experiences may have influenced their feelings and actions with each other, resulting in discrepancies between what they said (using conscious semantic memory) and what they did (based on preconscious somatic feelings, procedures and images).

Once when Mr Ruggles suggested that the nightly struggles with Rupert about homework could be avoided if they limited his homework time to 45 minutes, regardless of whether he completed the work or not, his wife countered that Rupert needed more time because of his disability. Mr Ruggles suggested asking the teacher and making a family chore chart. Mrs Ruggles immediately implemented both ideas by calling the teacher, who approved, and making the chart with sanctions for failure to perform. Family life became less stressful, the fighting was greatly reduced, and Rupert continued to do adequately in school.

Outcomes and reversal trial. At about this time, school was dismissed for summer and Mrs Ruggles decided the children should have a more relaxed schedule. She wanted the relaxed comfort she had missed in her childhood. She discontinued the chores chart – and family chaos ensued as before. It took only three weeks for the parents to decide to reinstitute the schedule. The final step was the parents' joint decision to follow the school's recommendation of individual treatment for Rupert to help his to cope with disability.

ADHD Type A strategy

The presenting problem

At 5 years of age, when Arthur's preschool teachers found him to be very active, Arthur was diagnosed with ADHD (with both inattention and hyperactivity), plus conduct disorder and various learning disabilities.

Historical context of the referral. Arthur's father had not wanted to have children and Arthur's mother was still very angry about that. During the time leading up to the diagnosis, the mother had been extremely fearful about the school rejecting Arthur, but couldn't talk to the father about it. The father was depressed and jealous of his wife's attention to Arthur; like his wife, he couldn't talk to her about it. In fact, they often spent weeks without talking at all.

A series of treatment attempts. When Arthur was 6, his psychologist initiated a set of CBT programmes with him, his parents, and his first grade teachers to lower his activity level. The programme with the teachers was the most effective, but only for short periods: every two to three months they complained again that the situation was unworkable.

Problems with violence. During first grade, Arthur was disruptive at school, including serious aggression that was threatened, but not carried out, against a male professional. By the end of the year, the clinical team had arranged for Arthur to receive individualized education and extra support school personnel. At the same time, the family consulted a centre that specialized in ADHD; Arthur was prescribed methylphenidate. The individual programme focused on his learning problems and was carried out with special educators.

A DMM family developmental assessment

By the beginning of third grade, Arthur's behaviour at school was becoming acceptable. At his mother's request, his parents saw another therapist for further assessment and support because, despite improvements, his mother still felt very anxious. The two therapists reframed Arthur's behaviour as indicative of high generalized anxiety, and decided on a DMM family assessment.

The parents' therapist gave each parent an AAI and Arthur an SAA. The mother's AAI was classified as disoriented with dismissed unresolved trauma regarding physical and emotional neglect and a coercive protective strategy. That is, she used a strong Type C strategy with both self-deception and also possible deception of others, with inattention to her childhood experience of neglect and overall confusion regarding whose perspective she was taking at any given moment, i.e., disorientation. This suggested both an angry, vengeful quality to her relationships and also an intense desire to keep relationships 'active', that is, not neglectful in any way. Her disoriented confusion suggested that she might confuse who should be punished for 'neglect' and who needed this active engagement; both might be shifted to someone else, possibly the teachers or her son or both. This would effectively keep her anger away from her marriage, without resolving either the anger or her on-going fear of neglect.

The father's AAI was classified as indicating preoccupation with the unresolved loss of his mother and with the unresolved trauma of separation and being sent to boarding school combined with a mixed strategy of idealizing his mother and using coercion. That is, the father mildly idealized his mother and dismissed his longing for her as a result of being sent to boarding school, which was followed by her death when he was 20. If he transferred this idealization and longing to his wife, it might interfere with his evaluation of her judgements about Arthur. He, too, demonstrated an angry treasuring of relationships, but less intensely than his wife. As a couple, they were set up for a struggle that held and confused them both and for her to be the leader even though she would be confused about where to lead.

Arthur's situation was more complex. His SAA was classified as indicating both disorganized unresolved trauma regarding parental violence and separation and also vicarious experience of his parents' traumas in a compulsive compliant and externally assembled self protective strategy, with suggestions of possible intrusions of forbidden negative affect that didn't actually occur in the SAA. His parents were a tight, but struggling, unit defined by his mother's fear of danger and his father's suggested aggression. In his fantasy stories, Arthur seemed to fear spousal violence and possible marital separation. But in addition, his parents deflected their feelings away from their true sources, making it difficult for Arthur to know what was relevant to him. Arthur seemed to reflect his mother's fear of his violence in his 'incipient' intrusions that were not actually enacted. He coped with his parents' mixed strategies and misdirected feelings by maintaining very high vigilance, obedience to any clear directive and acceptance of their judgement of him.

The critical dangers appeared to be different for the parents and for Arthur. The parents' relationship seemed threatened by Arthur's need for protection and comfort;

the parents defended their relationship blaming Arthur, and he worked to preserve at least their protection by dismissing his perspective.

Process of therapy and outcomes

Closing the therapy. Arthur's mother was still so afraid that he would hurt other children that she asked the teacher every day how he had behaved. Meanwhile, the father found that he disapproved of his wife's critical relationship with Arthur, but nevertheless sided with his wife when Arthur 'misbehaved'. Arthur would cry and apologize, but his father stayed angry for days to 'teach him'.

Each parent reported spousal problems, but they refused intervention on those. Nevertheless, each used individual sessions to complain about the other. The mother talked about how her husband didn't take charge of anything and that she didn't feel that their house was her own because her husband had had it before they met. The therapist sought to elaborate these semantic descriptions with sensory images, using hypnotic techniques. When asked to visualize herself in a secure place, the mother was surprised to find herself in her current living room. She was also surprised by an intense somatic image of 'pain/desire for comfort', in her left arm. Discussing these images led her to reconsider her negative view of her husband, recognizing instead his contributions to their marriage. Her imaged discovery of her own dismissed desire for protection, attention and comfort clarified what she wanted from her husband, but also what she could do herself to get it. She decided to fight less with Arthur and pass more information and parenting tasks to his father.

In the meantime, as a function of both the new family functional formulation and also the increased reflective potential of Arthur's maturing mind, Arthur's individual intervention changed radically. Arthur had insisted on using the sessions to play a computer game with his psychotherapist. His psychologist felt this wasn't productive to the point of considering termination of treatment. The two therapists, on the basis of the SAA classification, wondered whether Arthur might be using the predictability of the computer game to establish a safe basis for interaction. If so, this might require the therapist to abandon the therapist-led CBT approach in favour of taking a responsive stance. Could permitting Arthur to choose and direct the activity be conducive to an interactive experience if the therapist merely observed and responded to Arthur in empathic ways?

Using the computer game, Arthur began to talk about family problems semantically. Although his reasoning gravitated towards themes of duty, punishment, and right and wrong, the therapist helped him to recall specific episodes. By reflecting on these, Arthur learned to differentiate his own perspective from those of his parents, teachers and school mates.

The work with the father paralleled that with the mother, but with more emphasis on the father's childhood and regulation of the relationship between him and the therapist. The father tended to speak long, run-on sentences that touched many different topics, often far in the past. The topics oscillated: attention to spousal problems, problems with Arthur, past family, issues with the wife, then Arthur again.

When the therapist recognized that both parents ended up focusing on Arthur, he decided to suggest that they come together to sessions focused on how to deal with Arthur. In meetings with both parents, a strategy to introduce more positive contingency in their interaction with Arthur was discovered and implemented. Then suddenly, the father stated that these meetings were hopeless. Although everyone agreed that the new strategy had worked well, the father got angry and stood up, saying he had had enough. He lingered briefly, as if waiting to be stopped, then seeing no response, went out. The mother apologized, saying 'He wants all the attention.' Sessions were stopped for three months, until the father asked to resume personal work.

Ending treatment. Arthur's interpersonal treatment was concluded when he turned 12; he discontinued methylphenidate when he was 14. He had learned how to behave at school and his mother became less anxious after learning to cede responsibility for his behaviour at school to the school and at home to a shared responsibility with his father. His father, in the meantime, found that he could be warm with Arthur without waiting for his wife to change. With the boundaries between home and school better defined and when Arthur was old enough to think about and regulate his own behaviour, the diagnosis of ADHD no longer fit him.

Conclusions

Arthur changed much more than did his parents. Their unhappy and silent relationship remained largely out of the intervention's reach. This suggests why Arthur didn't organize a coercive Type C$^+$ strategy; he couldn't split and manipulate his parents. Instead, he organized a strategy of self-blame (which brought him into synchrony with their blame of him) and obedience (when their requests were concrete enough for him to follow). He also diverted attention away from their troubled relationship because this was too complex and alarming for him to deal with strategically. With this impenetrable 'no-go' zone, his treatment necessarily extended into adolescence when he had matured sufficiently to function with considerable independence.

A central process in the treatment was helping family members to transform implicit DRs into explicit statements, images, and episodes. This made communication and negotiation possible. Toward the end of the family sessions, Arthur was able to speak up humorously and use evidence to correct some of his parents' negative biases toward him. They were impressed by his maturity and ability to spot discrepancies between statements and actions. Arthur had to do most of the communicative work in the family, but he did so articulately and explicitly.

Viewing ADHD in a relational framework

Both of these cases indicate that ADHD needs to be viewed within a relational framework. The two cases, despite almost identical descriptive diagnoses, had courses and results of treatment that were substantially different. This might be explained by the differences in the children's self-protective attachment strategies, which in turn related to how the parents functioned. In fact, both cases showed how crucial the participation of the parents to the treatment was. However, to participate constructively, parents need reassurance that they are not being blamed for causing the ADHD and confidence to resist the dominant view that it is essentially a genetically based disorder. Forming a supportive relationship with the parents is essential; some individual work with each member of the family may assist with this, especially during the administration of DMM assessments. These can help focus on the critical dangers that family members are facing. This, in turn, can guide the therapist and reduce attention to proximal complaints that function as distractors from central problems.

Summary of constructs and treatment principles

Constructs

1 *Non-verbal DRs* (somatic states, procedures, sensory images): These implicit representations are processed quickly, yielding rapid and automatic protective responses. Endangered children rely preferentially on these DRs.

2 *Verbal DRs* (body talk, semantic prescriptions and descriptions, connotative language): Later-developed, more complex representations are derived from further processing of non-verbal DRs, can be evaluated before being implemented and assist more refined regulation of personal states and behaviour. Safe and comforted children are more advanced in these processes.

3 *Episodic DRs*: Non-verbal (somatic, procedural, and imaged) and verbal (body-talk, semantic, and connotative) DRs can be integrated in a representation of an episode that is relevant to the current circumstances of the self. This integrative episodic DR is structured verbally but also exists like an internal video in the mind. The features of the episodic DRs in terms of cognitive sequencing (making causal sense) and of affective imaging (conveying motivation of the actors) are shaped by the individual's self-protective strategy; the strategy determines completeness and possible distortions of the episodic DRs, thus increasing the probability that the episodic DR will dispose protective behaviour.

4 *Concrete logic*: Following cortical maturation at 5–7 years of age, school-aged children can think and understand linear causality underlying the concrete facts that they perceive directly (especially if the facts are personally relevant). On these instances, they can reflect on how the facts can be perceived by different perspectives, generating alternate solutions. Among these, the one that best fits the information available is selected to be implemented.

5 *Multiple DRs*: The availability of multiple DRs that dispose different, even incompatible, behaviours allows for strategic flexibility. Children are assisted by the parents to transform implicit DRs into verbal DRs and to reflect on the various DRs; without such assistance reflection and integration progress very slowly.

6 *Integration*: The mental processing for the selection of which DR will be acted upon, or for the combination of elements from various DRs to produce a more accurate and inclusive DR. Integrative processing becomes part of the overall self-protective strategy. When integration is conscious, it can be verbalized; this helps the selection of consistent and adaptive behaviour.

7 *School-aged exposure to new strategies*: The children's strategic specialization, reflecting an adaptation to their family condition, is now challenged by exposure to other children's and other adults' strategies. This can enlarge the children's strategic repertoire, fill in some unsatisfied attachment needs, or precipitate adaptation crises.

8 *Best friend and peer group*: The attachment relationship with the best friend is the first non-familial attachment relationship for many children. It resembles siblings' attachments for its symmetrical quality, and is the prototype for future non-familial, symmetrical and reciprocal attachments (spousal). It requires coordination with the more exploratory social relationships typical of this age period, such as the peer group affiliative relationships.

Treatment principles

1   The family's presented level of urgency for symptom reduction can be used as an indicator of the family's need to preserve the current balance. This predicts their likelihood of using intervention more for stabilization than for change. The need for balance might also be related to the difficulty for the family of identifying and addressing the critical danger (either because this is in the past, or is not considered changeable).

2   Siblings' strategies should be expected to differ meaningfully according to their birth order in the context of the family organization around the critical dangers.

3   In a family setting, enacted procedures and images (including special attention to somatic states) can be articulated and reflected on, employing techniques that allow self-observation of the family members (for example, video or switching roles).

4   Therapists might reserve a directive stance for the purpose of guiding patients to discover information about their DRs. Patients could then be encouraged to reflect on this information and make their own conclusions and judgements, and test these with the non-directive assistance of the therapist. In other words, the therapist's directiveness is best reserved to the precise application of exploratory techniques, and is best avoided when the patients try to generate and implement solutions to current problems.

5   When parents and children face different critical dangers, these can be compatible or in opposition. When what is safe for one member of the family is dangerous for another, changes of strategy might not be advisable or possible in treatment. The next best priority becomes promoting, among the currently open functional options for the family, those that allow for enough balance to leave open some potential for children's future independence and reproductive functioning. If this is not possible, separation of the family members might be the only way to protect everyone.

6 The school years: Learning, belonging, and identity

Being 11 is the best age of all! That's what Mary thinks as she lies back in the tall grass looking up at the sky. Sandy's next to her and they've been giggling about boys. But now they're both quiet, just taking in the warm sunshine, the chirping of the crickets, and the wonder of a beetle climbing up a stalk of grass. They don't think about it, but if a developmental psychologist were to peek into their little nest in the grass, she might note the beginnings of spontaneous reflective thinking. Mary and Sandy are beginning to think about themselves, about each other, and about their place on this planet. Of course, their thoughts were very concrete (how cute Jonny is and how gorgeous the beetle's colouring), but the beauty and expansiveness of it all have become a conscious part of their thinking.

Mary's mum and dad have changed too. They don't know exactly where Mary is, but they know that the limits they've set will be honoured and that Mary and Sandy are safe. In fact, both Mary and Sandy are sensible kids and their parents trust them. They'll be fine.

Mary's so competent! Physically skilled, she can ride her bike, climb trees, and, of course, cross streets by herself. Socially, she engages easily with friends, solving most of the problems that come up without needing recourse to an adult. Sandy is her best friend and they hang out together all the time, whispering their secrets to each other. When they aren't together, they text each other. Mary can't imagine how she'd feel if Sandy moved away. She's seen other kids move and she doesn't like thinking about it at all.

Mary has her own personality now and with it come her moods. Of course she has moods; we all do. But Mary also has ways to calm herself down and she doesn't get stuck in just one perspective. With a bit of time to herself or some cuddling from her mum, Mary can usually reach outside of herself, see things from someone else's perspective, and find a compromise. Academically, Mary has put her acquired skills to good use. She uses money wisely, without even thinking about the underlying arithmetic. She reads without even trying (the words just talk to her as soon as she sees them); a world full of information flows in all day long without her even noticing. Science class isn't on her mind, nor her book of common insects, but lying there in the grass, she knows all about photosynthesis, sunlight and rain, and the life cycle of beetles. Does it get better than this?

All in all, the family's anxiety about keeping Mary safe is about as low as it will ever be. It's freed her parents to attend to the younger children and the zillion tasks that keep a household running. In the few quiet moments when they're not busy, one or the other might notice that the romance of their early courtship is a distant memory. Instead, they feel comfortable together, like old slippers. When did this happen? They can't quite put their finger on it, but they are different too.

At the same time, Mary's parents are looking ahead. They've noticed that her body is beginning to change and they're thinking about 'the talk'. Mary's mum is paying attention to what Mary wears and how she moves. Mary's dad is beginning to think of his little girl as a young lady. They're both aware of a world of sexual dangers that are invisible to Mary and they want to protect and prepare her. They wonder why the best of life and the worst come bound together in sexuality. They know that this is the pause before the storm of puberty and they worry about how they'll handle what lies ahead. They also treasure these last moments of childhood.

Even in the infinity of lying hidden in the tall grass, time is flying forward – and Mary's parents know it.

Developmental processes: maturational change and new adaptations

Source memory

By about age 7, maturation enables several useful tools for integration. Source memory is children's ability to keep track of where they got information. Did they experience it personally? Did their mother say so? Or their teacher? Did they read it in a book? Or did their friend Rusty tell them? Knowing how you got information permits children to reflect on the quality of the source. Does mum know about these things – or is she telling how she wants it to be? Is Rusty a reliable source of information or does he tell tall tales? At the end of the school years – and into adolescence – children will come to understand that just because it's written does not make it true. Books can be wrong – so you must consider the writer as a source. Children's thinking will become more complex as they begin to understand that some of what you hear isn't true – and isn't an outright lie either.

Knowing the source of information makes fantasy possible. Where preschool-age children confuse fact and fantasy, school-age children want facts. How does Santa fly through the sky and fit down chimneys? If these things are impossible, then might Santa be impossible? What's the source of the Santa information? Should you always believe your parents or might *they* tell stories? Clearly, children are becoming discriminating thinkers and are not so easily fooled any more.

Fantasy

A special issue comes up when the source is one's own mind. How does a child decide whether her thoughts have an external reality or are internally generated, that is, a fantasy? It would seem straightforward that, when the source is sensory input, information/the thought has external reality, but in fact neurological processes are not so simple. Just as a dream can seem so real that one awakens confused, wakeful 'dreams', fantasy, can activate sensory neurons just as though incoming stimulation had done so (Damasio 2003). How does one tell the difference? Context and logic usually are sufficient: Was I asleep? Could it have really happened? Was it most likely a dream?

Fantasy is a wonderful tool! It can entertain, it can prepare, it can resolve. With fantasy, a child can reach into the future and have a look around without having to risk the consequences of a foolish response. Alternative scripts can be created and compared. Reflection can permit the child to select the sequence with the most favourable probable outcomes. Plus whole new sets of ideas can be generated. Scientists, inventors, politicians, and divorce mediators are being created here, in middle childhood.

But for some children this reflective process lets imaginary information slip through as if it were actual. Two conditions create vulnerability for this error. When parents –

or other caregivers – have not been scrupulous about the truth and children's feelings have dominated interpersonal processes (this is, when children have been using a Type C strategy) and when children feel they need something very much, then they may intensify their focus on themselves, imagining what they want in detail, until it seems, neurologically, just like real. The ability to deceive the self is born and with it will come the ability to deceive others. Moreover, once the self is deceived, the behavioural tell-tale signs of lying (which come from conflict between truthful and untruthful representations) recede: if the self is convinced of the truth of the fantasy, then there is no conflict – and no signs of conflict.

Alternatively, when reality is thin, believers and supporters are few, and the consequences of displaying DRs that are not approved of by parents or teachers are very great, a delusion might fit the bill. An imaginary life can fill the gap in reality that the child cannot fill in real life.

Understanding complex interpersonal causality

As children gather episodic information, they begin to draw conclusions about how they and others act. Putting these thoughts into words and communicating about them with others becomes crucial to finding discrepancy and correcting misattributions. This is a complex process that requires perspective-taking, holding incompatible ideas in mind at once, and thinking about how actions will affect others. At home, parents can encourage this process, but often do so in a prescriptive or didactic way. With friends, children have greater flexibility as they chat about other kids and why they do what they do. The understandings that result from these interactions explain children's behaviour to themselves and others. Slowly the skills and information needed to explain oneself in close and social contexts accumulate.

These points are important for family therapy. Family members' non-verbal DRs need to be acknowledged and included in the family discussion in all families, but when a family has young children, their non-verbal DRs are the only means of communication (Kozlowska and Hanney 1999). When school-aged children are involved, they should be helped to acknowledge the range of DRs that they have (see Figure 6.1), assisted to decide which to act upon, and helped to think about what they did and why they did it without self-negating censure. Young adolescents can be guided to think in terms of recurring patterns of responses (as opposed to the single instances that school-aged children can reflect upon). Finally, it must be kept in mind that adults are particularly likely to find it difficult to recall their own contributions when asked to provide a history about the onset of their child's problem (Byng-Hall 1980, 2002; Whittingham et al. 2009). This is especially true when these do not fit their self-image or when non-conscious DRs are involved. In recent years, FST has moved away from non-verbal processes (Dallos and Draper 2010) toward narrative-based treatment in which language is often taken at face value and non-verbal communication is given second priority. A developmental understanding of the role of language and recall suggests that semantic and episodic/ narrative treatment procedures might need to be augmented by non-verbal techniques that address both the form of the communication and also its meaning (to all individuals involved, acknowledging that this might be different).

When children and parents have been endangered, verbal representational and integrative processes are used less often, with implicit and somatic representations being

Dispositional Representations

Arousal	Temporal Order	Intensity
(Somatic information)	(Cognitive information)	(Affective information)
↓	↓	↓
Organic states	Procedural Memory	Imaged Memory
↓	↓	↓
Body Talk	Semantic Memory	Connotative Language
↓	↓	↓
	Episodic Memory	
	↓	
	Concrete Reflective Integration	

Figure 6.1 Dispositional representations used by school-aged children.

more important. To be able to develop and integrate different levels of awareness, children need to be in a comfortable state of moderate physiological arousal. Being too highly aroused or under-aroused will mean that the operation of the integrative (frontal cortical) regions of the brain is impeded. The same is true for their parents.

Learning from parents

Children learn from observing how their parents manage affect (Semin and Papadopoulou 1990; Mikulincer et al. 2003). Parents who are endangered or feel frightened often shift into flight–fight or shutdown states of arousal and are less able to help children to develop the reflective skills needed to integrate different representations of experience. During these intense states, the parents' social engagement system (eyes, muscles of the face, muscles of the middle ear, and laryngeal muscles) are not geared towards social engagement with their children, but, instead, toward defensive action or shutdown (Porges 2011). Physiologically, these states limit parents' opportunity to connect with children in a calm and soothing way and to help the child down-regulate his or her own arousal. Instead, the parent's body communicates danger or disconnection (de Gelder et al. 2004).

Family members have many different ways of coping, some of which can be quite complex and difficult for children to understand. This may leave children knowing information that they are not supposed to know, or not knowing what they are supposed to know. For example, parents may be so preoccupied with survival from danger, that they assume that the child understands these dangers and fail to explain them explicitly. Alternately, parents may not agree as to what constitutes danger or what to do about it. For example, Dániel was 8 years old when his family fled as refugees from the Hungarian revolution in 1956. His step-father needed to escape possible execution for recruiting guns for the revolutionaries, his mother wanted to stay with her mother and the life she knew. As a school-aged child, Dániel had some vague awareness that his parents disagreed, but was largely 'shielded' from the contradictions and conflicts his parents were experiencing.

In other cases, protective action may have been taken too precipitously to have become conscious, verbal, and be thought about; that is, it is not known to either the child or parent. Or what is known may be 'unspeakable', either because others (usually parents, but also teachers, religious authorities, political regimes, etc.) don't approve of people who act that way or because it conflicts too strongly with one's own self-image. In these cases, what is known is transformed by distortion, dichotomization, displacement, or denial into something more palatable.

Accurate self-awareness is a process, a life-long process. It is best accomplished when one is safe enough to have the time to think and reflect and when powerful other people (parents, teachers, and partners) are empathic and understanding about imperfection. When, instead, adults use phrases like 'You always [do that]!' or 'You are a bad boy/incompetent girl/fool/bully/so mean, etc.!', children learn these things about themselves as absolute and enduring states (rather than occasion-specific behaviour). As a consequence, they avoid thinking about themselves, thinking in semantic terms, and gathering and integrating DRs. To understand the functioning of these individuals, we need assessments that do not rely solely on semantic and episodic information.

Coping with rejection

Rejection is one of the most powerful and self-negating experiences in life (Eisenberger et al. 2003; De Wall and Bushman 2011). Three forms of rejection are important: rejection by parents, by peers (both best friends and groups), and by authorities. Once children go to school, social and institutional rejection become possible threats. The long-term effects of rejection are very concerning. Learning to cope with rejection is a crucial skill, one that has not, perhaps, been addressed sufficiently.

One lens on children's understanding of rejection is picture card 2 of the SAA (see Appendix 1). This card shows a group of children rejecting one child and has the caption 'The girl's (boy's) best friend is going to play with her (his) friends.' Children's responses to this card are informative. Many simply pretend the problem isn't there by changing the story plot to remove the rejection. When the interviewer brings them back to the picture and storyline, they show physiological distress (wiggling, looking around) and mumble unintelligible responses. Others use nice, cookie-cutter formats: 'So she asked if she could play and they said yes and they all played happily ever after.' In some cases, the child gives up immediately and goes home or away alone. A few leave sadly, then find another friend and play happily. A concerning observation is that children who are receiving psychological services are the most likely to give up and go away. It appears that, in the eyes of these children, situation-specific rejection is absolute and leaves them without any resource except accepting their exclusion.

Parents' development

By the mid-school years, many parents have two children in school and no children in diapers. Family life has changed. Everyone is busy – mostly with non-familial activities. Usually, both parents are working now. One or both might be dedicated to a career that spills out of the designated work day and into family time. Children are going hither and yon for extracurricular lessons, sports practice, and a host of other peer-related activities. Keeping up with everything can become a major scheduling challenge. Retaining family priorities can become lost in the hurly-burly of car pools and obligations. The outcomes range from close marriages with balanced spousal and caregiving priorities to child-focused marriages, troubled marriages, and breakdown of the couple relationship with separation or divorce ensuing. Parental separation with its inherent uncertainty of outcome may be the most difficult of these for children to manage (Crittenden et al. 2010; Neale and Flowerdew 2007).

Self-protective strategies in the school-aged years

Maturation, development, and new contexts give children the chance to change their strategy. Change can involve refining an existing strategy, acquiring an additional strategy, or escalating a strategy that isn't functioning effectively. Below, we describe the new strategies that can be organized in the school years by those children whose families leave their children at risk.

Types A5–6 and depression

Some children who have used compulsive caregiving (Type A3) or compulsive performance and compliance (Type A4) strategies find that these do not improve their family relationships. This can be because (1) their parents are reacting to each other – and not directly to their children (that is, the children are triangulated into the parents' relationships) or (2) the parents are too unpredictable in their use of negative outcomes for the child's behaviour to yield safety (this often accompanies parents' use of drugs or alcohol). In these cases, school-age children may try to pull out of relationships so as to avoid conflict by managing on their own. Because the do-it-by-myself strategy of compulsive self-reliance (Type A6) (Bowlby 1980) cannot succeed in the school years, its use by pre-adolescents is accompanied by depression. Alternatively, such children may seek other, non-intimate attachment figures out of home (Type A5, compulsive promiscuity); this strategy can be quite dangerous because unknown people bring unknown threats. Depression, in this context, marks both a cognitive awareness of their impotence to change anything and the futility of self-protective action and also an affective state of sadness.

Self-deception and coercion: the Types C5 and C6 strategies

Some children live in unpredictable contexts with parents who often twist the truth to get what the parents want without the negotiation or struggle of accurate communication. In the school years, children learn to do these things too. Because simple lying is easily discovered and punished, children learn to deceive. Deception, in the context of unpredictable outcomes, creates a probabilistic situation in which the children who become skilled at deception are often rewarded and only occasionally punished. If the odds are good enough, deception may become the preferred strategy.

Two forms of deception develop, yielding two new strategies which are given the short-hand labels of punitively obsessed with revenge (Type C5) and seductively obsessed with rescue (Type C6).

In Type C5, a vindictive, aggressive use of threat can create the appearance of invulnerability. This can be used to make other children (and parents too!) back down and give the aggressive child what he wants. This, of course, is bullying and girls can do it too. Because the appearance is built on a bluff, avoiding actual conflict is important. That's where gangs of allies come in.

Type C6 plays on the other half of the Type C strategy, the appearance of vulnerability. In these cases, the child appears endangered, at risk, and incompetent to protect herself; she needs someone to rescue her! Of course, there is risk in waiting for rescue while placing oneself in risky conditions. One might not get the rescue and might be harmed. The greater risk, however, is that one will be rescued and, as a consequence, will not learn to protect oneself. In addition, when this strategy is used by boys, it can elicit aggression from other children. In many cultures, being a sissy might be an effective aggression-reducing strategy at home, but it is rarely successful for boys at school (Wallien et al. 2010).

This pair of strategies is thought to develop when outcomes are uncertain but at least intermittently and unpredictably involve moderate danger. As with all Type C strategies, Types C5 and C6 are joined in an alternating good cop/bad cop style and, while one side of the strategy may appear dominant, in all cases the individual uses both the invulnerable appearance (Type C5) and the vulnerable one (Type C6). A crucial feature of Types C5–6 is self-deception about one's contribution to relationships and events; this makes psychological rationalization of extreme behaviour, including deception of others about one's motivations and actions, possible.

Physiological symptoms that have an interpersonal basis

Normative somatic regulation

Somatic symptoms of distress become more common in the school-aged years (Holden 1999; Berntsson and Kohler 2001) and are closely linked to the child's capacity to self-regulate. By the school years, children who have lived in safe and stable families have good self-regulation skills. They are able to settle their bodies and put body sensations into words. For these children, these complex skills have been learnt in a seamless way: upsets from each day have provided these children with many opportunities to become distressed and to practise body, mind, and interpersonal skills to shift their bodies and minds back to a calm state. Mary might pat the dog, distract herself by reading or seek comfort from her mother to settle herself down. In doing this, she shifts out of a state of sympathetic arousal to a calm state characterized by a predominance of parasympathetic activity – her heart slows down, her breathing slows down, her gut re-engages the process of digestion, her mind is able to think clearly again and she knows everything is alright. Once her body is settled, Mary will then have the opportunity to talk with her mother about what happened and she will plan how she might manage a similar situation in the future.

Danger and somatic regulation

Self-regulation is much more difficult for children who live in endangered families (Felitti 2009; Crittenden et al. 2010; Kozlowska et al. 2011; Rask et al. 2013). As noted previously, parents who are very distressed may shift in and out of fight and flight states, or even states of shutdown (Porges 2011): physiological states that signal danger (de Gelder 2006) and compromise the parents' capacity to connect with their child in a calm way and to assist the child to settle his or her body (Porges. 2011). Consequently, the child may experience frequent periods of overly high arousal and may become overly distressed even in response to normal daily stressors.

Many medically unexplained somatic symptoms are manifestations of increased physiological arousal and reflect the child's difficulty in shifting his or her body state to a calm state (Kozlowska 2013). Muscle pain, including headache, is often a result of activation of muscle spindles. Abdominal pain, nausea, bloating, and toileting irregularities may reflect the activation of defensive gut programmes reflecting the child's compromised ability to maintain a calm physiological state. Hyperventilation – breathing more than required in the context of anxiety – can cause sudden changes in blood physiology and can result in symptoms of dizziness, muscle cramping, blurred vision, and even fainting. Children who remain very aroused for long periods of time may present with burn out syndromes in adolescence – debilitating fatigue or chronic unremitting pain – which seem to reflect the body's long-term response to chronic arousal (Chrousos and Gold 1998). Finally, conversion symptoms – non-epileptic seizures, loss of motor-sensory function in a limb or limbs or odd contortions and posturings of the body – whose mechanisms have not yet been elucidated are activated in situations where the child feels threatened (Kozlowska and Williams 2009; Crittenden et al. 2010; Kozlowska et al. 2011).

Somatic symptoms and attachment

The function of somatic symptoms varies in different types of attachment relationships. Among children who use a compulsive strategy, the symptoms are often a burden because they interfere with the child's attempts to be perfect for the parents; such children do not want to stress the parents any further. Alternatively, for some compulsive children, somatic symptoms allow the child to seek comfort from the parent for a physical complaint without having to disclose their distressing feelings (Freud introduces similar ideas in 'Dora' and isn't too far from the self-protective functions of the DMM).

Among children using a Type C strategy, the children often use the somatic symptom to coerce the parents to attend to them more. When caregiving is not forthcoming, the children may demand substitutes like buying toys though this does not address the underlying problem of emotional and physiological discomfort. The unsoothed child may up the ante by signalling pain and disability in exaggerated ways, for example, by wailing incessantly or by limping in an exaggerated way (Kozlowska 2009). Such signals are difficult for parents to ignore and they may find their lives revolving around the physical needs of their child.

Interpersonal adaptations

Managing multiple relationships

Disputes and discord

By the middle school years, children have had considerable social interactions outside of the family. This has both allowed some development of independence from the family – friendships with other children, relating to alternate attachment figures such as teachers, getting to know different families – and at the same time, these new relationships make demands and pose emotional challenges. Children require the assistance and support of their parents to help them manage quarrels and falling out with friends, friends ganging up against them, disliking aspects of their friends, concern and worry about the well-being of friends and to assist the child to refine and possibly revise their attachment strategies.

Becoming part of a group

School-aged children both develop distinct personalities and also learn to tone down individuality so as to function as a member of a group (Buckingham et al. 2009). Managing these opposite processes is complex – and some children do not manage it well. Finding recognition in school is important and requires tactics that were not usually so essential at home. Does the teacher reward achievement? Some children will compete for excellence. But not all can be first or even second. Other children will compete for attention – by being the most helpful or, conversely, the most troublesome or needy or entertaining. What works for each child will have an enduring impact on his or her developing personality – and on the image that others form of his or her personality. Once that image is in place, other people's expectations will constrain a child's attempts to change.

Family processes

Cultural variation

Cultures view 6- to 12-year-old children differently. In Western societies, they are still very much children. Their energy and enthusiasm are invested in play, toys, and games and, though they are becoming physically stronger and more assertive, they are still highly dependent on their parents. In non-Western societies, they may already be involved in work and rather than objecting and resisting schooling, as many Western children do, they aspire to get an education. For example, in parts of India or Africa, only the most privileged, favoured or clearly able children receive the luxury of an education. In Western countries, child employment is strongly frowned upon; instead, school and preparation for adulthood are children's 'work'.

Variation in family dynamics

The normative (Western) assumption is that school-age children are still in the position of being cared for rather than looking after their parents' needs. However, things are not always so straightforward, and in many families conflictual relationships between parents create a context that is anxious and strained. Parents also begin to expect that the school-aged child now starts to act less like a child: tantrums, moody outbursts, childish whining become less acceptable. Various interpersonal patterns become discernible at this age.

Three patterns emerge in families in which the parents need excessive support from their children (Byng-Hall 2002; Butler and Ashbury 2005). Some children take on caregiver roles (Type A strategies); this is especially common in families where one or other parent is physically or mentally ill, drug-dependent, struggling to cope with demands of work, and so on. When parents do not consciously attend to children's priorities, children sometimes become too adult-like and lose the benefits of these childhood years.

In contrast, other children develop Type C strategies of forgetting, resisting, or refusing to do as adults require. Such children may come to use increasingly deviant and deceptive strategies to escape, confront, or delude authority. Frequently these children seem immature, but in fact deception requires highly sophisticated integrative functioning. These children also lose many of the advantages to development in the school years.

Yet another pattern involves children being triangulated into their parent's relationships. Because they need the emotional support of their parents and think in absolute ways, children cannot easily recognize this process. Needless to say, their parents cannot recognize it either. When all the sources of information are within the family, the situation may only come to attention when the child enters school and, when that happens, it may be the child who is seen as having a problem.

When there are problems

In this section, we focus on two cases of serious dysfunction, both tied to father absence. One addresses acting out behaviour; the other psychosomatic problems. In both cases, a DMM formulation added new options to the clinical management of the problems.

Rejection

Graeme is an example of the impact of rejection – on both mothers and their children. Graeme was living with his mother who had divorced his father and the continuing animosity between the parents meant Graeme had no contact with his father (see Figure 6.2). At age 5, Graeme was referred for psychiatric evaluation by his school where he was defiant, aggressive with his peers and very controlling. His mother had expected a diagnosis of ADHD, but instead she was offered parental support, which she accepted.

Graeme and his mother also participated in a research programme using a variety of assessments of anxiety, depression, life events, and attachment (PAA and SAA). Of course, the coders knew none of the history.

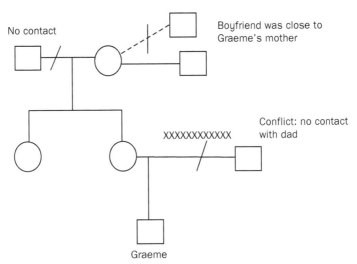

Figure 6.2   Genogram of Graeme and his family.

Graeme's attachment strategy. At 5 years old in a PAA, Graeme was classified as compulsively caregiving (A3) toward his mother. Six months later in his SAA, his basic strategy appeared to be the same (compulsive Type A), but now with a verbal assessment tool, more nuanced detail could be discerned regarding how satisfactorily the strategy functioned and what happened when it didn't work.

Graeme began by not wanting to say his name and age, but said his family was 'me mum, me dad, and nana.' He said twice, 'No, I don't have a best friend' and that he liked to play computer games alone.

For picture card 1, he was asked to tell a story about 'the boy going out alone'; he said he couldn't 'because I go out alone ALL the time'. He refused to tell about a recalled time. Asked what the boy on the card was doing, he said, 'He's walking off.' Why? 'They've had an argument?' This was a question, as if his answer needed the interviewer's approval. What did the boy feel? 'Annoyed.' How did his mum feel? 'Mmm mental.' What? 'Temperamental.' Arguing seemed to mean that someone must leave and mum seemed unpredictable. Mental and temperamental were connected in an unsettling way.

On card 2, he said the best friend wouldn't let the boy play with the group 'because the last game they played, he [the boy] didn't let them join in.' The rejection was the fault of the rejected boy! By this time, Graeme was flapping the card around and mocking 'saddo' children who feel scared by rejection. The interviewer asked him to recall a time when his friends wouldn't let him play and he placed the card on his head, saying 'Can you do this?' She asked him to concentrate and he said, 'It's boring.' Peer rejection really aroused him and he tried to minimize his feelings, deny feeling scared, avoid thinking about it, and, finally, he mislabelled it using a word that denied its arousing effect on him.

On the moving house card, Graeme became critical of something *so* 'stupid' as moving. Instead of making up a story, he discussed the difference between fiction and non-fiction. Then he said quietly, 'They are not going to let him move with them . . . because he has been cocky.' Having tried to dismiss and avoid the moving card, he ultimately said the boy's parents would abandon him – because he had a strong sense of his own worth.

By the bullying card, Graeme couldn't sit still and the card was flying toward the interviewer's face. He wanted to go directly to the next card and sounded cross so the interviewer got the card of the father leaving.

At first, Graeme tried to get rid of the card by saying it wasn't number 5, then spontaneously, he said, 'Maybe the boy's mam has been shouting at the dad . . . and now his dad's gone.' The boy was only 'quite upset', but his dad was 'really, really upset'. Asked about his own dad leaving, he said, 'Mmmmm . . . even worse' and fiddled with the microphone, before adding, 'My mam and her boyfriend had an argument and he smashed the living room door in.' This was when we discovered that his dad is not part of the family, in spite of what Graeme said at the beginning. Initially, it seems, he had offered us the family he wanted: mum, dad, and nana. Asked how he felt, he said 'My mam was crying' and fiddled with the microphone some more and began flapping the cards rapidly, before asking, 'Can we stop talking about it now?'

The interviewer moved to the boy running away card. 'Maybe it was because his mam made his dad go away . . . he's escaping.' He wouldn't talk about himself and began talking nonsense into the microphone. Running away seemed to really distress Graeme.

The final card was about the boy's mum going to hospital: 'Maybe she was so worried about the boy running off in the morning when she couldn't find him that she panicked. She died . . . cause she had a heart attack.' Suddenly Graeme turned the discussion to a detailed medical discussion of heart attacks. Brought back to the story, he said the boy was 'happy' and 'the dad didn't like the mum and he was really, really happy'. When the interviewer asked about the dad, Graeme snapped back, 'That's what I just said!' The interviewer asked why he ran off in the morning. 'At night! Don't you ever listen!' 'I thought you said in the morning.' 'No, I said in the morning when his mam was looking for him.' 'Why did the boy run away?' ''Cause he hated his mum.' 'Has anything like that ever happened to you?' 'N-O spells no!' In DMM terms, this is an intrusion of forbidden negative affect.

The interviewer said the cards were finished and asked what a happy card would look like for his family. Silence. Then 'My birthday', followed by 'Do you have to know about it?' The interviewer said no and mentioned that this had been hard for him. Graeme concurred.

There are several important features to this SAA. First, the seven cards are meant to address different threats that become salient in the school years, but for Graeme they all reduced to rejection. This suggests the second point: feeling rejected by one's parents colours everything else. A third point is that a number of Graeme's behaviours (e.g., flapping the cards, moving around, being interested in the recording equipment and not the questions) could be seen as symptoms of a psychiatric disorder or, conversely, as part of a Type C strategy. What is important from the DMM perspective is how the behaviour functioned for Graeme.

When the whole of the SAA is read with care, it becomes clear that the agitation marked Graeme's perception of danger and his off-topic focus reflected his attempt to keep negative affect from being displayed and, as a consequence of display, from disposing aggressive behaviour. In addition, he tried to regulate his feelings by omitting himself, minimizing his own feelings, and displacing negative feeling to 'the boy' and dad; these indicate a Type A strategy. When psychological strategies for regulating his rising anger and despair failed, Graeme intensified his agitated attempts to get off the topic of rejection by flapping the cards and playing with the microphone. But when he was brought back, he obeyed the interviewer and eventually reached a point where he couldn't manage any longer. He lashed out at the interviewer – who had exposed his vulnerability – in words that sounded very adult. Where had he learned that kind of cutting verbal aggression? Because his strategy was one of inhibiting anger or displacing his attention to other topics, Graeme's attacks on the interviewer were considered 'intrusions of forbidden negative affect' (see Hakim in Chapter 3, Denise in Chapter 4, and Arthur in Chapter 5).

Graeme's mother's attachment strategies. Graeme's mother told her story in an AAI. Her history of attachment-relevant experiences and the discourse with which she told her story provide a basis for understanding Graeme's pervasive sense of rejection.

In her opening statement about her family, she said she had a sister, mum, and dad and that her parents split up when she was 9. In the follow-up questions about her father's family, she said, 'But he doesn't really have anything to do with them.' In the next few responses, that phrase was repeated five times, referring to both her father (he) and also herself, her mother and her sister (we) having nothing to do with the paternal side of the family. Asked if there was anyone else she had been close to, she said, 'Erm . . . um . . . not really, just my mum, it were, like, my mum was on her own for quite a while and then she got wi with a guy who I became quite close to and then they split up, and then then she she got with somebody else who she is now married to.' Her dysfluence around these 'close' people is notable, as is her loss of the first 'guy' and rejection of his replacement, her step-father ('somebody').

The remainder of her AAI painted a picture of a strict mother whom she idealized and supported in an on-going triangulated struggle with her derogated and ousted father. Graeme's mother did not, of course, see that she was idealizing her mother, nor that her on-going rejection of her father's overtures (even in her adulthood) reflected her defence of her mother; she did not see that she was continuing the struggle that had split her parents years ago. In her recalled episodes, she complained at length about her dad making her eat food she didn't like, when, in fact, the episodes about needing care showed him, and not her mother, to be the protective and comforting parent. Indeed, when asked how her childhood had affected her adult personality, she almost knew that her father had been supportive:

> I think, I . . . I don('t) thi(nk), I know it sounds it sounds strange, but the way the way that my dad was strict with me, I think that did me good . . . really because . . . sounds dead strange cause you hated them for doing it. But, eh, it it's I I have never done, I have never gone the wrong way.

Nevertheless, despite the recognition of her father's strict parenting as caring, she said she had chosen not to bring Graeme up like her parents brought her up.

Information from the school. The principal reported that Graeme's behaviour had settled during a short period of time when he was regularly seeing his father. Conflict between his parents had caused this to deteriorate.

Functional formulation. It appeared that Graeme's mother had been drawn into her parents' conflict as her mother's ally and retained this role even as an adult and even in spite of information to the contrary. This meant losing her father as a support for herself, even though he had been more supportive than her mother and even though he continued to offer support in the present. She had also lost her whole paternal family. She had accepted her mother's first boyfriend and loved him, but her mother cast him away (as she had her father). When Graeme arrived, she unknowingly carried forward her distrust of men. She rejected Graeme's father, thereby depriving Graeme of a second attachment figure. Of course, she did not see how her mother's actions had interfered with her forming relationships to men – and possibly to young boys as well. She also did not see how rejected Graeme felt. The critical danger for Graeme's mother seemed to be losing her relationship to her own mother; she protects against it by actively rejecting male partners (her mother's, but also her own, with a confusion of persons that suggests unresolved trauma). The critical danger for Graeme seemed to be the same: losing his relationship with his mother. However, the efficacy of his protective strategy of caring for his mother was limited by mother's own protective strategy. The critical dangers for mother and son seem nearly incompatible.

The rest of the story. Five years later, Graeme, now 10 years old, continued to have behavioural difficulties at school and was seeing a psychotherapist. His father sought access through the courts, but Graeme said that he didn't want to see him because it made him (Graeme) too angry. Graeme's teachers understood that his angry outbursts were linked to the animosity between parents.

When Graeme was 12, his behaviour had deteriorated further, including self-harm through deep scratching when he was stressed and unable to cope (he said he felt like exploding). He was articulate and could talk about this. Social services began supervising the family. Graeme had repeated angry explosions at school that got him into trouble and made him feel bad; he wanted to talk with someone again about his life and his struggles. Unfortunately, there was no one who had contact with both of his parents. Graeme was about to move to senior school and everyone was worried about how he would cope.

By the time Graeme's mother met with a counsellor, she had begun to discover her childhood triangulation, idealization of her mother, and the struggle between her parents, recognizing that her mum still expected her support against her father. Having feedback on her AAI assisted the counsellor to focus on this and not be distracted to minor issues. The outcome was that Graeme and his mother gained a closer relationship with her father. Nevertheless she was unwilling to think about Graeme's father and adamant that he not be contacted.

For his part, Graeme struggled between trying to make his mum feel better and his violent outbursts. When his therapist changed job, things broke down. Graeme ran away several times, eventually ending up at his dad's. His dad and girlfriend took him in, after which he became stable, stopped self-harming, and worked productively with his new therapist. This therapist strongly supported the dad and spoke almost angrily about the mother – whom she had not met. Graeme chose to see his mum only intermittently because she blamed him for her distress. Then, unexpectedly, he began running from one home to the other, each time complaining about the parent he had just left. The professionals were in an uproar. This wasn't according to the plan.

Whose plan? Not Graeme's! Further, the various professionals were dichotomized into supporting one parent or the other. 'Absolutist' thinking and triangulating processes threatened Graeme's development on every side. But more than that, the relationships that the professionals formed with Graeme and his parents were very much linked with their own histories and attachment strategies. One of the key professionals formed a relationship with Graeme that involved him making her feel good and her needing to be seen as the person who has rescued him from his mum. This dynamic was difficult to change because she had such a personal investment in it and was not aware of it. Thus, it was not just dad demonizing Graeme's mum and the reverse, it was also that professionals got caught up in this too, for their own reasons.

In conclusion, we note the long reach of childhood attachment issues, even into selecting a spouse and ways of interacting with children and even into why professionals choose their profession. In this case, the mother's misunderstanding of her mother's adult relationships with men was generalized and contributed to the breakdown of her marriage and her unyielding refusal to let Graeme see his father. No attachment information was available on the father. Most unfortunately, the various therapists sided with one parent or the other; this probably maintained Graeme's intense distress and delayed his adaptation longer than necessary.

As we go to press, a family-based perspective is being proposed with assessment of the father and group meetings of family members and professionals in various combinations. The goals are to achieve fuller understanding of each parent and their relationship with Graeme (including what each has to offer Graeme and their limitations) and guidance to the parents on how to act like a respectful couple that is working together to solve problems in ways that will promote Graeme's development. Put that way, the focus is off resolving the parents' childhood problems, even though these interfere with their daily relationships now, and off them as a couple. Instead, they are being guided to fake appropriate collaboration for the sake of their son. The professionals are working to achieve a more realistic and nuanced understanding of each parent so as to defuse their own triangulating process. We note that meeting, assessing, and engaging the father earlier might have prevented the current situation.

Somatic signs of psychological and interpersonal distress

Joseph's history and history of treatment

Joseph was a 10-year-old boy who suffered from many medically unexplained somatic symptoms: headaches, fainting, non-epileptic seizures and paralysis. He was an only child and his childhood had been rocky: his father was alcoholic and his parents had fought frequently. Joseph's parents separated when he was 9. His father became very depressed: when intoxicated, he talked to Joseph about suicide. When Joseph's mother began to date another man, his father became very angry. Unable to cope with the escalating conflict between his parents, Joseph began to suffer from recurrent headaches. His mother sought medical help (see Figure 6.3).

Some months later, the mother's boyfriend became inconsolably depressed and committed suicide. Joseph started worrying more about the safety of his father who was drinking a lot and had lost his driver's licence. Would his father commit suicide also? What could he do to look after his father? How could he look after his mother? At around this time, Joseph's mother also became depressed and Joseph became increasingly anxious: he developed a fear of being kidnapped and began to suffer from frightening nightmares about monsters. His father was concerned that his mother chose partners who were dangerous for his son.

One day, when Joseph was being looked after by his father, his 15-year-old dog Mollie died. Joseph's father had brushed him off when Joseph begged him to take Mollie

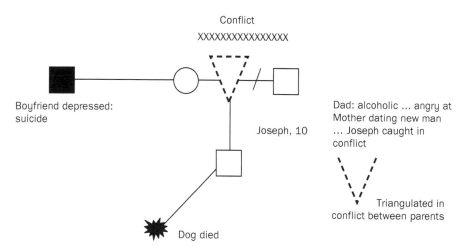

Figure 6.3   Genogram of Joseph and his family.

to the vet. Joseph was alone holding Mollie when she died. Following Mollie's death, Joseph began to suffer from frequent fainting episodes both at school and at home, his legs began to hurt all the time, he started to get panic attacks and was afraid of large crowds and open spaces. Although fainting can be triggered by fear or other strong negative emotions (Bracha 2004), this possible aetiology wasn't recognized.

Some months later, Joseph's fainting began to transform into extended non-epileptic seizures (Bowman and Markland 2005), accompanied by disorientation and visual hallucinations of bees buzzing around his head and spiders on his legs. His mother took him to the hospital repeatedly. A month later, Joseph developed paralysis and loss of sensation in his legs. Because all medical tests were normal, they were sent to child psychiatry.

Telling the family story was painful for both Joseph and his mother; they cried and cried. Joseph's Type A self-protective strategy – compulsive caregiving and the beginnings of self-reliance – together with unresolved loss (of his dog), and trauma (of parental conflict) were evident in his interviews. It was also very clear that Joseph's strategy was not working: both parents were so distressed that they were unable to provide either safety or comfort.

Joseph stayed in hospital for three weeks and was extremely compliant and adhered to every aspect of his treatment programme. He did physiotherapy to get his legs working. He took the prescribed medication to help decrease his body arousal so that he could sleep at night and to help contain his anxiety symptoms. He had sessions with his individual therapist to practise talking about what had happened and to explore his confused emotions and how these related to his somatic symptoms. Joseph found talking about negative family events and feelings very difficult. In an effort to keep everyone in a positive light, he clammed up and tried to manage his emotional pain and worry by himself. He also learnt a variety of arousal lowering strategies: breathing techniques to maximize vagal control of the heart, use of distraction when his worries became too intense, and talking to his mother when he was emotionally upset so that she would hug him and give him comfort. These strategies helped, but Joseph could not use them when he was very, very upset. Any sign of parental conflict upset him greatly. Then he would faint or have a non-epileptic seizure.

Joseph's father came to meet with the hospital treatment team only once. During this meeting, he was not able to acknowledge his own contribution to Joseph's suffering. He did not visit Joseph at the agreed times and could not be reached on his phone. Every time Joseph experienced another let-down from his father's absence, his legs would work less well or he would faint or he would have a non-epileptic seizure. An important topic of family sessions was to help Joseph talk about how complex and sad things were for his mother, his father, and him. These meetings allowed Joseph to acknowledge that at times he felt frightened and unsafe when his parents fought and when his father was drunk.

Slowly, Joseph became more aware and verbal about intra- and interpersonal states, including his anger. When Joseph's mother heard him express his emotional pain, distress and anger in words, and when she realized that Joseph's physical symptoms were being caused by these negative emotions, she experienced an 'aha moment'. Her strong feelings of distress combined with understanding (integrated affect and cognition) motivated her to treat her own depression so that she could function better as a mother, provide Joseph with comfort, and stabilize their family by completing the financial separation.

After discharge from hospital, the treatment team continued therapy sessions with Joseph and his mother. Although well most of the time, Joseph's symptoms recurred after contact with his father: a relapse being likely if Joseph's father was intoxicated or lost his temper. Joseph and his mother found themselves in an irresolvable predicament: Joseph loved his father and wanted to spend time with him – when he was not drunk – but he was unable to maintain sobriety and safety, and Joseph's somatic symptoms were re-triggered by contact visits.

After one particularly frightening visit when his father became exceedingly drunk and oblivious of his needs, Joseph suffered a very severe relapse: he had intermittent leg paralysis and recurring non-epileptic seizures for six weeks. The treating team became so worried that they notified child protection and considered another hospital admission. During this time, Joseph became openly very angry with his father and refused to see him or to take phone calls from him. He told the treating team that he loved his father and wanted him, but that he had decided that he could not see his father if he was drinking and that he did not want to talk to him on the phone when he was drunk. For Joseph, this meant never seeing his father and not taking his calls.

When discussing the decision with the team, Joseph wept openly. The treatment team felt powerless to help Joseph and discouraged with regards to their failed efforts to engage Joseph's father. They were also angry that the father continued to act in ways that were harmful to Joseph. In this therapeutic impasse, the team supported Joseph's mother to accept Joseph's decision in the short term, to initiate formal divorce proceedings in family court and to base her negotiations about contact around the issue of safety.

Gradually, all parties involved seemed to converge on the father as the critical danger for Joseph. Despite showing the greatest ambivalence about this formulation, Joseph was also the one to articulate it openly. The mother, who had decided to separate from the father in the first place, had Joseph's blessing and the support of the clinical team in completing all aspects of the separation. At this point it was unclear what motivated the father or why Joseph's mother had chosen an alcoholic partner and suicidal boyfriend. That is, the 'backstory' was incomplete.

The SAA was administered at this point in the treatment intervention to assist in treatment planning – referral to outside therapists to increase support was being explored – and when Joseph's story was chosen for inclusion in this volume.

The SAA and classification. The SAA was formally (blindly) coded a few months later, when this case was being prepared for inclusion in this chapter. Joseph's transcript was classified as indicating partial depression, unresolved trauma in both preoccupied and dismissed forms about parental fighting and a depressed response to the loss of his dog, plus an anticipation of losing his father together with a mixed protective strategy of compulsive caregiving, self-reliance, and delusional idealization of his mother (i.e., A^+) and triangulated coerciveness regarding his parents as a couple (i.e., C^+).

That is, Joseph was partially convinced that his situation was futile and was traumatized by his parents' on-going conflict and the loss of his dog. He also feared that his father might die from alcoholism. He used a caregiving strategy with his mother and idealized her unrealistically; in addition, however, he tried to rely only on himself, as if believing that she could not manage even with his help. Finally, he was furious with both of his parents for drawing him into their fighting, but he could only express this in relation to 'the boy' on the picture cards and not in personal recalled experiences.

Joseph's Type A strategy was very clear. Although he habitually cut off all negative affect, it was clear that he wanted his father very badly, was very concerned about his mother's well-being, and was very afraid that he might have no functional parents at all. In addition, his sense of being the problem seemed implicit in what he stated about his birth (card 7, mother going to hospital): 'I had to be cut out with a, I was stuck.' This response was seen as a summative statement about his life predicament because: (1) it occurred on the most threatening card; (2) it was his spontaneous response; (3) it contained a cut-off phrase (how would he be cut out?); and (4) it had a stark imaged quality (cut, stuck). Being stuck in birth and immobilized by non-epileptic seizures and paralysis seem analogous; they all suggest that Joseph thinks that he is the problem, needs extra-familial help, and faces a life-and-death dilemma.

The issue of a Type C strategy was less clear. Linguistic markers of Type C were present in the imagined stories about 'the boy' and rarely in the recalled episodes that Joseph told about himself though they 'seeped in' on the last two, very threatening cards. In the imaged stories, the boy (1) used angry evocative language with regards to the father, 'and he's just being all mean and, got the cranks and just went, just said "that's it, I'm leaving" and just stormed out the door'; (2) defended his mother while putting down his father (triangulation); (3) created magical rescues, (4) presented himself in a heroic, self-aggrandizing manner; and (5) twice told a story about the father getting cancer after smoking and drinking too much (punishment), and the boy – when older – refusing to see him because the father had treated him badly.

A revealing moment occurred in the imagined story in the 'father leaving' card. The imagined story was about the boy's father going to hospital with cancer because he drank and smoked. The coder interpreted this as punishing the father for behaviour that upset him and his mother. The interviewer had asked what the mother was thinking about the father's absence and Joseph had 'the boy' say: 'she was thinking if the boy is gonna be upset or if he's gonna, if she's gonna go nuts without someone helping'. The cut-off suggested Joseph's emerging awareness – albeit not conscious – that his upsets were expressed as non-epileptic seizures, but, if that was his meaning, he both displaced it to the boy and also cut it off rather than stating it. On the other hand, Joseph was clear that if the boy gets upset, his mum will need outside help to avoid going 'nuts'. This passage highlights that there are different ways of knowing and implicit somatic knowledge is among them. One effect of eight months of treatment may have been to bring somatic and verbalized semantic knowledge closer together.

The Type C discourse suggested that changes were taking place in Joseph's DRs. In contrast to his self-protective organization at the time of referral (which had relied on the omission of all negative information), Joseph was now preoccupied with both his extreme anger and also his intense longing for his father. He seemed to hold his father more responsible than his mother and to both fear his father's death and also punish him with it.

Formulation, taking the history into account. As often happens when children are caught between psychiatrically troubled and disputing parents, Joseph was at risk of losing both and felt he had to choose between them. Like most such children, he chose his residential parent who was also the parent who could not refuse to participate in treatment unless she was willing to risk having her child put in care. Making this choice, as a 10-year-old, required that he distort his DRs to reduce the apparent complexity of the situation. Joseph allied with and idealized his mother and derogated his father. His action was distorted by the lack of contingency to his father's state of being sober or inebriated and enhanced by the clinical team's support of his mother.

Long-term change. Joseph's father became very distressed that his son was afraid to see him and agreed to meet the treating team. Although the team acknowledged the importance of the father–son relationship, they said they could only support the relationship in their letters to the court if the relationship was safe. Joseph's father could not understand why Joseph became upset by seeing him pull out a beer bottle. The team offered to help if he wanted assistance for his alcohol problem. Following this meeting, Joseph's mother with her solicitor negotiated short two-hour access visits with the father, contingent upon his being sober. In the subsequent three months, Joseph saw his father fortnightly without any further incidents. This was the first extended period of time that Joseph had been symptom-free in two years.

Joseph's father, like most such fathers, did not live daily with his son's suffering and did not face the immediate consequences of refusing to accept external intervention. Like Joseph's mother initially, he saw the problem as medical, not interpersonal. However, when Joseph's decision created consequences for him, he took immediate action, renewing efforts to negotiate with his ex-wife to protect his access to his son. In terms of critical causes, it was only when faced with yet another loss (son, after wife) that he took action. The team supported his decision-making by framing the situation simply and clearly so that he could make a meaningful decision and take action on it.

Joseph's decision fits a caregiving strategy (i.e., his mother should have made the decision) and had the effect of differentiating his relationships with his parents (Bowen 1978). It is worth noting, however, that without the treatment team's support, Joseph could not have done this.

The take-home lessons

The cases of Graeme and Joseph were selected for different reasons: one to illustrate rejection and one to explore somatic representations of interpersonal problems. Although it was not sought, both hinged on triangulated parental discord that was experienced by children, but beyond their comprehension and control. Moreover, in both cases, the children resorted to distorted DRs that functioned as short-cuts to by-pass the impasse in between their parents. Moreover, in the absence of fathers, both boys became involved with caring for their vulnerable mothers and rejecting their desired fathers. This emphasizes the importance of fathers and their relationships with mothers. Finally, the professionals became active participants in the families' functioning; when children are seriously threatened, a decision that reduces irresolvable complexity must be taken.

Short-cuts in professionals' DRs

Why did the professionals use less complex formulations than the DMM assessments suggested were needed? For Graeme, we could ask why a diagnosis was sought for the boy and his parents' histories and current functioning were not explored. The answer would likely be the huge demands on professionals' time, the limited resources for such in-depth assessment, and the 'in-your-face' quality of the boy's behaviour compared to the invisible quality of his caring parents' contribution. In retrospect and after five years of increasing trouble, the cost of early family evaluation seems small. Maybe having a triangulating and rejecting pattern in mind early on could enable other such cases to receive thorough family-level evaluation sooner.

For Joseph, it is easy to point to the father's intransigence and the mother's cooperation as explanations or even justifications for the failure to engage the father. But these, we think, are short-cuts that overlook the complexity of the situation. Fathers are more often missing from families than mothers and, when children are in trouble, non-residential parents are less easily engaged. The frequency of this situation suggests that cultural values and practices are operating. The data on children with absent fathers suggest the need to seek alternative solutions to this problem. Clinicians working with such children need to be aware of the bias toward residential parents and to engage the non-residential parent in creative ways.

Children's transitional DRs

In the best of worlds, mothers and fathers would work productively with therapists to reduce the demands that their animosity places on their children. In reality, when parents don't simplify the situation, the child's mind must do so. When that doesn't solve the problem, their strategies break down: that can appear as anger, defiance, or physical illness. Without therapy, Graeme's problems escalated. With therapy, Joseph became conscious of his predicament, transformed it to words, and protected himself by taking a drastic decision. To do this, however, he needed the treating team's support and, even so, the best he could do was to use the short-cut of excluding his father entirely. One role for members of the treating team might be to keep this distortion clear in their own minds and to remind Joseph that this might be the best solution 'for now', but that, as he grows older, he might want to reconsider. Learning the provisional and flexible quality of strategies is good for everyone. Fortunately for Joseph, once his mother had negotiated contact visits that were safe, she was able to help Joseph to modify his decision and maintain contact with his father.

Reaching fathers

At many institutions, especially those who do not work within a family systems framework, fathers are not invited to the initial meeting. When this happens, the professionals have already engaged with the mother and will have lost neutrality (Selvini et al. 1980). Fathers may be invited into the therapy once the professionals discover that the problems extend to the father. That is, blame lies just out of sight, under the surface of an invitation. It is not surprising that they may be hesitant to engage under these conditions. Moreover, the inviting professionals are usually women and they work the same hours that the men do. Possibly having more men in the frontline services and having the option of meeting in the evening or on weekends would be helpful. A more flexible approach, combined with early DMM assessments to identify the role of fathers, would help.

Repairing breaches

Finally, it might be worth looking at how these cases were developed for this book. Graeme was easy – because the research team was not invested in the process of change with the family. They remained outside the family system, being neither helpful, nor caught up in the story. Working out Joseph's story was much more complex. The treatment team wrote their story with residual anger at Joseph's father and needed time to integrate their treatment experience with the blinded coders' perspective. They also struggled to reconcile the Type C discourse markers in Joseph's transcript with his clinical presentation: Joseph had never behaved like a coercive child. In the end, the problems were resolved by treating different sources of information as each valid and also potentially distorted, keeping the dialogue open by asking questions, and trusting one another. Without trust, the discussion among professionals could have replicated the family's triangulation.

Our points are that: (1) problem resolution strategies are essential in all human relationships; and (2) offering treatment involves becoming part of the family process; that changes one's perspective, highlighting some things and hiding others. Doing research keeps one neutral, but also ignorant of important process information. The confluence of different perspectives and dialogue between them produced the clearest understanding of what could be helpful to families. When resolution was reached, everyone's perspective had value, even the perspective of people who were not present, and a way forward became visible.

Summary of constructs and treatment principles

Constructs

1   *Middle childhood*: Adequate practical ability to stay safe means a lower level of anxiety for children, which in turn allows them to practise concrete reflective functioning around regulation of their own behaviour, arousal and body state.
2   *Source memory*: A specialized type of episodic DR that records how information was gained. It is important to integrative functioning where the evaluation of the reliability of the source of information affects selection of the best behavioural response. Source memory also enables children to differentiate fact and fantasy.
3   *Priority of self-protection*: Endangered family members often focus on self-protection rather than assisting one another; parents who feel endangered are less able to help children to learn to reflect. This can lead to discordant and incompatible DRs held by a single person or by different family members.
4   *Compulsive promiscuity and self-reliance (Types A5, A6)*: When compelled behaviours directed to the attachment figures fail to increase safety, new strategies may be organized. The compulsively promiscuous (Type A5) strategy compels the approach to strangers in hope of finding protection or comfort: this involves inhibition of fear of strangers and incurs the risks of dealing with unknown people for safety and comfort. The compulsively self-reliant (Type A6) strategy is based on the construction of the self as the cause of the failure and can compel self-reliance to the point of isolation in the face of danger.

Although the child can conceptualize and desire to use these strategies, neither is functionally possible in school-age (because both require independence).

5   *Punitive and seductive coercion (Types C5–6)*: the punitive-seductive strategy (C5–6) is based on adding falsified cognitive information to the Types C3–4 strategy, in order to increase the effectiveness of the strategy by leaving the attachment figures unaware of the child's plans and thus less able to foil them. In the punitive (Type C5) half of the strategy, deception creates an appearance of invulnerability (thus, often avoiding the actual conflict). In the seductive (Type C6) half of the strategy, deception creates an appearance of vulnerability (thus, eliciting rescue and avoiding responsibility for self-protection).

6   *Depression*: a state that involves, cognitively, an awareness of the futility of self-protective action (cf. Seligman's (1975) learned helplessness), affectively, the feeling of sadness, and somatically, a state of lowered arousal. Any strategy can be in a depressed form, with Type B least likely and Type A^+ most likely.

Treatment principles

1   Treatment should guide people to acknowledge their non-verbal DRs *before* requesting and assisting integration: if integrative processes neglect non-verbal DRs (usually more attuned to major and early dangers), behaviour and understanding are likely to be incomplete and, possibly, non-adaptive. Semantic and episodic/narrative treatment procedures might need to be preceded by approaches that address preconscious representations.

2   Reflection-based treatments should be adapted to children's development: school-aged children can work on DRs of specific instances; adolescents can consider recurring patterns of responses. Adults can think in terms of life narratives and their on-going contribution to children's problems, but these can, nonetheless, be hard to acknowledge and verbalize.

3   Treatment can help parents to assist their children in the development of integrative skills about danger but only after the parents' non-verbal DRs have been acknowledged and understood. If parents are aware of their preoccupation with danger, they can be reminded to be explicit about their experience with danger with their children. Disagreements about danger between the parents can be addressed explicitly (with or without the children present). Conditions that render knowledge about danger 'unspeakable' should be acknowledged and addressed before the transformations of this information are rectified.

4   When children use strategies involving substantial distortion of information, and treatment cannot change their context towards greater safety, it might not be possible or advisable to work to change children's strategies. Two important goals are then to help children recognize their strategy as provisional, flexible, and matched to specific features of their context and assist them to practise more balanced functioning in the treatment context, identifying the contextual features that make the new strategy appropriate. For example, children using Type A strategies can be helped to cope with rejection by focusing on its situation-specific features, undoing its absolute quality by finding acceptance in therapy. Children using Type C strategies might be guided to use more direct

verbalization with the therapist and to experience and state what works with whom.

5   'Absent' members of the family should be included even if only through promoting awareness of their role by asking family members to reflect integratively on the absent member's behaviour. Professionals need to be more assertive and flexible in accessing fathers.

6   Triangulations: when dealing with triangulated families, professionals can choose to 'stay out' or 'get inside', by making explicit or implicit alliances with parts of the family or not doing so. 'Stuck' families whose members are in danger may require therapists who enter the family system to induce movement. Staying out reduces the bias in professionals' information and works best when family members are engaged and active.

7   Achieving a functionally balanced stance involves an on-going ability to attend to discrepancies in the treatment process.

7 Growing and healing: DMM-FST integrative treatment

What we have offered

A major contribution of this volume is to offer clinicians and other mental health professionals a nuanced understanding of development and the development of individual differences in self-, partner-, and child-protective strategies, as they are applied to dangers experienced in the present and also those in the personal, familial, and cultural past.

We have explored the processes needed to understand psychological distress and interpersonal dysfunction and to generate therapeutic responses for individuals and their families. These processes begin with observation and proceed to attribution of meaning, to an interpersonal dialogue about behaviour and meanings, and then to exploration of means of forming positive connections between people through temporal contingencies, affective attunement, and somatic awareness.

We have also reviewed the literature to generate new systemic formulations of important psychological disorders that are not effectively treated with current understandings. The most important aspect of these new formulations is their systemic quality that not only takes into account influences on adaptation from many levels (genes to families to cultures), but also identifies the reciprocal processes among them. These include autism, ADHD, and non-medical somatic symptoms. It is our hope that our ideas can assist therapists to facilitate change in families who have one or more members suffering from these conditions.

Finally, several ideas have crossed our chapters and case examples. The most central is that exposure to danger organizes brain structure and DRs (for both families and professionals). The way that family members deal with danger (current or past, impending or unlikely) is a useful perspective to the family's level of adaptation. We propose that crucial components of a family functional formulation are: (1) consideration of which danger or dangers are likely to underpin the family problem (what we call 'critical dangers'); and (2) defining how to assist families to change their functioning in the most effective and efficient manner (what Crittenden and Ainsworth 1989 call the 'critical cause' of change).

Other ideas that connect the chapters include the importance of placing people in both their current and past context in order to understand their behaviour, the importance of adapting intervention to each individual's ZPD (including the therapist's), and the on-going quality of change in all life processes. Although change can be daunting – and it is what those with psychological distress or behavioural dysfunction handle least well – it is the basis for hope. Optimism is so basic to mental health that all our efforts should promote hope.

A few central themes

The single most important theme of this volume is to show that people, *all* people, use learned, organized self-protective strategies that reflect both the meaning of their experience to them and also their efforts to cope with the threatening aspects of that experience. This is true for all of us. Our personalities are not stamped upon us; instead they develop across our lives out of the interaction of genes, maturation, and experience. The simple statement that we *learn* to become ourselves is crucial because it opens all developmental pathways to the possibility of change and roots this possibility in universally human developmental processes.

To modify this developmental process, as mental health professionals seek to do, we need a thorough understanding of human development and variations in development. This volume has been structured developmentally to give professionals a clear understanding of what is possible at different ages from birth to pre-puberty. Without this information, there is a tendency to work at the therapists' developmental level (in adulthood) and to direct the therapeutic dialogue to family members who are able to communicate similarly, through language and concepts. Often, this has meant that family therapy is largely directed to families with school-age or adolescent children.

We think that family therapy is most needed in the first years of life when infants and young children are laying down the fundamental preconscious neural pathways that will structure their thinking and response to threat for all their lifetime. Consequently, we have emphasized the importance of the earliest non-verbal learning, in the first weeks and months of life, as creating the basis of each individual's style of learning and responding.

For mental health professionals, this means reading non-verbal communication (in infancy and all older ages as well) and including infants and children actively in the therapy (just as they are active in their families). Ian and Kate (Chapter 1) are an example of a young family that could not articulate their problems (they said, 'she can't play', but they meant 'we fear domestic violence'.) But their baby clearly indicated that 'what you hear in words is not what we the family live with'. Denise (Chapter 4) provides another example. She used a parent-pleasing strategy of compulsive caregiving and everybody was happy – except Denise. Her distress wasn't noticed until her strategy broke down and she expressed her distress as both intrusions of forbidden negative affect and the dangerous refusal of her insulin therapy. Fortunately, her therapist was quick to see that his initial approach was not working and to seek the father's 'back-story', that is, the developmental influences on his parenting behaviour. With a new approach to treatment centred on the father's ZPD, Denise's father became able to change his behaviour quickly – within four sessions. If he (or the therapist) had been rigid, the consequences for Denise could have been severe. To resolve the problems of families who cannot articulate their problems using language, we need to read their behaviour, including that of infants and young children who do not talk well or at all. If we want to prevent the escalation of distress to very complex interpersonal states that we might not know how to resolve, we need to offer family intervention to families with infants and young children.

The second most important theme is that this learning is interpersonal. This includes the learning of behaviour that makes up the symptom clusters that define psychiatric diagnoses. In both the DMM and family systems theory, such behaviour is part of each person's learned repertoire of self-, partner-, and child-protective strategies.

Although every person is born primed to respond to other humans, it is the repeated pattern of responses from attachment figures that shapes what is learned about how to live a safe and comfortable life. There is no single moment when this learning occurs; to the contrary, it occurs in the accretion of moment-to-moment interactions, especially those when the infant or child feels distressed and unsafe. It is in those moments that parents are most likely to by-pass their semantic values and verbally stated intentions and revert to the short-cut of preconscious routines in response to preconsciously perceived images and somatic states (for example, Cecilia, Chapter 2, whose play with Juan was just fine until he raised his arm unexpectedly and rapidly). If these moments reflect danger in their own childhood, they may not be able to protect and comfort their infants adequately. This has consequences for all family relationships.

Our third important theme is that typical development and troubled development arise through the same dynamic process of individuals' genes (G) being applied in a sequence defined by maturation (M) to each person's experience (E) in unique ways (G × M × E). Our evolved genetic heritage enables the same fundamental developmental principles to yield a diversity of outcomes, depending upon differences in context and experience. Humans adapt to an extremely wide range of contexts, from those that are safe and comforting to those that are marked by pervasive danger and the absence of comfort. Strikingly, the genes that are most closely associated with psychological dysfunction are found in all humans and are tied to normative brain development (as opposed to being anomalous genes that disrupt brain development). Is it nature? Surely nothing is possible without our genes. Is it nurture? Surely genes yield nothing without a context in which to be expressed. Of course, it is the dynamic interaction of genes activated in maturational sequence with contexts (G × M × E) that produces the wide range of adaptations necessary for survival under a wide range of conditions. The point is that there is no 'we', the category of adapted, normal people, and 'they', the category of disordered, diseased, or genetically flawed people; we all are on a dynamic continuum of adaptation to the context we are living in. Even when the danger to our bodies is massive (such that we might not survive, e.g., Mrs Freeman's daughter in Chapter 1 and Alexander in Chapter 2) or the context delivers almost none of the expected experiences (such that we can hardly connect to others, e.g., some children exposed to institutional deprivation, Chapter 3), we still attach and, in this attachment, we organize the most adaptive strategy that we can discover. Attachment, in other words, is among the last of human processes to break down when life is imperilled – because it is the process by which we elicit protection and learn to protect ourselves.

But circumstances change. In addition, maturation changes our potential to adapt to circumstances. Therapists are in the business of intervening dynamically in the interaction of individuals with their context to nudge development in more adaptive directions.

Adaptation, however, is a complex construct. It is not the 'right' behaviour, for example, it is not necessarily security of attachment. Instead, it is the best solution for the immediate conditions (short-term adaptation) that also does not foreclose different adaptation to other conditions (long-term adaptation) and that leads to an optimistic frame of mind regarding the possibility of adapting to future conditions (mental health). Mental health is hope, based on processes of change in perception, attribution of meaning, and response to other people and the context.

'Conditions' is a crucial word. One's parents and siblings constitute the most powerful of conditions whereas extra-familial conditions may facilitate or constrain what family members can do. Some parents bring a harrowing history of surviving danger. Some cultures do as well; all cultures reflect the history of many families' survival in spite of the dangers they have faced in their communities across decades (the short term) and centuries (the long term). Disabling conditions compromise some individuals' development; these instances remind us of the importance of a strategy with a self-protective function in the short term, for without that, there is no long term. Mental health, of course, is a separate issue: given what has been learned individually, within families, and by members of cultural groups, in the short and long term, can family members adapt to the current conditions so as to raise their child in a way that promotes future adaptation?

Crucial developmental and treatment processes

Information processing

Using transformations of information to adapt

To understand how any specific person, born into any specific family, in any of the infinite set of contexts that humans could experience, will be able to adapt in the future, we need to understand information processing. Repeatedly, as we described troubled development in the preceding chapters, the information available to family members about the dangers that they and family members experienced was incomplete or distorted or both. Furthermore, the processes used to generate meaning from information were distorted by omission, distortion, error, falsification, denial, and delusion. Don't get us wrong! Everyone uses and *needs* distorted transformative processes; one could not be safe if they did not know how and when (conditions, again!) to distort information. Remember how Denise's therapist used an erroneous explanation of the meaning of her behaviour to soothe and engage her step-mother? However, when distorting transformations of information are used under safe conditions and without awareness, both adaptation and mental health are put in jeopardy.

Short-cuts and development

When transformed information is applied to future situations without recognition of the transformation, a mental short-cut is taken. For example, a child beaten by the father may take the short-cut of thinking that the father is always threatening – or that all fathers or all men are always threatening. The outcome is an absolutist perspective that both holds and distorts truth. A child who was abandoned and grew up in care may take the short-cut of concluding that all strangers are safe and good. Such short-cuts can prevent close relationships or lead to dangerous consequences.

Children are especially likely to develop short-cuts in their information processing when they face complex circumstances. Because most of life is too complex for infants and young children to understand, early exposure to danger can change information processing in ways that will affect neural organization and, thus, thinking, feeling, and acting far into the future.

Nevertheless, the ability to use short-cuts is good because we would freeze in our tracks if we had to think freshly about everything. Sometimes, however, the short-cut omits information that will be needed in the future. The minds skips forward and thinks it has solved the problem – because it has not looked carefully at what was cut out by taking the short-cut. It is a matter of which short-cuts are used, whether they are adaptive under future conditions, and whether the mind alerts and reconsiders when faced with the discrepancy of unpleasant and unexpected outcomes.

Using reflection and consciousness to change how one acts

Awareness becomes the key to changing how the accumulation of interpersonal moments shapes a baby's developing mind. Maturation makes processes possible, but interaction determines the specific processes that will affect each infant's psychological development. Leaving aside those infants with no interactant at all (so dangerous a condition that many infants die; Spitz 1946), all human minds are shaped by the accumulation of moments when one person interacts with the contingencies and attunement of another person in ways that produce somatic ease or various forms of dis-ease. Contingency, affect, and somatic state derive their meaning from the innumerable moments of connection with another person in a reciprocal process that shapes both minds (Siegel 2012). For example, the baby of an anxious mother is affected by the mother's non-contingent, escalating negative arousal, and uncomfortable body. The mother is affected by the baby's incessant (i.e., non-contingent) crying (i.e., escalating negative affect) and rigidly jerky body (i.e., somatic discomfort), but the impact on her is less because she perceives the baby through existing DRs whereas the baby is forming his or her initial DRs. Mother and infant travel together, linked in the process of making meaning, toward the child's 'anxiety disorder' and the family's distress.

In treatment, the crucial issues are delaying integrative work until the individuals are in a moderate state of arousal (Brown and Curhan 2013) and have relatively accurate information available to reflect upon and integrate into new behavioural and strategic alternatives. Integration that precedes correction of highly transformed information is unlikely to be useful because its basis does not accurately represent the current self, dangers, or context. The too early formulation with Denise's father and step-mother (Chapter 4) is an example of premature 'integration'' that the therapist offered without yet knowing that Doug was working on the basis of mis-information and mis-attributions of causality, that is, assuming Denise was responsible for the family's problems without understanding his own contribution.

Family processes

Men and the boys who will become men

Of all the things that we could say about families, we think the most important message for current families is about the importance of fathers. Mother–infant dyads are not usually isolated units. Where's Dad? WHERE IS DAD?!

Fathers can change the whole process of the mother–baby dyad. They can be a second attachment figure who provides a different set of 'innumerable moments' for the baby, either by taking over the role of primary caregiver or by caring directly for the mother in ways that promote her potential to approach their baby differently. The absence of this opportunity is one reason that single mothers and their children are at greater risk of psychological dysfunction than mothers with partners (Lipman et al. 1997; Crosier et al. 2007). With a third to half of children born to single parents, about half of all marriages breaking down and 80 per cent of all unmarried partners separating, with 8 per cent of European married couples divorcing before the child's fifth birthday versus 48 per cent of cohabiting couples separating, most children spend some time in a home without a father (Social Justice Policy Group 2007; Benson 2010; Centers for Disease Control and Prevention 2013). If our case stories tell us anything, it is that DAD IS IMPORTANT. We leave him out of families and out of the treatment with troubled families at the peril of everyone.

We wish also to emphasize the importance of how we raise boys. The women's movement has improved conditions for girls greatly; we wouldn't want to diminish that. But our boys seem not to have benefitted; indeed, they seem less well off than 50 years ago. Boys are particularly vulnerable to being diagnosed with autism as early as toddlerhood and ADHD, particularly when they go to school. Our review of these conditions suggests a strong, but unrecognized, influence from family conditions. Before we 'blame' mothers, let's note that they and other women (daycare providers, teachers, etc.) have both been left to raise children all the way into late adolescence (where are the men?) and also have the opportunity to become conscious of the unintended consequences so as to change what they do. Possibly boys need a greater range of experience and expression than they currently have (Courtenay 2000). This could mean more acceptance of – and adaptation of institutions like schools to – boys' greater activity level, aggressiveness, and hierarchical group behaviour. It might also mean greater acceptance of boys' vulnerability, that is, their desire for comfort and occasional fearfulness. Maybe we need both more men helping to raise boys and also broader standards that permit greater variation in how masculinity is expressed. For sure, without healthy and happy boys, we are unlikely to have strong and competent men who are prepared to become active and supportive husbands and fathers.

For providers of mental health services, this means that we need to become more flexible. When we designate a child as eligible for services, we need this to include both parents. To reach fathers, we need to broaden our work hours so that working men do not have to lose work time to meet with us. We also need to give fathers the respect that they expect when they define themselves as head of household. Anything less will undermine the work we do with mothers and children. Ideally, we would welcome and seek the participation of fathers.

Compulsive strategies

The compulsive strategies are strategies for pleasing powerful adults, for example, parents and teachers. When adults are pleased, they don't look for problems or refer children for evaluation and treatment. Nevertheless, children using compulsive strategies are often distressed, especially if the strategy isn't fully adaptive. When compulsive strategies don't fully protect children, but adults are oblivious of the problem, the strategy may break down, leaving the child expressing their distress through intrusions of forbidden negative affect and somatic signs or medical symptoms. Both are signals of serious problems and, more than compulsive behaviour, they attract adults' attention. Among our cases, all children except Billy (Chapter 4) and Rupert Ruggles (Chapter 5) used a compulsive A strategy! Two used A/C strategies: Ana (who couldn't go to her grandmother's overnight, Chapter 4) and Joseph (who had pseudo-paralysis and pseudo-seizures, Chapter 6). We think it is very important for mental health professionals to learn to recognize these strategies. In his agonizing autobiography, the film director Ingmar Bergman wondered 'whether there are, or ever will be, instruments which can measure a neurosis that so effectively gave the appearance of normality [as mine did]'

(Bergman 1987). We think there are (the DMM assessments), but someone must ask for them.

Unresolved trauma and loss

Most strategies can function adequately in the context in which they were organized. Alexander and Bonnie (both in Chapter 2) and Maija and Ana (both in Chapter 4) used adaptive strategies, given their context. Strategies are at greatest risk of failure when there are unresolved traumas or losses. By 'unresolved', we mean processing that is so full of short-cuts and transformations of information that the connection between the information and the present context is tenuous at best and maladaptive at worst. Mrs Freeman (Chapter 1), Cecilia (Chapter 2), Maija's mother and father, Billy's mother (both in Chapter 4), Denise's whole family (Chapter 4), Arthur (Chapter 5), and Graeme and Joseph (both in Chapter 6) were all characterized by carrying distorted ideas and intense feelings from past traumatizing experiences or losses to current circumstances where they not only did not fit, but also generated new problems.

Triangulation

Dads are not a panacea to family problems and sometimes their presence creates problems. When the bond of a couple opens, creating a place for a baby, a family is born. A triangle is the basic structure upon which families are built. The triangle connects the members of the family, but, as every student of geometry knows, triangles come in many shapes.

In some families the bond between the mother and father cannot easily accommodate the arrival of a child. A 'triangulated' family pattern reflects a parental struggle in which one or both parents appropriate the child as their ally against their partner, the child's other parent (for example, Denise, Chapter 4, Graeme, Chapter 6). When this happens, both parents and children distort information in a way that tends to dichotomize the character of each parent, that is, idealizing one parent while derogating the other. Absolutist positions are taken. Until the triangulating process is changed, problem resolution is almost impossible.

In other families, the children are needed to enhance the functioning of the parents through giving care to the parents or performing in ways that reassure the parents of their competence (e.g., Bonnie's and Ana's caregiving, Chapter 4, and Hakim's compliance, Chapter 3). When children organize around their parents' needs, it can be very difficult for adults to find an interpersonal problem; instead the child's symptomatic behaviour appears inexplicable. As a consequence, a child-based intervention is often sought. Further, because adults are pleased by the child's caregiving or performing behaviour, problems tied to inhibition or over-attention to the perspectives of others are usually picked up quite late (as opposed to early for oppositional behaviour, autism and ADHD, in which the parents or teachers are made uncomfortable).

Finally, in some cases, the two parents are so dependently interdependent that there is no place for a baby, that is, there is no connective triangle (Arthur, Chapter 5). The child's experience is of being excluded from the parents' endless struggle or from their mutual caregiving. Either way, the parents don't notice the child's clear communication (Type B strategy), distorted negative affect (Type C strategy), or compulsive behaviour (Type A strategy). There is no strategy that can engage the parents in protecting and comforting the child because they are absorbed with their own needs. Children of such parents often become symptomatic, but neither they, nor we the professionals are able to identify the reason (e.g., Graeme, Chapter 6); self hatred and self-injury become possibilities. Rejection is the most detrimental experience for humans, exceeding the negative outcomes of all forms of abuse. Rejection by one's parents is the most harmful form of rejection and the earlier it occurs in life, the more detrimental it is.

Cross-generational patterning

All parents bring their history to bear on their parenting. We all seek to do some things the same and some differently from what our parents did with us. But when we rely on non-verbal and not conscious representations to guide our behaviour, there can be a discrepancy between our conscious intentions and our preconsciously organized behaviour. This is particularly likely if we grew up facing dangers that were beyond our developmental capacity to understand. The discrepancy yields two types of outcome, pendulum parenting (usually in cases of mild to moderate danger) and trauma-based parenting (usually in cases of severe danger). Pendulum parenting reflects the attempt of parents using Type A or C strategies to apply a 'corrective script' (Byng-Hall 1995), but over-shooting the balanced middle and thus swinging to the opposite distortion of the one used by their parents (Crittenden 2008). In trauma-based parenting, we repeat harmful patterns from our childhood experience without awareness of how the accumulation of tiny high-intensity moments that are mis-attuned to the present affects the brain development and psychological organization of our children (e.g., both Ian and Kate, Chapter 1, and Cecilia and Juan, Chapter 2). In such families, it is as though the family had invisible members who coached from behind the parents, making their behaviour discordant and maladaptive with current conditions.

Parents' strategies

In every one of our cases, the parents had non-Type B strategies. Understanding the child's situation was dramatically improved once the therapist understood the parents' strategies, unresolved traumas and transformations of information. Every one of the parents in our cases of troubled children had a back-story; knowing it, especially when it was revealed in a dialogue (an AAI, for example), made it possible for the therapist to be genuinely compassionate with the parent. It reduced the therapist's absolutist thinking.

Once the dangers (past and present) facing all family members were explicit and understood adequately by the therapist, therapy that was compassionate with everyone and productive to everyone could begin. This is not blaming parents. All parents bring what they have learned to their children; some of it is helpful, some is not. The real message here is that parents of infants and young children have the power to realize their hopes for their children through understanding themselves.

Physiological conditions

A theme throughout this book has been responding to the compromised somatic state of family members when one member of the family suffers from an organic medical disease. Sometimes it is the parents who are unable to fulfil all essential aspects of the parent role (e.g., Mrs Freeman's daughter and son-in-law who have cerebral palsy and severe learning difficulties, Chapter 1.) At other times it is the child whose development is compromised (e.g., Bonnie's early heart murmur, Chapter 2, Alexander's massive organ dysfunction, Chapter 2, and Denise's diabetes, Chapter 4). In the case of parents with cerebral palsy and intellectual deficit, it is amazing – and reassuring – that the essential survival processes of attachment and reproduction functioned as they would with any adults. Of course, these parents would not be able to raise their son, but he was born and that creates hope. In Bonnie's case, the danger was in the past and she knew nothing about it; it was her mother's continuing worry that affected her interaction with Bonnie and that, in turn, shaped Bonnie's self-protective strategy of compulsive care-giving. Alexander's body was massively impaired, but he too managed to engage his mother to protect him using a caregiving strategy. Finally, Denise had a chronic condition that she appropriated (without awareness) as a means of communicating her distress to her parents. The points are that mind and body work together in many different ways and that attachment is so fundamental to survival that it functions even when almost every other function has failed.

Medical conditions affect the whole family and we have sought to highlight the need to consider their effects on both the couple relationship and siblings. The issue of providing what every family member needs, even if one cannot fulfil all their desires, is crucial in families with a sick member whose well-being depends upon having a well-functioning family. The obvious and pressing needs of the medically compromised individual can obscure the equally important needs of other family members. The outcomes of such unbalanced use of limited family resources can be the breakdown of the parents' relationship (e.g., Alexander's parents) or appropriation of a child to meet a parent's needs (e.g., Maija's caregiving to her father after the loss of a previously born twin and the severe disability of the surviving twin, Chapter 4). On the other hand, the appearance of physical distress can be misleading; although Joseph (Chapter 6) could not say it in words, his 'paralysed' leg and 'seizures' expressed his distress at the impasse and the danger in his family. Assessment was needed both to rule out organic disease and also to identify the interpersonal roots of his condition.

Assessment of family relationships

All of these issues bring us back to knowing, what is known, and discovering how to know. If one cannot rely solely on what people say the problem is and if symptoms can have different meanings in different people, then how does one discover what needs to be treated? We think a family assessment is needed.

Family assessment

The first and most important thing to know about assessment of relationships is that it does not give answers. To the contrary, it is a way of approaching understandings. Further, unlike inventories, psychological measures, and psychiatric diagnoses, it requires input from another person and results in an approximation of 'truth', one that almost certainly will change as the therapy evolves. Nevertheless, assessment of relationships is like a stake in the ground, a spot both from which one can view the past and the near-term future and also to which one can return later to see what distance has been travelled in the therapy. That is, early assessment of relationships can focus the process of therapy and provide a gauge of the effects of therapy.

A particularly important contribution of assessments of attachment is their attention to non-verbal communication. This is important because implicit and forbidden-to-be-known meanings are often expressed at least partially through non-verbal means. Moreover, young children have only non-verbal means of communicating. Working effectively with families with infants and young children requires attention to non-verbal meanings.

Standardized assessment and family systems therapy (FST)

Early family systems theorists suggested that an assessment of family dynamics needed to be based upon a study of the patterns of information processing in families. Specifically, this involved attempts to explore patterns of communication in terms of the use of explicit verbal and implicit non-verbal communication (Watzlawick et al. 1967; Satir 1972). One approach was to examine the patterning on a case-by-case approach, another to look for patterning of communication across families which could be related to different types of problems, for example, emotionally 'enmeshed' families as connected to development of psychosomatic problems or eating disorders (cf. Satir 1972; Minuchin 1974; Epstein et al. 1978; Olson et al. 1989). However, this search for connections between types of problems and standardized assessment procedures has not been accepted or implemented regularly by family systems theorists or therapists. Possibly the task was too daunting and the early instrumentation disappointingly simplistic (cf. FACES, Olson et al. 1989) or complex (cf. Bandler and Grinder 1975; Grinder and Bandler 1975). Instead, attachment theory yielded the first standardized assessment for looking at the state of a relationship, specifically Ainsworth's Strange Situation (Ainsworth et al. 1978) for the infant–mother relationship. This was both helpful and limiting.

It was helpful because it began with infancy, providing a sound observational and developmental base upon which to build assessments at older ages. Attachment researchers soon did just that by generating a series of developmentally attuned assessments from the neonatal period through toddlerhood, the preschool years, school years, adolescence, and adulthood. Following Ainsworth's lead, the assessments all focused on functioning in moments of uncertainty and threat. Further, they were all observational in nature and developmentally attuned. With the assessments came guidelines for identifying and attributing meaning to non-verbal information (including implicit information in verbal discourse) and classificatory systems for clustering similar relationships.

The limitations were the dyadic or individual focus of the assessments, the inherent reductionist quality of classifications, and the effort and expertise needed to code and classify the assessments. Further, these assessments, being used primarily in research, gave the appearance of being factual or deterministic. Although attachment theorists would consider the classifications assays or working models, the negative point of being reductionist and determinist has continued to concern family therapists who work daily with the unique features of families. The issue is to find a level of patterning that provides a useful clustering while recognizing that each pattern has infinite variations. We need to ask of assessment what it can provide, that is, a useful guide to fundamental processes in individuals and families, and not what is impossible, that is, a complete understanding of each person, dyad, or family. Good assessment is a jump-start to understanding, not the end point.

The absence of standardized assessment in family therapy might have resulted in three problems for FST. The first is the absence of a focus for evaluating adaptation. In attachment, this is clearly protection and comfort together with the information processing used to generate protective strategies, or conversely the dangers, both past and present that threaten individuals and elicit their self-protective strategies. FST does not have this focus and is, therefore, more wide-ranging about what can be treated. The question is whether the focus on danger and information processing on protective strategies can clarify what needs to be treated and, thereby, expedite the treatment.

In our examples, it did – or could have. Ian and Kate in Chapter 1 provide the clearest example of the therapists needing to focus on danger in order to protect Kate from violence, Ian from loss of his family and self-respect, and their baby from loss of his father and the effects of spousal violence on his mother. Without this focus, ten weeks of family therapy were wasted and, in fact, the situation became more volatile, resulting in violence shortly after the conclusion of therapy. Had Kate not called the therapists, they would never have even known this! As it was, the therapists' work was too rigidly organized for *them* to adapt to the danger they had helped to elicit.

Follow-up assessment is crucial to therapists' understanding of the outcomes of their work (see Denise, Chapter 4, for the benefits of following up). We wish every therapist checked back after the treatment was concluded; how else can *we* learn from the short- and long-term effects of our work? How else can we avoid repeating mistakes that we didn't notice during the treatment?

In less striking ways, a focus on danger was needed to understand Hakim's compulsive compliance (Chapter 3) and Ana's 'shyness' that really signalled fear for her mother's well-being (Chapter 4). On the other hand, Cecilia and Juan (Chapter 2) benefitted from early assessment of their attachment and a consequent focus on danger, in this case Cecilia's childhood danger and the danger in her relationship with her imprisoned partner, Juan's father. In the case of Denise's behaviour problems and lack of compliance with her insulin therapy (Chapter 4), an early focus on the history of parental danger redirected the whole treatment, yielding a good conclusion quite quickly. This is a reminder that big problems don't always mean long therapies; when therapists find the critical cause of change and parents are ready to change, change can occur quickly. Similarly, the therapists working with Rupert Ruggles (Chapter 5) used a family assessment to move beyond Rupert's symptoms of ADHD to the discomfort experienced by both Rupert and Rob in the context of their parents' permissive unpredictability – and the basis of that in each parent's childhood attachment. This therapy of enacting new strategies in a home-like dinner table task produced a balancing change in only a few sessions. Doing, as opposed to thinking and talking, was effective. The case of Joseph (Chapter 6) stands out for having the focus on danger from the beginning and using it to see past the dramatic medical presentation of leg paralysis and non-epileptic seizures and the 'rights' of each parent to see their child. Joseph needed to be safe in his relationships and lack of safety was generating dangerous symptoms. In this case (but not in all cases with somatization), the symptoms themselves captured opposite effects of his self-protective strategy: the stuck paralysing quality of his family situation (the inhibiting Type A) and its overwhelming stressfulness to him (the arousing Type C).

The second problem for family systems treatment is the absence of an unbiased means of describing the state of families at the beginning of treatment. Without this, therapists become dependent upon the families' statement of the problem, but families often do not know what the problem is (e.g., Ian and Kate, Chapter 1) or they have unspeakable information (e.g., Maija and her father, Chapter 4) or both. Without an independent assessment, mental health professionals are sometimes reduced to addressing symptom behaviours in an individual (for example, CBT for Rupert's ADHD symptoms) or taking excessive amounts of time to discover the unstated problem that is critical to relieving family members' distress (for example, 6–7 years for Graeme, Chapter 6).

The third problem for FST is the difficulty of demonstrating the effectiveness of FST when standardized pre- and post-treatment assessment is unavailable. In the absence of such studies, CBT has taken the field. Nevertheless many therapists feel that CBT and the measures of its effectiveness reflect both publication bias and also short-term effects that are not enduring (cf. So et al. 2013). Because FST has not provided enough methodologically sound outcome studies, it may be less likely that other therapists will discover the benefits of a family-in-danger approach and, thus, families may not be offered family therapy when it could be the most effective treatment.

Thus, while acknowledging the limitations of using standardized attachment assessments for understanding family functioning, we nevertheless think that these assessments provide both useful information and also a model upon which to build family-focused assessments. That is, dyadic assessment may have been a necessary step to thinking about the complexity of families with children of many different ages.

A particularly important aspect of using formal assessments of attachment in family therapy is the relational benefit that comes from the process of the assessment. When the therapist and family member(s) engage in this process, the therapist comes to share knowledge about the inner aspects of the family member(s). Even before the assessment is coded and classified (and even if it never is), the collaborative process of engaging in the assessment can improve the outcomes of treatment. In part, this is because the therapist becomes privy to sensitive, personal information that is given in a way that elicits feelings (as checklists or history-based interviews do not). The non-temporal, context-based approach to eliciting recall is crucial to unlocking hidden information. Sharing this process creates the beginning of a bond between the interviewer-therapist and the speaker. Indeed, sometimes the AAI is the first time that a person has ever told their story; the person who hears and accepts it (that is, accepts the story *and* the speaker) necessarily becomes very important to the speaker (Kozlowska et al. 2012). In addition, because these assessments activate the speaker's self-protective strategy, the interviewer-therapist has an opportunity not only to view the strategy, but more importantly to explore responses on their part that can assist the speaker to moderate the strategy. Thus, sharing the experience of assessment can initiate the process of building a therapeutic relationship and help the therapist to learn quickly how best to interact therapeutically with the family members(s). Finally, asking pertinent questions, without guiding the speaker's responses, sets the speaker's mind in motion (Main et al. 1985). Indeed, almost all people who are given an SAA, Transition to Adulthood Assessment of Attachment (TAAI), or AAI continue to recall experiences of danger and distress and safety and comfort for several days thereafter and, often, they begin spontaneously to reflect upon the meaning to themselves of the experiences. The information that emerges – and continues to emerge from this process – can then be integrated into the family functional formulation.

Family functional formulation. As the array of attachment assessments is being administered and coded and especially when all are completed, the therapist or team of therapists begins their process of reflective integration. The process of administering the assessments has permitted the therapist to 'feel' each person's strategy in interaction with the 'home base' of the therapist, that is, his or her own strategy. Important information is gained by comparing that interpersonal process with other such experiences. The formal coding of the assessments has pointed to hidden or inexplicit problems that might affect family members; it has also revealed the transformations of information used by each family member and for what probable purposes. Finally, each person's self-protective strategy has been estimated and, for the parents, their partner- and child-protective strategies have been tentatively identified. It should be understood that, though formal standardized assessments are carried out at one point in time, assessment is an on-going and interpersonal process that increasingly involves the family in the process of drawing conclusions.

The reflective process seeks both continuities among the different assessments of family members and also discrepancies among them, especially inexplicable discrepancies that point to something misunderstood by the therapist, missing from the coding, unknown to the family members, or known but hidden away very deeply (i.e., the 'unspeakable'). The outcome of this reflective process is a 'family functional formulation'. The family functional formulation reflects the confluence of what is currently understood about family members' exposure to danger, transformations of information, and attachment strategies around the critical cause of dysfunction and, more important, the likely critical cause of change in the family (Crittenden and Ainsworth 1989). In all clinical discussions, we identified what we called the 'critical danger(s)' as the likely source of the family members' strategic functioning. This then was the therapist's entry to identifying a potential 'critical cause of change' which, in turn, would guide the therapist's behaviour.

Again, it is important to note that assessment, formulation, and treatment planning are all evolving and provisional processes. Still, having these, in written and dated form, provides a systematic way to think about what has happened in the treatment and what might be helpful next. This is in contrast to simply launching the treatment around the presenting problem and hoping it will be solved; Ian and Kate demonstrate an unfortunate outcome of that process, in spite of their having had faculty co-therapists and a student reflecting team. Without a focus on danger, understanding of non-verbal communication, and attention to the baby, the team did not have the needed information for their reflection. Ian and Kate are also a reminder that family members are often unable to articulate – or face – their central issues. Until they feel safe in the therapy, it will not be possible for family members and therapists to have similar understandings about the therapy and safety is not possible as long as family members are hiding the aspects of their lives that distress them. It is ironic that therapists sometimes think they offer a 'safe base' whereas family members know intuitively that, because they are not truly known by the therapists, they cannot be safe with them. However, the therapist can facilitate the development of this sense of safety and understanding by communicating that they are interested in finding out about the person(s) and not rushing in to impose premature interpretations or being overly organized by theory.

Formal assessment, formulation, and planning are also in contrast to manualized treatments, specifically because these are meant to be applied uniformly and without variation, even as family members and therapists learn more about their work together.

Formulation is a dynamic and evolving process and needs to be amenable to assimilate new information as it emerges in the process of the clinical work. Clinical interventions can be regarded as 'experiments' which will hopefully foster some change but, importantly, always provide information. This is consistent with a consolidated tradition in cognitive psychotherapy: from Beck's notion of therapeutic relationships as a form of 'collaborative empiricism' (Beck 1979) to the idea of 'behavioural experiments' as a crucial component of therapeutic work (Bennett-Levy et al. 2004), the focus has been on methods of gaining and using information to increase adaptation. Over time, the formulation is expected to change and, increasingly, to include family members in the planning until the time when they take over and carry on with ordinary, real life in which independent and adequate parents assess their family's functioning, identify their own needs and resources and meet the needs of their children.

We think that formal assessment speeds the process of understanding the family dynamics, reduces risk of harm, and is a guide for the therapist. However, assessment needs to be paced and fit the family's processes and attachment dynamics. For example, assessment of the parents' own childhood experiences can be experienced as implying blame for their child's problems if initiated without preparation and explanation to the parents. In addition, when administered by the therapist, it facilitates the process of coming to know the person with enough detail for the therapist to be accepted as a transitional attachment figure.

DMM-FST integrated treatment

Whoever said that life has no dress rehearsal was not thinking about mental health treatment. Treatment is the combination of hope with reflection and purposeful practice. Hope makes treatment possible. Reflection and practice are the processes that can change a person's array of DRs, meanings, and behaviours. That is, they can change how life is lived.

Therapy is like a rehearsed and repeatedly rewritten play as opposed to the flowing story or narrative of real life that cannot be turned back or reworked. In this practised drama, the family members and therapist address 'Danger-past' and 'Danger-present', all the while preparing for 'Danger-future' (with apologies to Charles Dickens). Unlike real-life situations, in treatment one can explore new perspectives on old experiences, try different responses, practise useful routines until they become automatic, and then vary them to fit different situations.

Moreover, in therapy, everyone can try on different masks and play different roles. For family members, it can mean taking each other's role to try to understand one another. More important, it offers an opportunity to try out being the person they'd like to become. For Graeme's parents (Chapter 6), who could not stop fighting and degrading each other, learning to *act* appropriately in front of Graeme would have helped him. It might also have taught his parents something about resolving problems, but that was not the immediate goal: Graeme needed to see his parents acting in a more balanced way and, for his sake, they might have tried a charade.

Choosing roles is especially important for therapists who must combine a genuine presentation of themselves as transitional attachment figures with an artificial professional self who functions more thoughtfully and without the personal baggage of their full selves. Of course, no one fully checks their history and 'self' at the door of the office, but therapists do consciously structure their behaviour in ways that minimize the influence of detrimental aspects of themselves and highlight features of themselves that facilitate meeting the needs of people who seek their help. Further, this therapeutically fabricated self is adapted differently for each family and family member. It's like real life (in which we change a bit for each person that we are with) and, at the same time, it is done with such conscious awareness of leaving huge chunks of self outside the therapy room that it is a form of play acting. Stepping into the role as one steps into the office gives mental health professionals the authority to play their part in the therapy as someone 'better' than they are in their own daily lives, which, of course, are fraught with the same array of concerns as other people have! A credible authority, then, could be claimed by the therapists not so much on the 'right way to lead a good life', but more believably on 'how to find useful information and to practise changing ways of living'. The families should be guided to be or become the ultimate authority on what way of life fits their circumstances best.

The ideas we offer in this volume developed from our cases, and our cases, were selected to represent the array of ordinary cases facing mental health professionals in ordinary public, private, and hospital settings. We sought cases where we made progress, but not necessarily stellar successes – because those do not reflect therapists' daily business. We included a few failures – because everyone has those too. We sought a breadth of presenting problems and a range of treatment settings. The principles that we elucidate below have a long history in the literature, but most convincing to us, they reflect the families we have worked with.

General principles of DMM-FST integrative treatment

Before describing the differences in treatment strategies for different families and family members, we want to emphasize several general principles of treatment based on both attachment and FST that can be considered the basis of what we called DMM-FST integrative treatment in the Introduction to this book.

1   *Danger and safety*: First and foremost, the DMM focuses attention on danger (past, present, and future). Behaviour (both enacted and psychological information-processing) is considered 'adaptive' (even if not secure) to the extent that it promotes the safety and comfort of the self, one's partner, and one's progeny. One might say that addressing safety is not really psychotherapy, but if people are not safe in the immediate short term, there might be no long-term 'psychological' adaptation to worry about. Further, if they don't feel safe, they might not be able to focus on anything else and the 'therapy' will be lost. Achieving safety, including stabilizing somatic conditions of acute threat, is an essential first step for the family. Because safety is so important, somatic signals should be evaluated carefully early on. Understanding the nature of the danger, from each family member's perspective, is an urgent and on-going process for mental health professionals regardless of their discipline or role. Comfort is another issue, one that is both less urgent and also impossible to achieve at the outset.

2   *Therapists as transitional attachment figures*: Therapists will be most effective at promoting adaptation when they function as transitional attachment

figures who help to bridge the gap between the frightening perception of current conditions and a more accurate understanding of them. (It is not a psychological problem when people react to serious and real dangers; return to point No. 1.) To reduce the gap between perception and reality, therapists should display compassion for the experience of each family member while maintaining a balanced understanding of the entire current situation. The DMM-AAI for adults, the TAAI for adolescents and young adults, and the SAA for children (see Appendix 1) are particularly suited to initiating the process of establishing a therapeutic relationship because these assessments cut through presenting complaints and procedural defences to reveal aspects of the individual's inner self. Acceptance by the therapist of this vulnerable and imperfect inner self is crucial to establishing a transitional attachment relationship. Of course, there is complexity in doing this for family members who are in conflict, but demonstrating how to manage such complexity is central to guiding the parents to do the same.

3   *Regulating arousal*: When they are present, modifiers (such as depression, intrusions of forbidden negative affect, disorientation, and expressed somatic signs) need to be addressed early on in order to provide sufficient motivation and stability of arousal to proceed with the treatment. When family members' bodies are not stable (because arousal is too low, too high, or has extreme fluctuations), then individuals do not have sufficient access to conscious mental processes to benefit fully from treatment. Sometimes medication can induce stability and permit work to be done that will enable the individual to both recognize that the threat is less intense or imminent than they had thought and also learn to regulate themselves. But if the threat is real, medication will not resolve it. Further, if medication is treated as the solution and work is not undertaken on estimating threat more accurately and learning to regulate arousal, then medication can mask the presence or even become part of an on-going problem.

4   *Quieting traumatic responses to current conditions*: Next, unresolved traumas and losses require enough exploration to make them explicit and open to discussion; this reduces the potential of current sensory stimulation to produce peaks or plunges in the individual's arousal. Again, the DMM-AAI the TAAI, and the SAA provide a basis for identifying unresolved traumas and losses without either long periods of hesitation and lack of recall or, conversely, such torrential flows of information that crucial events are buried in the debris. It is notable that the most disruptive forms of lack of resolution are those that are dismissed (e.g., Arthur, Chapter 5), denied (e.g., Ian and Kate, Chapter 1), or displaced onto other family members (e.g., Denise as the 'family problem', Chapter 4); these need special attention from therapists.

With arousal largely under control, the individual's pre-existing strategy can function again and could be considered 'repaired'. This is good because everyone feels safer with a functional and effective strategy. On the other hand, if family members are content with a repair, they remain at risk of another 'breakdown' of the strategy whenever the context calls for a different strategy. That is, there is more work to be done than simply repairing the existing strategy by reducing the unresolved traumas and losses. Family members are more likely to move forward beyond the alleviation of the symptoms if they each have a comfortable attachment relationship with the therapist. Conversely, the relative comfort achieved at this point in treatment may mislead people into thinking they are finished and can end the therapy. It is important that therapists be clear about what was accomplished and what might still be done in the future, if availability of resources and cost/benefit ratios allow it. In other words, therapists should let the family make informed choices, to ensure that, if the family decides to come back for more services, this doesn't happen with an unnecessary sense of failure.

5   *Increasing family members' repertoire of protective strategies*: Many family members still need to acquire additional strategies that are better suited to their current situation than are their childhood strategies. Some families will be able to manage this on their own, once the crisis that brought them to treatment is resolved. Others will need continued work with a professional in change processes, that is, with a mental health professional. The outcome of this phase of therapy is establishment of: (1) new connections between sensory aspects of the environment and arousal (such that arousal is at comfortable levels except in the presence of current danger); and (2) new procedures to replace out-of-date habitual responses. When these steps have been accomplished, most individuals are symptom-free and can manage most aspects of their lives (work, marriage, raising children). Nevertheless, without a final integrative phase, they remain vulnerable to relapse if conditions were to deteriorate sharply and in ways they have not experienced previously.

6   *Reaching coherence and resilience*: The final step is reflective and integrative. Many families will not reach this step, either because they are satisfied with being comfortable on a daily basis or because funding is not available once the immediate problems are resolved. Integration can, of course, occur without a therapist, but a dialogue can be very helpful and reflective approaches to therapy provide that. When it is possible to address integrative functioning, it can yield great personal rewards while yielding the greatest safety under the greatest range of conditions for families. Integration as an on-going process yields resilience in the face of new problems and increases the probability that all family members will be safe, comfortable, and happy. Because it involves complex cortical processing, full integration is not possible before late adolescence.

Integration involves reconsidering one's experience, both past and present, from multiple perspectives to gain an understanding of what one has experienced, how one used that experience to develop self-protective strategies, the influence of change in oneself (including maturation) and in one's context on the adaptiveness of one's strategies, and, finally, one's emerging ability to regulate the process of development in the future. The outcome of this iterative integrative process is greater flexibility, greater satisfaction in one's entire developmental progress, a more compassionate understanding of the limitations of important other people such as one's parents, and optimism that one could face new adversities and still protect oneself and one's loved ones. Hope and comfort are key to enduring mental health and they are best achieved through an on-going, life-long process of reflection and integration.

This sequenced list (talk, do, talk about what we did) is meant to assist therapists to map their progress with families. It should be expected that progress through these 'stages' will not be linear. The tasks will overlap, at times they will be revisited from a new perspective, and treatment will often be terminated before completion of them all. Whatever the reason, many families – and individuals – address this progression of tasks sequentially over time, often with different therapists. One might say they give themselves time for integration of the most recent accomplishments in treatment before moving forward. We hope that therapists will keep this progression in mind with the goal of preparing the family members for an on-going process of learning about themselves and learning how to live with themselves and each other. In addition, we hope that therapists will think of families who are coming to treatment in terms of their current and past status with this progression. This can promote a reframing of the return to treatment not as another failure, but as readiness to move forward through the next step in adaptation.

Adapting the principles of DMM-FST integrative treatment to specific families

But what shall I do with this family?

General principles are fine and dandy, but every family is unique. How does one decide how to implement the principles in specific circumstances? Well, we think we've outlined that. First, assess while engaging family members, including the men and non-symptomatic siblings. Then work through the sequence of processes outlined above, attending to both the families' stated priorities (i.e., their desires) and also the therapist's evolving understanding of their needs. The desires/needs distinction is an important point: what the therapists might see as family members' desires could be perceived by the family as a need, reflecting their attempt to protect themselves from a critical danger that is not visible to the therapists (or not present at all anymore, except in some family members' minds!). This gives family members a sense of the framework: 'We can do this bit here now, but to do X and Y, you may need more time or even a different service.' Children's immaturity and constant maturational change can mean that a different sort of assistance may be needed later. Families can be prepared to think of life (and therapy, i.e., the dress rehearsal for life) as evolving and changing. When they understand that no one is 'fixed' for all of life, they will be better prepared to attend to each family member's development in the context of the changing vicissitudes of life.

In sum:

1   Don't get preoccupied with the presenting problem or symptoms.
2   Organize your thinking around real and perceived danger.
3   Work in the zones of proximal development of each family member.
4   And – very important – remember that families are like boats: they float or sink together.

As a therapist, you want to help *all* family members equally (even absent fathers) so that their family boat will float, sustaining everyone.

Choosing techniques

Good treatment uses whatever techniques will best fit the goals of the treatment. That is, good therapists do not limit themselves to the techniques introduced by their school of therapy. Instead, they use everything that works when it is the best solution for the circumstances (when 'circumstances' means the problem, the family members, and the therapist). These techniques include methods to elicit discovery, foster exploration, or encourage practice.

The dialogue between the therapist and family members is the most flexible and powerful tool of all. In the same way that discourse analysis of the AAI, TAAI and SAA reveals meanings that were not made explicit in words, the dialogue within therapy can be managed with attention to surface, explicit meanings and also underlying meanings contained in phrasing, omissions, changes of topic, non-verbal accompanying behaviour, and so forth. Including infants and young children in this dialogue is important and requires therapists' ability to track non-verbal behaviour. Finally, part of the therapist's role is to decide which of these to address and which to let go or save for later.

This includes selecting which family members should be present for which parts of the process. While seeing the family together is essential, always having everyone present at once can be harmful. Some families need a strong parental subsystem; seeing the parents alone can both mark this feature and also permit discussion of it in ways that the children should not hear. Couples with problems between them, especially sexual problems, should address these without the children; houses have bedroom doors because it is appropriate to have privacy. Similarly, children have private lives that cannot be revealed adequately with parents or siblings present. Managing trust when seeing family members is not so different from parents' managing trust within the array of family relationships.

Of course, therapy is live and not everything can be perceived, far less decided consciously before the therapist speaks or acts. This leads to two important points. First, improvisation is essential because this 'play' is not written in advance. Everyone is playing a part, but it's being made up in the moment. Therapists often function on the basis of intuitive hunches (implicit functioning regulates most of everybody's behaviour all the time). Therapy works best when the therapist has time to reconsider what he or she did, making the hunch explicit, and evaluating the outcomes. Yes, we know: no one has time to think; the next case is waiting already. But it remains true that reflection yields clarity and direction that cannot be derived entirely from intuition. Experience, however, moderates this. The more reflection there was early on – in training and early supervision – the more reflection itself will become procedural, the faster it will operate, and the broader the base for informed hunches will be. The broader base is improved pattern recognition: quick recognition of more aspects of an interpersonal pattern, recognition of increasingly subtle differences among patterns, and recognition of discrepancies that require conscious attention. For those of us who like identifying wild flowers, it's the difference between seeing and naming a familiar flower and pulling out the guidebook to work through the sequence of season, colour, leaf shape, number of petals, etc. until we identify the plant. It's just like with patients! The more you do it, the better and faster you become at doing it. (Back to learning; this too is learned.)

To conclude: we have tried to focus on the art of the possible, knowing that chasing perfection will necessarily lead to failure for both families and clinicians. Good enough will do!

The second point is the value of a dialogue among professionals. This can be supervision with recordings of therapy. It can be a reflecting team. It can be using a co-therapist and discussing recent sessions. The point is to have someone with both a different perspective and also independent information. Supervision without video or audio support is the weakest form of dialogue because errors or distortions in the therapist's recall of the therapy cannot readily be identified and therefore cannot be addressed.

That brings us to planning. As we said above, it's important to have a plan, but equally important not to follow it. The plan is a map that tells you where you started and where you're going; without knowing these things, one is lost. Nevertheless, the journey reveals much about the terrain that was not known initially: there are mountains that block your progress here, going through the valley can get you there faster and less stressfully. Let' name the mountain and go through the valley. The plan should be revised to accommodate these discoveries. Further, life keeps rolling forward even while treatment is in progress. Stuff happens – and the plan must be changed. Have a plan, but don't follow it.

But does it work?

We hope you are excited by the ideas of DMM-FST Integrative Treatment. But does it work? There are three aspects to this crucial question.

The first is defining how we would know whether a form of treatment was effective. This is a methodological question. Until recently, randomized control trials (RTCs) have been the 'gold standard' and have been used largely by CBT researchers. However, recent reviews have identified that most RTCs do not use assessment that is independent of the patient, therapist, or originator of the method being tested (Crighton and Towl 2007; de Maat et al. 2013; So et al. 2013) and even fewer use long-term follow-up. Strikingly, there are very few studies that assess harmful outcomes even though evidence is accumulating that treatment can produce negative effects (Lilienfeld 2007). Long-term follow-up is needed and it should address not only the initial behaviour symptoms, but also symptom substitution in either the person who received the treatment or other family members. It is also necessary to assess not just individual, but also relational changes, for example, one family member might display problems experienced by all family members or treating the displayed problems might shift the distress to a different family member.

CBT has contributed more to the existing evidence base than other forms of treatment. However, the large majority of the studies have methodological problems including being carried out by researchers who are invested in treatment success, using self-report inventories, not being double blind and not having long-term follow-up data. In addition, CBT has some limitations, specifically, it does not address non-conscious functioning, relies excessively on prescriptive semantic learning (Whittingham et al. 2009), is overly individual-focused, does not take account of systemic processes, does not address the developmental causes of problems, and is applied with as much fidelity as possible across therapists. The last point limits the functioning of the therapist as a transitional attachment figure and makes modification of the treatment to match individual differences unlikely. On the other hand, CBTs do attempt to offer treatment packages for people with different psychiatric disorders.

Psychoanalytic treatment and short-term psychodynamic psychotherapy have contributed a large number of outcome studies as well (Shedler 2011; Abbass et al. 2012; de Maat et al. 2013). Immediate post-treatment symptom reduction from long-term psychoanalytic treatment was good and, though it was substantially less, there was also an effect for long-term personality change (de Maat et al. 2009). In addition to having similar methodological difficulties to CBT, these findings are often compromised by not having comparison groups. Psychodynamic treatment has been criticized for being too long, varying from person to person (thus not being replicable), and for not addressing psychiatric diagnostic categories. Nevertheless, even these findings are compromised by being limited to individuals who completed treatment.

More broadly, when compared with each other, there is little overall difference between the efficacy of different therapies, e.g., CBT versus psychodynamic therapy (Fonagy and Roth 1997; Thoma et al. 2012). More crucially, the majority of efficacy studies may be irrelevant to ordinary psychotherapy. Most are limited to individuals who completed treatment; given that 40 per cent of people coming to treatment drop out, this provides a major distortion to the knowledge base (Kazdin and Blasé 2011). In addition, there is a strong bias against submitting and publishing studies that report no effects. Finally, most ordinary treatment is not part of a study and that which is, is often university-based and carried out with extra funding (Kazdin and Blasé 2011). In other words, most outcome studies are not methodologically sound, negative findings are rarely published, and efficacy studies address a particular subpopulation that is unlike the caseloads of ordinary psychotherapists. Finally, aggregated group-based data obscure important individual differences in responses to the therapy.

The second point is deciding when full studies that meet these methodological standards are warranted. Carrying out a methodologically sound study, with double-blind, independent, observational or functional assessment, with attention to symptom or patient substitution and follow up of a year or more is very expensive. It would not be feasible to carry out such studies without reason to believe that the outcome would be positive.

We suggest a process of validation that begins with: (1) clinical experience and observation that proceeds to (2) descriptive specification of possible patterns (both strategic patterning and patterns of change over time); (3) theoretical explanation of the processes and causal factors (including familial and extra-familial conditions that maintain the behaviour); (4) clinical case studies (Yin 1994; Kazdin and Blasé 2011) which are elaborated and lead to publication; (5) case study series or clinical trials to explore crucial aspects of the cases; (6) published pilot comparative studies; and, finally, (7) methodologically sound large-scale outcome or process studies that address the causes of problems, outcomes and the active ingredients of change. Because the treatment process might not be identical for all individuals, process designs are needed to test outcomes.

The assessments of attachment can be especially useful in process designs because they have fully developed methods for assessing verbal and non-verbal communication. These could be applied quite easily to audio- or video-recorded therapy sessions. Although doing this might feel uncomfortable for a while to therapists who do not do this already, it is standard practice in mother–infant treatment. Besides generating an evidence base, when checked weekly, it can give therapists feedback that cannot be processed when one is live in the session and also identify the active components of change.

The third point is that our integrative approach to treatment already meets some of the above standards and is ready for further examination. Here and elsewhere (Dallos 2006; Ringer and Crittenden 2007; Crittenden 2008; Dallos and Vetere 2009) we have published formulations for autism, ADHD, somatic disorders, post-natal depression, eating disorders, child sexual abuse, etc. All use the same set of theoretically coherent constructs. There is also an expanding base of case studies employing a DMM framework that similarly use a range of research methods (see Appendix 2). Research studies of family therapy have incorporated some or several aspects of these criteria. They have incorporated case study evidence of family members' experience of therapy, analyses of changes in overall family functioning as well as individual changes in the family members, observational studies of family communicational dynamics and explorations of the processes of change (Dallos and Draper 2009). In addition, there is already a substantial base of comparative studies using DMM constructs, for example, the role of exposure to danger, and patterning, of both strategies and change over time (see Appendix 3).

Finally, a particularly important point is that DMM-FST Integrative Treatment is open to using whatever form of intervention best meets the needs outlined in the family functional formulation. Hence the formulation might include family therapy alongside individual-focused methods. We argue that our framework can assist in clarifying what may be the most effective integration of treatment approaches. This is a dynamic process and the developmental/maturational emphasis of our model encourages a flexibility of approach based on feedback as the course of treatment unfolds.

Choosing the form of treatment

Although there has often been an implicit assumption that one type of treatment or another was best, that is changing. Consideration was given to whether different treatments were better for different people (Fonagy and Roth 1997). A different approach has been taken by those who have tried to integrate different forms of treatment. In response to the criticisms listed above, CBT is becoming more interpersonal and increasingly similar to more dynamic and interpersonal therapies (Kahl et al. 2012). Dialectical behaviour treatment (DBT) (Linehan 1993) is an example: it is a lengthy treatment that is individualized, relies on the relationship with the therapist, and addresses both affect and non-conscious processes (but see McMain et al. 2012, for the absence of long-term benefits). Other 'Third Wave' cognitive treatments, e.g., schema therapy, acceptance and commitment therapy, mindfulness-based cognitive therapy, metacognitive therapy, address other of the criticisms. Correspondingly, psychodynamic treatment has been incorporated into aspects of other treatment approaches, for example, cognitive analytic therapy, gestalt therapy, transactional analysis, systemic psychotherapy, and mindfulness therapy; notably some of these have cognitive or behavioural roots as well.

Possibly there are a few universal processes essential to good therapy, regardless of the label. We think these include a close relationship with the therapist (as a transitional attachment figure), attention to both cognitions and feelings and also temporal contingencies and arousal, and, in most cases, attention to non-conscious functioning. To these, DMM-FST Integrative Treatment would add exposure to danger, together with individuals' developmental state and response to exposure to danger, and the systemic effects of exposure to danger within families; these can both inform behaviour in the present and suggest causal pathways that frame current dysfunction as explicable and adaptive at earlier ages.

The point is that formally named treatment approaches are beginning to integrate ideas from several different schools of therapy. This is good! But it comes with the continuing limitation that therapists are expected to use a specific therapy with commitment and fidelity. We think it is time to acknowledge what most experienced therapists know implicitly and do regularly: all (or almost all) forms of treatment have something to offer that is useful. Which tool one uses depends upon what is needed at specific points in a course of treatment with specific patients and therapists.

That brings us back to thinking about the goals of therapy. DMM-FST Integrative Treatment focuses therapists on the role of exposure to danger in shaping information processing, multiple DRs, and the process by which these shape self-, partner-, and child-protective behaviour. With good assessment, the therapist can construct a plan for correcting those DRs that do not fit current circumstances. The plan can be implemented by selecting the treatment strategy that best addresses each part of the process, from arousal regulation to quieting trauma responses to strategy repair to recognition of one's own strategies and family members' strategies, to acquiring new context-adapted strategies, and ultimately, taking a reflective stance regarding one's own functioning and that of family members.

To accomplish this, the therapist will need access to the full array of possible treatment tools, together with a rationale for employing them. We hope that DMM-FST Integrative Treatment (with its focus on protection, information processing, strategic behaviour, and interpersonal processes) can provide a logical and utilitarian framework to enable mental health practitioners to employ as many psychotherapeutic tools as possible, when and where they are likely to be most effective. Process analysis can confirm or disconfirm these choices relatively quickly, thus freeing therapists to explore other approaches and refine the choices they make, based on immediate person-specific evidence (cf. Crittenden 1991). That, of course, is what adaptive humans do every day in their regular lives. The people who come to psychotherapy, however, do not know how to do this. Instead, they live lives defined by threat. For this reason, therapists are neither service managers, sending clients to specialist services, nor technicians who select treatments; instead their most crucial role is to function as a transitional attachment figure to guide and accompany family members on the journey from threat and distress to greater safety and comfort.

Therapy is about hope in the presence of danger. Danger that is brought into the therapy and also the danger of therapy. Initially, therapy is not serene, contemplative, reflective or revitalizing. Nevertheless, if one is lucky, family members will receive their lives back, finding again all the potential they held at birth – and the newfound ability to realize this potential. But little about the experience of therapy itself gives any hint of that. No more than the labour of birth hints at the baby to come.

We began our book with a lyrical song – and a baby was born. The stories of development in childhood have been told, together with the dramas of distress and the replays and rehearsals of therapy. Now we close at the end of childhood in a transient interlude before the second act of life: sexuality, romantic love, and reproduction.

Appendix 1: Assessments

Standardized assessment can assist professionals to understand the complex state of families. The following DMM assessments are developmentally attuned, and focus on accurate observation of behaviour (recorded to preserve its structure), interpreted functionally in relational context.

The Infant CARE-Index (C-I)

The *CARE-Index* (C-I) (Crittenden 1981; Crittenden 2007a) is a videotaped three to five minute free play observation in which the adult is asked 'to play with your child as you usually would'. It highlights the connections between parent and child behaviour, but because the procedure does not contain any threat, it tends to show parents at their best. Moreover, adults do what they think is the right thing to do with children, thus, giving an assessment of the best of their potential interaction at times of low stress. It is not an assessment of attachment, but it predicts the pattern of attachment at 12 and 18 months.

The infant C-I is unique because it can be used *from birth* to 15 months (after which the Toddler version should be used) and with adults who are not the child's parents. It is also flexible in where it can be carried out, e.g., home, office, laboratory. The videotapes are coded by reliable coders who are blind to the facts of the case.

Adults are evaluated in terms of sensitivity, control, and unresponsiveness; children in terms of cooperation, compulsivity, difficultness, and passivity. The outcome includes a rating of dyadic synchrony. This is tied to the degree of risk to the child's future development. The C-I was designed as a screening tool and should always be considered in the light of other evidence.

There are many publications supporting the validity of the C-I, including those addressing its use in situations of maltreatment and maternal psychiatric disorder (Farnfield et al. 2010).

The Toddler CARE-Index (TC-I)

The Toddler *CARE-Index* (TC-I) (Crittenden 2007b) uses the same procedure as the Infant C-I with the addition, after three minutes of free play, of a frustration and resolution task administered to the child by the parent. It but is coded with a different system, that takes into account the developmental changes and yields, as well as the same aspects evaluated by the Infant C-I, proxy patterns of attachment, i.e., the DMM Types A, B, C, A/C patterns. As the procedure does not contain threat to the child, it cannot be considered a proper assessment of attachment but the frustration and resolution task activates some conflict management and resolution strategies that allow more insight into the attachment strategies. It is, however, much simpler than the Strange Situation Procedure, and therefore can be useful as a screening tool. There are two studies validating the toddler system (Crittenden 1992a; Kunster et al. 2010), but considerably more on the infant system on which it is based.

The Strange Situation procedure

The Strange Situation (Ainsworth et al. 1978, Ainsworth 1979) is the classic assessment of attachment, the one upon which all other assessments of attachment are built and validated. It consists of a sequence of eight three-minute episodes. Initially, the baby and mother are together in a room with toys and two chairs. After three minutes, an unfamiliar person, the 'stranger', enters and, after a minute or so of chatting with the mother, she tries to play with the baby. At the sound of a knock, the mother leaves and the stranger is alone with the baby for three minutes. The mother watches her baby through a one-way mirror. The mother returns. The mother and baby have three minutes to settle, then at the sound of a second knock, the mother goes out leaving the baby alone. After three minutes (or when the baby cries a lot), the stranger returns; she comforts the baby if needed, then sits down. After three minutes (or less if the baby is crying), the mother returns. This final three-minute reunion is crucial to determining the baby's attachment strategy.

The baby's response in the two reunions is important for understanding his pattern of attachment. Most babies with a Type B strategy welcome the mother. Babies with a Type A strategy tend to ignore the mother. Babies with a Type C strategy often protest while approaching the mother.

The DMM coding method (Crittenden 2003) expands on the revision of Ainsworth's original method made by Crittenden with Ainsworth in 1983. It is particularly sensitive to nuances of attachment behaviour in high-risk contexts.

The Preschool Assessment of Attachment (PAA)

The Preschool Assessment of Attachment (PAA) (Crittenden 1992a, 2004) uses the modified Strange Situation Procedure that accommodates preschoolers' ability to walk, talk, and open doors. It assesses a child's self-protective strategy in an attachment relationship, indicating (1) whether the child identifies the parent as a source of danger or protection or both, and (2) what strategy he or she uses for self-protection.

The PAA identifies all the Ainsworth patterns (Types A1–2, B, C1–2), plus Types A3, A4, C3, C4, A/C, as well as modifiers of depression and intrusions of forbidden negative affect. It has been validated in terms of maltreatment status, maternal sensitivity, developmental quotient, and maternal attachment strategy (Farnfield et al. 2010). Based on published studies (see below), the PAA is currently the best assessment of attachment in children aged 2–5 years old with evidence that it differentiates maltreated and emotionally troubled children as well as children of troubled mothers from more normally developing children. Although there is another classificatory method for the Strange Situation with preschool-aged children, the Cassidy-Marvin method, it accounts for much less variance in outcomes and predicts future development less well than the PAA (Crittenden et al. 2007; Spieker and Crittenden 2010).

The School-Age Assessment of Attachment (SAA)

The School Age Assessment of Attachment (Crittenden 1997–2005; Crittenden and Landini 1999) is a semi-structured interview which is administered to school-aged children between the ages of 6 and 13 years. The interview is tape-recorded then transcribed verbatim. It is then coded using the DMM discourse method (Crittenden and Landini 2011) and classified with the DMM model of attachment, identifying all the Ainsworth patterns plus Types A3-4, C3-6, A/C, unresolved traumas and losses and modifiers. Most interviews take 30–45 minutes to administer.

The SAA uses seven picture cards depicting increasing levels of danger about which the child is asked to tell first a made-up story and then to talk about a similar time in their own life. Once s/he has told a story (fantasy or real), the interviewer explores the child's understanding of their feelings and motives and their understanding of the perspectives of others, particularly attachment figures.

This is a new procedure and therefore there are few published empirical studies to date (Crittenden et al. 2010; Kwako et al. 2010). There are also articles using the SAA in case studies (Crittenden and Kulbotton 2007; Kozlowska and Williams 2009).

The Transition to Adulthood Assessment of Attachment (TAAI)

The Transition to Adulthood Attachment Interview (TAAI) (Crittenden 2005) is a procedure for assessing older adolescents' and young adults' self-protective strategies. The assessment uses a modified version of the Adult Attachment Interview (AAI) (George et al. 1985–1996), the DMM-AAI (Crittenden and Landini 2011). The modification is designed to address the competencies and salient issues of young adults during the transition to adulthood (~16–25 years).

Like the Adult Attachment Interview, the TAAI consists of a series of questions that ask the speaker to consider their childhood experience and how this might affect their thoughts and behaviour in the present. Importantly, the TAAI probes for the same information in multiple ways; this permits exploration of conflicting ideas that could motivate incompatible behaviours. In addition, the TAAI explores possible past traumas that could trigger extreme behaviour.

The TAAI is audio-recorded and then transcribed verbatim. Information is gained by attending both to the individual's speech and their relationship with the interviewer. The TAAI is analysed using the DMM method of discourse analysis in which the content of the interview (what happened) is less important than how the speaker thinks about their childhood, as an adult. It identifies the same patterns and modifiers as the SAA, with the addition of the Type A5–6 strategies.

The Adult Attachment Interview (AAI): the DMM method

The Adult Attachment Interview (AAI) (George et al. 1985–1996) and the DMM-AAI (Crittenden and Landini 2011) consist of a series of questions that ask the speaker to consider their childhood experience and how this might affect their thoughts and behaviour in the present, especially as parents. Like the TAAI, it asks for the same information in multiple ways, and the topics are ordered starting from the most neutral and going towards the most dangerous. Most interviews take between 60 and 90 minutes.

The AAI is audio-recorded and then transcribed verbatim. The DMM-AAI is analysed using the DMM discourse analysis method in which the content of the interview (what happened) is less important than how the speaker thinks about their childhood, as an adult. Information is gained by attending both to the individual's speech and their relationship with the interviewer. The DMM-AAI is then classified yielding a self-protective strategy (all the DMM strategies, singularly or combined), a list of unresolved dangerous events (losses or traumas, that can be unresolved in different ways) and modifiers of the basic strategies (depressed, disoriented, reorganizing, intrusions of forbidden negative affect, expression of somatic symptoms).

The DMM-AAI has been validated in a number of empirical studies focusing on fMRI associations, infant Strange Situation Procedure associations and cross-generational patterning in normative samples, as well as on a variety of clinical issues (Farnfield et al. 2010).

The Parents Interview (PI)

The Parents Interview is a one-hour, semi-structured interview that is given to the parent(s) with the children present (Crittenden 1981). Before beginning, the parents are asked to keep an eye on the children and to handle any problems that come up. Managing multiple stressful situations all at one time during the interview simulates the conditions that elicit parenting problems.

The PI itself consists of a series of questions that ask the parents to consider: (1) their childhood experience; (2) their functioning together; and (3) how they work together to raise the child(ren). The PI asks for the same information in multiple ways; this permits exploration of conflicting ideas that could motivate incompatible behaviours. Parents with less integration of thought and feeling, i.e., with varied and incompatible answers to the same question, are more likely to behave in unexpected and sometimes maladaptive ways than individuals with greater awareness of how past experience motivates their current behaviour. The PI explores how the parents work together in their relationship by looking at how they work together to answer the questions.

The PI is audio-recorded and then transcribed verbatim. Information is gained by attending to each individual's speech, their relationship to each other, and their relationship with the interviewer. The PI is analysed using the DMM-AAI method of discourse analysis (Crittenden and Landini 2011) in which the content of the interview is less important than how the speaker thinks about their childhood, as an adult, and how they interact with their partner and the interviewer. The one published study using the PI indicated that the PI could differentiate four groups of parents: abusing, neglecting, marginally maltreating, and adequate (Crittenden et al. 1991).

The PI yields: (1) an approximation of an attachment strategy; (2) an over-riding distortion of the strategy such as depression; (3) a brief developmental history of each speaker; and (4) a level of parental reasoning (LPR), i.e., how the parent thinks about making caregiving decisions for the children. The levels range from inarticulate to simplistic to complex interpersonal decision-making. The LPR suggests the flexibility and sensitivity with which the parent will be able to interpret and respond to the child's behaviour. The PI does not address trauma or loss.

Appendix 2: Published DMM case studies

Baldoni, F. (2011) The adaptive value of desperation in a case of psychosomatic breakdown following child sexual abuse. *DMM News*, 11: 4–5.

Chisholm, K. (2000) Attachment in children adopted from Romanian orphanages: two case studies, in P. Crittenden (ed.) *The Organization of Attachment Relationships: Maturation, Culture, and Context*. New York: Cambridge University Press, pp. 171–89.

Chudleigh, C., Kozlowska, K., Kothur, K., et al. (2013) Managing non-epileptic seizures and psychogenic dystonia in an adolescent girl with preterm brain injury. *Harvard Review of Psychiatry*, 21: 163–74.

Crittenden, P.M. and Kulbotton, G.R. (2007) Familial contributions to ADHD: an attachment perspective. *The Norwegian Journal of Psychology*, 10: 1220–9.

Crittenden, P.M. and Poggioli, D. (2011) PTSD in the context of childhood endangerment: implications for assessment and treatment, in V. Ardino (ed.) *Post-traumatic Syndromes in Childhood and Adolescence*. Chichester: Wiley-Blackwell.

Gullestad, S.E. (2003) The Adult Attachment Interview and psychoanalytic outcome studies. *International Journal of Psychoanalysis*, 84: 651–68.

Haapasalo, J., Puupponen, M. and Crittenden, P.M. (1999) Victim to victimizer: the psychology of isomorphism in a case of a recidivist pedophile. *Journal of Child Sexual Abuse*, 7: 97–115.

Hans, S.L., Bernstein, V.J. and Sims, B.E. (2000) Change and continuity in ambivalent attachment relationships from infancy through adolescence, in P.M. Crittenden and A.H. Claussen (eds) *The Organization of Attachment Relationships: Maturation, Culture, and Context*. New York: Cambridge University Press, pp. 277–99.

Kozlowska, K. (2007) Integenerational processes, attachment and unexplained medical symptoms. *Australian and New Zealand Journal of Family Therapy*, 28: 88–99.

Kozlowska, K. (2010a) Family-of-origin issues and the generation of childhood illness. *Australian and New Zealand Journal of Family Therapy*, 31: 73–91.

Kozlowska, K. (2010b) The bowl of terror: a case study of an adolescent perpetrator of sexual abuse. *Australian and New Zealand Journal of Family Therapy*, 31: 43–59.

Kozlowska, K. (2012) Transition to society: the school-age years and the School-Age Assessment of Attachment, in M. Stokowy and N. Sahhar (Eds) *Das dynamische Reifungsmodell der Bindung und Anpassung – DMM und seine Anwendungen*. Gießen, Germany: Psychosozial-Verlag, pp. 87–112.

Kozlowska, K., English, M., Savage, B., et al. (2013) Multimodal rehabilitation: a mind-body, family-based intervention for children and adolescents impaired by medically unexplained symptoms. Part 2: Case studies and outcomes. *American Journal of Family Therapy*, 41: 212–31.

Kozlowska, K. and Foley, S. (2006) Attachment and risk of future harm: a case of non-accidental brain injury. *Australian and New Zealand Journal of Family Therapy*, 27: 75–82.

Kozlowska, K., Foley, S. and Crittenden, P.M. (2006) Factitious illness by proxy: understanding underlying psychological processes and motivations. *Australian and New Zealand Journal of Family Therapy*, 27: 92–104.

Kozlowska, K., Foley, S. and Savage, S. (2012) Fabricated illness: working within the family system to find a pathway to health. *Family Process*, 51(4): 570–87.

Landini, A., Kozlowska, K., Davies. F. and Chudleigh, C. (2012) Adolescence and the Transition to Adulthood Attachment Interview, in M. Stokowy and N. Sahhar (eds) *Das dynamische Reifungsmodell der Bindung und Anpassung – DMM und seine Anwendungen*. Gießen, Germany: Psychosozial-Verlag, pp. 113–40.

Nørbech, P., Crittenden, P.M. and Hartmann, E. (2013) Self-protective strategies, violence and psychopathy: theory and a case study. *Journal of Personality Assessment*, Aug. 27 [Epub].

Purnell, C. (2011) The application of the Dynamic-Maturational Model of Attachment to psychotherapy and some reflections on practice. *Attachment*, 5: 209–25.

Wilkinson, S. (2012) Another day older and deeper in therapy: can the DMM offer a way out? *Clinical Child Psychology and Psychiatry*, 15: 423–33.

Appendix 3: Published DMM comparative studies

Empirical studies using the Care-Index

Risk studies

1. Adolescent mothers

Pacquette, D., Bigras, M., Zoccolillo, M., Tremblay, R., Labelle, M-È, and Azar, R. (2001) Comparison de la sensibilité parentale entre des mères adolescentes et des mères adultes peu scolarisées. *Revue de Psychoéducation et d'Orientation*, 30: 283–98.

See also Cassidy et al. (1996), Leadbeater et al. (1996) and Linares et al. (1999), below.

2. Drug abusing mothers; drug-exposed infants

Ciotti, F., Lambruschi, F., Pittino, B. and Crittenden, P. (1998) La valutazione della relazione precoce madre-bambino in una popolazione di madri con una storia di tossicodipendenza attraverso l'uso del CARE-Index. *Psicoterapia Cognitiva e Comportamentale*, 4: 53–9.

See also Linares et al. (1999), below

3. Maternal psychiatric disorder

Ayissi, L. and Hubin-Gayte, M. (2006) Irritabilité du nouveau-né et dépression maternelle du post-partum. *Neuropsychiatrie de l'Enfance et de l'Adolescence*, 54(2): 125–32.

Cassidy, B., Zoccolillo, M. and Hughes, S. (1996) Psychopathology in adolescent mothers and its effects on mother-infant interactions: a pilot study. *Canadian Journal of Psychiatry*, 41: 379–84.

Kemppinen, K., Kumpulainen, K., Moilanen, I. and Ebling, H. (2006) Recurrent and transient depressive symptoms around delivery and maternal sensitivity. *Nordic Journal of Psychiatry*, 60: 191–9.

Leadbeater, B.J., Bishop, S.J. and Raver, C.C. (1996) Quality of mother-toddler interaction, maternal depressive symptoms, and behaviour problems of adolescent mothers. *Developmental Psychology*, 32: 280–8.

Leventhal, A., Jacobsen, T., Miller, L.J. and Quintana, E. (2004) Caregiving attitudes and at-risk maternal behaviour among mothers with major mental illness. *Psychiatric Services*, 55: 1431–3.

Mullick, M., Miller, L.J. and Jacobsen, T. (2001) Insight into mental illness and child maltreatment risk in mothers with major psychiatric disorders. *Psychiatric Services*, 52: 488–92.

Ostler, T. (2010) Assessing parenting risk within the context of severe and persistent mental illness: validating an observational measure for families with child protective service involvement. *Infant Mental Health Journal*, 51: 467–85.

4. Handicapping conditions

Crittenden, P.M. and Bonvillian, J.D. (1984) The effect of maternal risk status on maternal sensitivity to infant cues. *American Journal of Orthopsychiatry*, 54: 250–62.

Hubin-Gayte, M. and Ayissi, L. (2005) Sensibilité et réprésentations des mères de nouveau-nés irritables. *Neuropsychiatrie* de l'Enfance et de l'Adolescence, 53(1–2): 78–85.

Killen, K. (2006) Tidlig mor-barn-samspill i norske familier. *Tidsskrift for Norsk Psykologforening*, 7: 694–701.

5. Maltreated infants

Crittenden, P.M. (1981) Abusing, neglecting, problematic, and adequate dyads: differentiating by patterns of interaction. *Merrill-Palmer Quarterly*, 27: 1–18.

Crittenden, P.M. (1984) Sibling interaction: evidence of a generational effect in maltreating families. *International Journal of Child Abuse and Neglect*, 8: 433–8.

Crittenden, PM (1985) Social networks, quality of child-rearing, and child development. *Child Development*, 56: 1299–313.

Crittenden, P.M. (1987) Non-organic failure-to-thrive: deprivation or distortion? *Infant Mental Health Journal*, 8: 56–64.

Crittenden, P.M. (1988) Distorted patterns of relationship in maltreating families: the role of internal representational models. *Journal of Reproductive and Infant Psychology*, 6: 183–99.

Crittenden, P.M. (1992) Children's strategies for coping with adverse home environments. *International Journal of Child Abuse and Neglect*, 16: 329–43.

Crittenden, P.M. and DiLalla, D.L. (1988) Compulsive compliance: the development of an inhibitory coping strategy in infancy. *Journal of Abnormal Child Psychology*, 16: 585–99.

Jacobsen, T. and Miller, L.J. (1998) Compulsive compliance in a young maltreated child. *Journal of the American Academy of Child and Adolescent Psychiatry*, 37: 462–63.

Leadbeater, B. and Bishop, S.J. (1994) Predictors of behaviour problems in preschool children of inner city Afro-American and Puerto Rican mothers. *Child Development*, 65: 638–48.

Ward, M.J., Kessler, D.B. and Altman, S.C. (1993) Infant-mother attachment in children with failure to thrive. *Infant Mental Health Journal*, 14: 208–20.

6. Prematurity

Baldoni, F., Facondini, E., Minghetti, M., Romeo, N., Landini, A. and Crittenden, P.M. (2009) Family attachment and psychosomatic development in preterm-born children. *Panminerva Medica*, 51(3 suppl. 1): 7.

Baldoni, F., Facondini, E., Romeo, N., Landini, A. and Crittenden, P.M. (2010) Precursori dell'attaccamento e adattamento di coppia nella famiglia con bambino nato pretermine: uno studio italiano, in L. Cena, A. Imbasciati and F. Baldoni (eds) *La relazione genitoro-bambino. Dalla psicoanalisi infantile alle nuove prospettive evoluzionistiche dell'attaccamento.* Milan: Springer Verlag, pp. 194–200.

Fuertes, M., Faria, A., Soares, A. and Crittenden, P. (2009) Developmental and evolutionary assumptions in a study about the impact of premature birth and low-income on mother-infant interaction. *Acta Ethologica*, 12: 1–11.

Muller-Nix, C., Forcada-Guex, M., Pierrehumbert, B., Jaunin, L., Borghini, A. and Ansermet, F. (2004) Prematurity, maternal stress and mother-child interactions. *Early Human Development*, 79: 145–58.

7. Toddlers

Künster, A.K., Fegert, J.M. and Ziegenhain, U. (2010) Assessing parent-child interaction in the preschool years: a pilot study on the psychometric properties of the Toddler CARE-Index. *Clinical Child Psychology and Psychiatry*, 15: 379–90.

8. Institutionalization

Muhamedrahimov, R.J., Palmov, O.I., Nikforova, N.V., Groark, C.J. and McCall, R.B. (2004) Institution-based early intervention program. *The Infant Mental Health Journal*, 25: 488–501.

Pleshkova, N.L. and Muhamedrahimov, R.J. (2008) Attachment in family and orphanage children. *Defectology*, 2: 37–44.

Normative studies

Cantero, J. and Cerezo, J. (2001) Interacción madre-hijo como predictora de conductas de apego: evaluación de dos modelos causales. *Infancia y Aprendizaje*, 24(1): 113–32.

Hautamäki, A. (2010) Attachment and sensitivity in a low-risk Finnish sample: the avoidant and unresponsive Finns?, in P. Aunio, M. Jahnukainen, M. Kalland and J. Silvonen (eds) *Piaget is Dead, Vygotsky is Still Alive, or? Honorary Book for Professors Airi and Jarkko Hautamäki*. Jyväskylä, Finland: Finnish Educational Research Association, Jyväskylä University Press, pp. 149–82.

Kemppinen, K., Kumpulainen, K., Moilanen, I., Raita-Hasu, J. and Ebling, H. (2006) Continuity of maternal sensitivity from infancy to toddler age. *Journal of Reproductive and Infant Psychology*, 24: 199–212.

La Sala, G.B., Gallinelli, A., Fagandini, P., et al. (2003) Developmental outcomes at one and two years of children conceived by intracyctoplamic sperm injection. *International Journal of Fertility and Women's Medicine*, 49(3): 113–19.

Mosheim, R., Hotter, A., Steiner, H-J., Kemmler, G., Biebl, W. and Richter, R. (2001) Une étude pilote sur le congré parental de pères au Tyrol. *Paternité et santé mentale* 26: 118–35.

Paavola, L., Kemppinen, K., Kumpulainen, K., Moilanen, I. and Ebling, H. (2006a) Characteristics of mother-infant communicative interaction: relations to the rating of maternal sensitivity and infant cooperation. *Journal of Early Childhood Research*, 4: 203–22.

Paavola, L., Kemppinen, K., Kumpulainen, K., Moilanen, I. and Ebling, H. (2006b) Maternal sensitivity, infant cooperation and early linguistic development: some predictive relations. *European Journal of Developmental Psychology*, 3: 13–30.

Pleshkova, N.L. (2006) Quality of attachment in young children, in S.F. Sirotkin and M.L. Melnikova (eds) *Attachment and Early Intervention Psychology*, July 3–4 International Research Seminar Materials (pp. 40–6). Ijevsk, Russia: NIPC 'ERGO'.

Simó-Teufel, S., D'Ocon, A. and Dolz, L. (2002) Comparación entre los patrones interaccionales madre-hijo y la calidad del apego a los 15 meses de edad: un análisis de validación. *Metodología de las Ciencias del Comportamiento*, 12: 516–20.

Simó-Teufel, S., D'Ocon, A. and Pons-Salvador, G. (2002) Evaluación de la calidad del apego a los 15 meses de edad: análisis de la concordancia entre observadores. *Metodología de las Ciencias del Comportamiento*, 12: 512–15.

Simó-Teufel, S., Rauh, H. and Ziegenhain, U. (2000) Mutter-Kind-Interaktion im Verlaufe der ersten 18 Lebensmonate und Bindungssicherheit am Ende des 2. Lebensjahres. *Psychologie in Erziehung und Unterricht*, 47: 118–41.

Predictive longitudinal studies

Crugnola, C.R., Albizzati, A., Caprin, C., Di Filippo, L. and Sagliaschi, S. (2004) Modelli di attaccamento, stili di interazione e responsivita nello sviluppo della relazione tra madre e bambino: elementi di adeguatezza e di rischio. *Eta Evolutiva*, 78: 66–76.

Forcada-Guex, M., Pierrehumbert, B., Borghini, A., Moessinger, A. and Muller-Nix, C. (2006) Early dyadic pattern of mother-child interaction and outcomes of prematurity at 18 months. *Pediatrics*, 118: e107–14.

Simó-Teufel, S., Rauh, H. and Ziegenhain, U. (2000) Mutter-Kind-Interaktion im Verlaufe der ersten 18 Lebensmonate und Bindungssicherheit am Ende des 2.

Lebensjahres. *Psychologie in Erziehung und Unterricht*, 47: 118–41.

Ward, M.J. and Carlson E.A. (1995) The predictive validity of the Adult Attachment Interview for adolescent mothers. *Child Development*, 66: 69–79.

Intervention studies

Barlow, J., Davis, H. and McIntosh, E. (2007) Role of home visiting in improving parenting and health in families at risk of abuse and neglect: trial and economic evaluation results of a multicentre randomised controlled health in families at risk of abuse and neglect: *Archives of Disturbed Children*, 92: 229–33.

Bigras, M. and Pacquette, D. (2000) L'interdépendance entre les sous-systèmes conjugals et parentals: une analyse personne-processus-contexte. *Psicologia: Teoria e Pesquisa*, 16: 91–102.

Cramer, B., Robert-Tissot, C., Stern, D.N. and Serpa-Rusconi, S. (1990) Outcome evaluation in brief mother-infant psychotherapy: a preliminary report. *Infant Mental Health Journal*, 11: 278–300.

Crittenden, P.M. (1985) Maltreated infants: vulnerability and resilience. *Journal of Child Psychology and Psychiatry*, 26: 85–96.

Linares, L.O., Jones, B., Sheiber, F.J. and Rosenberg, F.B. (1999) Early intervention for drug-exposed infants in foster care, in J. Silver, B.J. Amster and P. Haecker (eds) *Young Children and Foster Care*. Baltimore, MD: Brookes, pp. 373–97.

Pacquette, D., Zoccolillo, M. and Bigras, M. (1999) L'efficacité des interventions en foyers de groupe pour mères en difficulté d'adaptation. *Défi Jeunesse*, VI: 30–5.

Priddis, L. and Howieson, N.D. Insecure attachment patterns at five years: what do they tell us? *Early Child Development and Care*, 182: 45–58.

Robert-Tissot, C., Cramer, B., Stern, D., et al. (1996) Outcome evaluation in brief mother-infant psychotherapies: report on 75 cases. *Infant Mental Health Journal*, 17: 97–114.

Svanberg, P.O. and Jennings, T. (2002) The Sunderland Infant Program (U.K.): reflections on the first year. *Signal*, 9: 1–5.

Svanberg, P.O., Mennet, L. and Spieker, S. (2010) Promoting a secure attachment: a primary prevention practice model. *Clinical Child Psychology and Psychiatry*, 15: 363–78.

Empirical studies using the infant Strange Situation: DMM

Baldoni, F., Minghetti, M. and Facondini, E. (2012) Trasmissione dell'attaccamento e Modello Dinamico-Maturativo, in L. Cena, A. Imbasciati and F. Baldoni (eds) *Prendersi cura dei bambini e dei loro genitori. La ricerca clinica per l'intervento*. Milan: Springer-Verlag.

Crittenden, P.M. (1985a) Maltreated infants: vulnerability and resilience. *Journal of Child Psychology and Psychiatry*, 26: 85–96.

Crittenden, P.M. (1985b) Social networks, quality of child-rearing, and child development. *Child Development*, 56: 1299–313.

Crittenden, P.M. (1987) Non-organic failure-to-thrive: deprivation or distortion? *Infant Mental Health Journal*, 8: 56–64.

Crittenden, P.M. (1988) Relationships at risk, in J. Belsky and T. Nezworski (eds) *The Clinical Implications of Attachment*. Hillsdale, NJ: Lawrence Erlbaum, pp. 136–74.

Hautamäki, A. (2010) Transmission of attachment across three generations: continuity and reversal. *Clinical Child Psychology and Psychiatry*, 15: 347–54.

Hautamäki, A., Hautamäki, L., Neuvonen, L. and Maliniemi-Piispanen, S. (2010) Transmission of attachment across three generations. *European Journal of Developmental Psychology*, 7: 618–34.

Pleshkova, N.L. and Muhamedrahimov, R.J. (2010) Quality of attachment in St. Petersburg (Russian Federation): a sample of family-reared infants. *Clinical Child Psychology and Psychiatry*, 15: 355–62.

Shah, P.E., Fonagy, P. and Strathearn, L. (2010) Exploring the mechanism of intergenerational transmission of attachment: the plot thickens. *Clinical Child Psychology and Psychiatry*, 15: 329–46. (Also uses the AAI.)

Empirical studies using the PAA

Chisholm, K. (1998) A three year follow-up of attachment and indiscriminate friendliness in children adopted from Romanian orphanages. *Child Development*, 69: 1092–106.

Crittenden, P.M., Claussen, A.H. and Kozlowska, K. (2007) Choosing a valid assessment of attachment for clinical use: a comparative study, *Australian and New Zealand Journal of Family Therapy*, 28: 78–87.

DeVito, C. and Hopkins, J. (2001) Attachment, parenting, and marital dissatisfaction as predictors of disruptive behaviour in preschoolers. *Development and Psychopathology*, 13: 215–31.

Fagot, B.I. and Pears, K.C. (1996) Changes in attachment during the third year: consequences and predictions. *Development and Psychopathology*, 8: 325–44.

Fisher, L., Ames, E.W., Chisholm, K. and Savoie, L. (1997) Problems reported by parents of Romanian orphans adopted to British Columbia. *International Journal of Behavioural Development*, 20: 67–82.

Gunnar, M.R., Morison, S.J., Chisholm, K. and Schuder, M. (2001) Salivary cortisol levels in children adopted from Romanian orphanages. *Development and Psychopathology*, 13: 611–28.

Hans, S.L., Bernstein, V.J. and Sims, B.E. (2000) Change and continuity in ambivalent attachment relationships from infancy through adolescence, in P.M. Crittenden and A.H. Claussen (eds) *The Organization of Attachment Relationships: Maturation, Culture, and Context*. New York: Cambridge University Press, pp. 277–99.

Hautamäki, A. (2010) Transmission of attachment across three generations: continuity and reversal. *Clinical Child Psychology and Psychiatry*, 15: 347–54.

Hautamäki, A., Hautamäki, L., Neuvonen, L. and Maliniemi-Piispanen, S. (2010) Transmission of attachment across three generations. *European Journal of Developmental Psychology*, 7: 618–34.

Kwako, L.E., Noll, J.G., Putnam, F.W. and Trickett, P.K. (2010) Childhood sexual abuse and attachment: an intergenerational perspective. *Clinical Child Psychology and Psychiatry*, 15: 407–22.

Kidwell, S.L., Young, M.E., Hinkle, L.D., Ratliff, A.D., Marcum, M.E. and Martin, C.N. (2010) Emotional competence and behaviour problems among preschoolers: differences across preschool attachment classifications. *Clinical Child Psychology and Psychiatry*, 15: 391–406.

Moilanen, I., Kunelius, A., Tirkonnen, T. and Crittenden, P. (2000) Attachment in Finnish twins, in P.M. Crittenden and A.H. Claussen (eds) *The Organization of Attachment Relationships: Maturation, Culture, and Context*. New York: Cambridge University Press, pp. 125–40.

Rauh, H., Ziegenhain, U., Müller, B. and Wijnroks, L. (2000) Stability and change in infant-mother attachment in the second year of life: relations to parenting quality and varying degrees of daycare experience, in P.M. Crittenden and A.H. Claussen (eds.) *The Organization of Attachment Relationships: Maturation, Culture, and Context*. New York: Cambridge University Press, pp. 251–76.

Sajaniemi, N., Makela, J., Saolkorpi, T., von Wendt, L., Hamalainen, T. and

Hakamies-Blomqvist, L. (2001) Cognitive performance and attachment patterns at four years of age in extremely low birth weight infants after early intervention. *European Child and Adolescent Psychiatry*, 10(2): 122–9.

Spieker, S.J. and Crittenden, P.M. (2010) Comparing the validity of two approaches to attachment theory: disorganization versus danger-informed organization in the preschool years. *Clinical Child Psychology and Psychiatry*, 15: 97–120.

Teti, D.M. (2000) Maternal depression and child-mother attachment in the first three years: a view from the intermountain west, in P.M. Crittenden and A.H. Claussen (eds) *The Organization of Attachment Relationships: Maturation, Culture, and Context*. New York: Cambridge University Press, pp. 190–213.

Teti, D.M. and Gelfand, D.M. (1997) The Preschool Assessment of Attachment: construct validity in a sample of depressed and non-depressed families. *Development and Psychopathology*, 9: 517–36.

Teti, D.M., Gelfand, D.M., Messinger, D.S. and Isabella, R. (1995) Maternal depression and the quality of early attachment: an examination of infants, preschoolers, and their mothers. *Developmental Psychology*, 31: 364–76.

Von der Lippe, A. and Crittenden, P.M. (2000) Quality of attachment in young Egyptian children, in P. Crittenden and A.H. Claussen (eds.) *The Organization of Attachment Relationships: Maturation, Culture, and Context*. New York: Cambridge University Press, pp. 97–114.

Vondra, J.I., Hommerding, K.D. and Shaw, D.S. (1999) Stability and change in infant attachment in a low-income sample, in J.I. Vondra and D. Barnett (eds) *Atypical Patterns of Attachment in Infancy and Early Childhood*; Monographs of the Society for Research in Child Development, Serial No. 258. Malden, MA: Blackwell, pp. 119–44.

Vondra, J.I., Shaw, D.S., Swearingen, L., Cohen, M. and Owens, E.B. (1999) Early relationship quality from home to school: a longitudinal study. *Early Education and Development*, 10: 163–90.

Vondra, J.I., Shaw, D.S., Swearingen, L., Cohen, M. and Owens, E.B. (2001) Attachment stability and emotional and behavioural regulation from infancy to preschool age. *Development and Psychopathology*, 13: 13–33.

Ziegenhain, U., Müller, B. and Rauh, H. (1996) Frühe Bindungserfahrungen und Verhaltensauffälligkeiten bei Kleinkindern in einer sozialen und kognitiven Anforderungssituation. *Praxis der Kinderpsychologie und Kinderpsychiatrie*, 45(3–4): 95–102.

Empirical studies using the SAA

Crittenden, P.M., Kozlowska, K. and Landini, A. (2010) Assessing attachment in school-age children. *Child Clinical Psychology and Psychiatry*, 14: 185–208.

Kwako, L.E., Noll, J.G., Putnam, F.W. and Trickett, P.K. (2010) Childhood sexual abuse and attachment: an intergenerational perspective. *Clinical Child Psychology and Psychiatry*, 15: 407–22.

Empirical studies in adolescence using the TAAI/AAI

Black, K.A., Jaeger, E., McCartney, K. and Crittenden, P.M. (2000) Attachment models, peer interaction behaviour, and feelings about the self: indications of maladjustment in dismissing/preoccupied (Ds/E) adolescents, in P.M. Crittenden and A.H. Claussen (eds) *The Organization of Attachment Relationships: Maturation, Culture, and Context*. New York: Cambridge University Press, pp. 300–24.

Kozlowska, K. (2010) The bowl of terror: a case study of an adolescent perpetrator of sexual abuse. *The Australian and New Zealand Journal of Family Therapy*, 31: 43–59.

Wilkinson, S. (2003) Another day older and deeper in therapy: can the DMM offer a way out? *Clinical Child Psychology and Psychiatry*, 15: 423–33.

Empirical studies using the AAI (DMM)

Baldoni, F., Baldaro, B., Minghetti, M., Surcinelli, P., Landini, A. and Crittenden, P.M. (2012) La trasmissione dell'attaccamento tra madre e figlio: uno studio nella prospettiva del Modello Dinamico-Maturativo, in L. Cena, A. Imbasciati, and F. Baldoni (eds) *Prendersi cura dei bambini e dei loro genitori. La ricerca clinica per l'intervento*. Milan: Springer-Verlag.

Crittenden, P.M. and Newman, L. (2010) Comparing models of borderline personality disorder: mothers' experience, self-protective strategies, and dispositional representations. *Clinical Child Psychology and Psychiatry*, 15: 433–52.

Hautamäki, A., Hautamäki, L., Maliniemi-Piispanen, S. and Neuvonen, L. (2008) Kiintymyssuhteen välittyminen kolmessa sukupolvessa – äidinäitien paluu? [Transmission of attachment across three generations: the return of grannies?]. *Psykologia*, 6: 421–42.

Hautamäki, A., Hautamäki, L., Neuvonen, L. and Maliniemi-Piispanen, S. (2010a) Transmission of attachment across three generations. *European Journal of Developmental Psychology*, 7: 618–34.

Hautamäki, A., Hautamäki, L., Neuvonen, L. and Maliniemi-Piispanen, S. (2010b) Transmission of attachment across three generations: continuity and reversal. *Clinical Child Psychology and Psychiatry*, 15: 347–54.

Hughes, J., Hardy, G. and Kendrick, D. (2000) Assessing adult attachment status with clinically-orientated interviews: a brief report. *British Journal of Medical Psychology*, 73: 279–83.

Ringer, F. and Crittenden, P. (2007) Eating disorders and attachment: the effects of hidden processes on eating disorders. *European Eating Disorders Review*, 15: 119–30.

Shah, P.E., Fonagy, P. and Stratearn, L. (2003) Exploring the mechanism of intergenerational transmission of attachment: the plot thickens. *Clinical Child Psychology and Psychiatry*, 15: 329–46.

Stratearn, L., Fonagy, P., Amico, J.A. and Montague, P.R. (2009) Adult attachment predicts mother's brain and peripheral oxytocin response to infant cues. *Neuropsychopharmacology*, 34: 2655–66.

Worley, K.O., Walsh, S. and Lewis, K. (2004) An examination of parenting practices in male perpetrators of domestic violence: a qualitative study. *Psychology and Psychotherapy: Theory, Research, and Practice*, 77: 35–54.

Zachrisson, H.D. and Kulbotton, G. (2006) Attachment in anorexia nervosa: an exploration of associations with eating disorder psychopathology and psychiatric symptoms. *Eating and Weight Disorders*, 11: 163–70.

Zachrisson, H.D., Sommerfeld, B. and Skårderud, F. (2011) What you use decides what you get: comparing classificatory procedures for the Adult Attachment Interview in eating disorder research. *Eating and Weight Disorders*, 16: 285–8.

Other empirical studies

Christopoulos, C., Bonvillian, J.D. and Crittenden, P.M. (1988) Maternal language input and child maltreatment. *Infant Mental Health Journal*, 9: 272–86.

Crittenden, P.M. (1983) The effect of mandatory protective daycare on mutual attachment in maltreating mother-infant dyads. *International Journal of Child Abuse and Neglect*, 3: 297–300.

Crittenden, P.M. (1984) Sibling interaction: evidence of a generational effect in maltreating families. *International Journal of Child Abuse and Neglect*, 8: 433–8.

Crittenden, P.M. and Craig, S. (1990) Developmental trends in child homicide. *Journal of Interpersonal Violence*, 5: 202–16.

Crittenden, P.M. and DiLalla, D. L. (1988) Compulsive compliance: the development of an inhibitory coping strategy in infancy. *Journal of Abnormal Child Psychology*, 16, 585–99.

Crittenden, P.M., Lang, C., Claussen, A.H. and Partridge, M.F. (2000) Relations among mothers' procedural, semantic, and episodic internal representational models of parenting, in P.M. Crittenden and A.H. Claussen (eds) *The Organization of Attachment Relationships: Maturation, Culture, and Context*. New York: Cambridge University Press, pp. 214–33.

Crittenden, P.M. and Morrison, A.K. (1988) Preventing maltreatment of infants: a hospital screening procedure. *Pediatric Nursing*, 14: 415–17.

Crittenden, P.M., Partridge, M.F. and Claussen, A.H. (1991) Family patterns of relationship in normative and dysfunctional families. *Development and Psychopathology*, 3: 491–512.

Crittenden, P.M. and Snell, M.E. (1983) Intervention to improve mother-infant interaction. *Infant Mental Health Journal*, 4: 23–41.

DiLalla, D.L. and Crittenden, P.M. (1990) Dimensions in maltreated children's behaviour: a factor analytic approach. *Infant Behaviour and Development*, 13: 439–60.

Jean-Gilles, M. and Crittenden, P.M. (1990) Maltreating families: a look at siblings. *Family Relations*, 39: 323–9.

Kozlowska, K., Brown K.J., Palmer, D.M. and Williams, L.M. (2013) Specific biases for identifying facial expression of emotion in children and adolescents with conversion disorders. *Psychosomatic Medicine*, 75: 272–80.

Kozlowska, K., Scher, S. and Williams, L.M. (2011) Patterns of emotional-cognitive function in pediatric conversion patients: implications for the conceptualization of conversion disorders. *Psychosomatic Medicine*. 73: 775–88.

References

Abbass, A., Town, J. and Driessen, E. (2012) Intensive short-term dynamic psychotherapy: a systematic review and meta-analysis of outcome research. *Harvard Review of Psychiatry*, 20(2): 97–108.

Abrahams, M.F. (1994) Perceiving flirtatious communication: an exploration of the perceptual dimensions underlying judgments of flirtatiousness. *Journal of Sex Research*, 31: 283–92.

Achenbach, T.M., McConaughy, S.H. and Howell, C.T. (1987) Child/adolescent behavioral and emotional problems: implications of cross-informant correlations for situational specificity. *Psychological Bulletin*, 101(2): 213–32.

Adamson, L.B., Bakeman, R., Deckner, D.F. and Nelson, P.B. (2012) Rating parent-child interactions: joint engagement, communication dynamics, and shared topics in autism, Down Syndrome, and typical development. *Journal of Autism and Developmental Disorders*, 42(12): 2622–35.

Ainsworth, M.D.S. (1979) Infant-mother attachment. *American Psychologist*, 34: 932–7.

Ainsworth, M.D.S. (1984) Attachment, in N.S. Endler and J. McVicker Hunt (eds) *Personality and the Behavioral Disorders* (2nd edn, Vol. 1). New York: Wiley.

Ainsworth, M.D.S. (1993) Attachments and other affectional bonds across the life cycle, in C.M. Parkes, J. Stevenson-Hinde and P. Marris (eds) *Attachment Across the Life Cycle*. London: Routledge.

Ainsworth, M.D.S., Blehar, M.S., Waters, E. and Wall, S. (1978) *Patterns of Attachment: A Psychological Study of the Strange Situation*. Hillsdale, NJ: Erlbaum.

Ainsworth, M.D.S. and Wittig, B.A. (1969) *Attachment and Exploratory Behavior of One-Year-Olds in a Strange Situation*. London: Methuen.

Akinbami, L.J., Liu, X., Pastor, P.N. and Reuben, C.A. (2011) Attention deficit hyperactivity disorder among children aged 5–17 years in the United States, 1998–2009. *National Center for Health Statistics Data Brief*, 70: 1–8.

Ammon Avalos, L., Galindo, C. and Li, D.K. (2012) A systematic review to calculate background miscarriage rates using life table analysis. *Birth Defects Research. Part A, Clinical Molecular Teratology*, 94(6): 417–23.

Andersen, T. (1987) The reflecting team: dialogue and meta-dialogue in clinical work. *Family Process*, 26(4): 415–28.

Arns, M., van der Heijden, K.B., Arnold, L.E. and Kenemans, J.L. (2013) Geographic variation in the prevalence of attention-deficit/hyperactivity disorder: the sunny perspective. *Biological Psychiatry*, 74(8): 585–90.

Auerbach, J.G., Atzaba-Poria, N., Berger, A., et al. (2010) Dopamine risk and paternal ADHD symptomatology associated with ADHD symptoms in four and a half-year-old boys. *Psychiatric Genetics*, 20: 160–5.

Avenanti, A., Bueti, D., Galati, G. and Aglioti, S.M. (2005) Transcranial magnetic stimulation highlights the sensorimotor side of empathy for pain. *Nature Neuroscience*, 8: 955–60.

Baker-Ericzn, M.J., Brookman-Frazee, L., Stahmer, A. (2005) Stress levels and adaptability in parents of toddlers with and without autism spectrum disorders.

Research and Practice for Persons with Severe Disabilities, 30(4): 194–204.

Bandler, R. and Grinder, J. (1975) *The Structure of Magic: A Book About Language and Therapy*. Palo Alto, CA: Science and Behavior.

Barkley, R.A. (1980) The parent-child interactions of hyperactive children and their modification by stimulant drugs, in B.D. Knights (ed.) *Treatment of Hyperactive and Learning Disabled Children*. Baltimore, MD: University Park Press, pp. 219–36.

Barkley, R.A. (1997) Behavioral inhibition, sustained attention, and executive functions: constructing a unifying theory of ADHD. *Psychological Bulletin*, 121(1): 65–94.

Barkley, R.A. (2002) International consensus statement on ADHD: January 2002. *Clinical Child Family Psychology Review*, 5(2): 89–111.

Barkley, R.A., Fischer, M., Edelbrock, C. and Smallish, L. (1991) The adolescent outcome of hyperactive children diagnosed by research criteria—III. Mother-child interactions, family conflicts and maternal psychopathology. *Child Psychology and Psychiatry*, 32(2): 233–55.

Barlow, D.H. (2010) Negative effects from psychological treatments: a perspective. *American Psychologist*, 65(1): 13–20.

Baron-Cohen, S., Golan O. and Ashwin, E. (2009) The transporters: animation to teach children with autism to recognise emotions. *Autism Spectrum Quarterly*, Winter: 15–18.

Battle, E.S. and Lacey B. (1972) A context for hyperactivity in children, over time. *Child Development*, 43: 757–73.

Baumrind, D. (1971) Current patterns of parental authority. *Develpmental Psychology*, 4: 1–103.

Beck, A.T. (1979) *Cognitive Therapy of Depression*. New York: Guilford.

Bell, S.M. and Ainsworth, M.D. (1973) Infant crying and maternal responsiveness, in

L.D.F. Rebelsky (ed.) *Child Development and Behavior* (2nd edn). Oxford: Alfred A. Knopf.

Benedetti, F. (2011) Meeting the therapist: a look into trust, hope, empathy, and compassion mechanisms, in *The Patient's Brain: The Neuroscience Behind the Doctor-Patient Relationship*. Oxford: Oxford University Press, pp. 124–79.

Bennett-Levy, J., Butler, G., Fennell, M., Hackmann, A., Mueller, M., and Westbrook, D. (2004) *Oxford Guide to Behavioural Experiments in Cognitive Therapy*. Oxford: Oxford University Press.

Benson, H. (2010) *Married and Unmarried Family Breakdown: Key Statistics Explained*. Bristol: Bristol Community Family Trust. Available at: http://www.bcft.co.uk/2010%20Family%20policy,%20breakdown%20and%20structure.pdf (accessed 10 Sept. 2013).

Bergman, I. (1987) *The Magic Lantern: An Autobiography*. (J. Tate, trans.). Harmondsworth: Penguin.

Bernstein, B.B. (1971) *Class, Codes and Control: Theoretical Studies Towards a Sociology of Language*. London: Routledge.

Berntsson, L.T. and Kohler, L. (2001) Long-term illness and psychosomatic complaints in children aged 2–17 years in the five Nordic countries: comparison between 1984 and 1996. *European Journal of Public Health*, 11(1): 35–42.

Bidwell, L.C., Willcutt, E.G., McQueen, M.B., et al. (2011) A family based association study of DRD4, DAT1, and 5HTT and continuous traits of attention-deficit hyperactivity disorder. *Behavior Genetics*, 41(1): 165–74.

Biederman, J. (2002) Influence of gender on attention deficit hyperactivity disorder in children referred to a psychiatric clinic. *American Journal of Psychiatry*, 159: 36–42.

Biederman, J., Keinan, K., Benjamin, J., et al. (1992) Further evidence for family-genetic risk factors in attention deficit hyperactivity disorder: patterns of comorbidity in probands and relatives in psychiatrically and pediatrically referred samples. *Archives of General Psychiatry*, 49: 728–38.

Biederman, J., Mick, E. and Faraone, S.V. (2000) Age-dependent decline of symptoms of attention deficit hyperactivity disorder: impact of remission definition and symptom type. *American Journal of Psychiatry*, 157(5): 816–18.

Biederman, J., Munir, K. and Knee, D. (1987) Conduct and oppositional disorder in clinically referred children with attention deficit disorder: a controlled family study. *Journal of the American Academy of Child and Adolescent Psychiatry*, 26(5): 724–7.

Blehar, M C., Lieberman, A.F. and Ainsworth, M.D.S. (1977) Early face-to-face interaction and its relation to later infant-mother attachment. *Child Development*, 48: 182–94.

Block, R.W., Krebs, N.F., American Academy of Pediatrics Committee on Child Abuse and Neglect and American Academy of Pediatrics Committee on Nutrition. (2005) Failure to thrive as a manifestation of child neglect. *Pediatrics*, 116(5): 1234–7.

Bowen, M. (1978) *Family Therapy in Clinical Practice*. Northvale, NJ: Jason Aronson.

Bowlby, J. (1953) *Child Care and the Growth of Love*. London: Penguin.

Bowlby, J. (1969) *Attachment and Loss* (1st edn, Vol. 1). New York: Basic Books.

Bowlby, J. (1973) *Separation: Anxiety and Anger*. New York: Basic Books.

Bowlby, J. (1980) *Attachment and Loss* (2nd edn). London: Hogarth and Institute of Psycho-Analysis.

Bowlby, J. (1982) *Attachment and Loss*. New York: Basic Books.

Bowlby, J. (1988) *A Secure Base: Clinical Applications of Attachment Theory*. London: Routledge.

Bowman, E.S. and Markland, O.N. (2005) Diagnosis and treatment of pseudoseizures. *Psychiatric Annals*, 35(4): 306–16.

Bracha, H.S. (2004) Freeze, flight, fight, fright, faint: adaptationist perspectives on the acute stress response spectrum. *CNS Spectrums*, 9(9): 679–85.

Braunschweig, D. and Van de Water, J. (2012) Maternal autoantibodies in autism. *Archives of Neurology*, 69(6): 693–9.

Brown, A.D. and Curhan, J.R. (2013) The polarizing effect of arousal on negotiation. *Psychological Science*, 24: 1928–35.

Buckingham, D., Willett, R., Bragg, S. and Russell, R. (2009) Sexualised goods aimed at children: a report to the Scottish Parliament Equal Opportunities Committee. Edinburgh: Scottish Parliament Equal Opportunities Committee. Available at: http://oro.open.ac.uk/25843/2/ (accessed 10 Sept. 2013).

Buhrmester, D., Whalen, C.K., Henker, B., MacDonald, V. and Hinshaw, S.P. (1992) Prosocial behavior in hyperactive boys: effects of stimulant medication and comparison with normal boys. *Journal of Abnormal Child Psychology*, 20(1): 103–21.

Bush, D., Schafe, G.E. and LeDoux, J.E. (2009) Neural basis of fear conditioning, in G. Berntson and J. Cacioppo (eds) *Handbook of Neuroscience for the Behavioral Sciences* (Vol. 2). Hoboken, NJ: Wiley, pp. 762–4.

Butler, A.H. and Ashbury, G. (2005) The caring child: an evaluative case study of the Cornwall Young Carers Project. *Children and Society*, 19(4): 292–303.

Byng-Hall, J. (1980) Symptom bearer as marital distance regulator: clinical implications. *Family Process*, 19(4): 355–65.

Byng-Hall, J. (1995) *Rewriting Family Scripts: Improvisations and Systemic Change*. London: Guilford.

Byng-Hall, J. (2002) Relieving parentified children's burdens in families with insecure attachment patterns. *Family Process*, 41(3): 375–88.

Byng-Hall, J. (2009) Foreword, in R. Dallos and A. Vetere (eds) *Systemic Therapy* and Attachment Narratives: Applications in a Range of Clinical Settings. London: Routledge.

Campbell, S.B. (1975) Mother-child interaction: a comparison of hyperactive, learning disabled, and normal boys. *American Journal of Orthopsychiatry*, 45: 51–7.

Campbell, S.B. and Ewing, L.J. (1990) Follow-up of hard-to-manage preschoolers: adjustment at age 9 and predictors of continuing symptoms. *Journal of Child Psychology and Psychiatry*, 31: 871–85.

Carlson, E.A., Jacobvitz, D. and Sroufe, L.A. (1995) A developmental investigation of inattentiveness and hyperactivity. *Child Development*, 66(1): 37–54.

Cassel, T.D., Messinger, D.S., Ibanez, L.V., Haltigan, J.D., Acosta, S.I. and Buchman, A.C. (2007) Early social and emotional communication in the infant siblings of children with autism spectrum disorders: an examination of the broad phenotype. *Journal of Autism and Developmental Disorders*, 37(1): 122–32.

Castellanos, F.X., Lee, P.P., Sharp, et al. (2002) Developmental trajectories of brain volume abnormalities in children and adolescents with attention-deficit/hyperactivity disorder. *Journal of the American Medical Association*, 288(14): 1740–8.

Caudill, W.A. and Schooler, C. (1973) Child behavior and child rearing in Japan and the United States: an interim report. *Journal of Nervous and Mental Disease*, 157: 323–38.

Centers for Disease Control and Prevention(2012) *Community Report from the Autism and Developmental Disabilities Monitoring (ADDM) Network: Prevalence of Autism Spectrum Disorders (ASDS) Among Multiple Areas of the United States in 2008*. US Department of Health and Human Services. Available at: http://www.cdc.gov/ncbddd/autism/documents/addm-2012-community-report.pdf (accessed 10 Sept. 2013).

Centers for Disease Control and Prevention. (2013) *FastStats: Unmarried Childbearing*. Available at: http://www.cdc.gov/nchs/fastats/unmarry.htm (accessed 9 Sept. 2013).

Charach, A., Dashti, B., Carson, P., et al. (2011) *Attention Deficit Hyperactivity Disorder: Effectiveness of Treatment in At-Risk Preschoolers: Long-Term Effectiveness in All Ages and Variability in Prevalence, Diagnosis, and Treatment*. Rockville, MD: Agency for Healthcare Research and Quality.

Chrousos, G.P. and Gold, P.W. (1992) The concepts of stress and stress system disorders: overview of physical and behavioral homeostasis. *Journal of the American Medical Association*, 267(9): 1244–52.

Chrousos, G.P. and Gold P.W. (1998) A healthy body in a healthy mind—and vice versa—the damaging power of 'uncontrollable' stress. *Journal of Clinical Endocrinology and Metabolism*, 83(6): 1842–5.

Clarke, A.R., Barry, R.J., McCarthy, R. and Selikowitz, M. (2001) EEG-defined subtypes of children with attention-deficit/hyperactivity disorder. *Clinical Neurophysiology*, 112(11): 2098–105.

Cole-Turner, R. (1998) Do means matter?, in E. Parens (ed.) *Enhancing Human Traits: Ethical and Social Implications*. Washington, DC: Georgetown University Press, pp. 136–50.

Courtenay, W.H. (2000) Constructions of masculinity and their influence on men's well-being: a theory of gender and health. *Social Science and Medicine*, 50: 1385–401.

Crighton, D.A. and Towl, G.J. (2007) Experimental interventions with sex offenders: a brief review of their efficacy. *Evidence Based Mental Health*, 10: 35–7.

Crittenden, P.M. (1981) Abusing, neglecting, problematic, and adequate dyads: differentiating by patterns of interaction. *Merrill-Palmer Quarterly*, 27: 1–18.

Crittenden, P.M. (1991) Strategies for changing parental behavior. *APSAC Advisor*, Spring: 9.

Crittenden, P.M. (1992a) Quality of attachment in the preschool years. *Development and Psychopathology*, 4: 209–41.

Crittenden, P.M. (1992b) The social ecology of treatment: case study of a service system for maltreated children. *American Journal of Orthopsychiatry*, 62: 22–34.

Crittenden, P.M. (1993) New perspectives on child neglect, in *1993 Conference Papers: Disability and Child Abuse: Acts of Omission*. Ninewells, UK: British Association for the Study of Prevention of Child Abuse and Neglect.

Crittenden, P.M. (1997) Toward an integrative theory of trauma: a dynamic-maturational approach, in D. Cicchetti and S. Toth (eds) *The Rochester Symposium on Developmental Psychopathology: Risk, Trauma, and Mental Processes* (Vol. 10). Rochester, NY: University of Rochester Press, pp. 34–84.

Crittenden, P.M. (1997–2005) School-age assessment of attachment coding manual. Miami, FL (on file with author).

Crittenden, P.M. (1999) Danger and development: the organization of self-protective strategies. *Monographs for the Society for Research on Child Development*, 64(3): 145–71.

Crittenden, P.M. (2000) A dynamic-maturational model of the function, development, and organization of human relationships, in R.S.L. Mills and L. Duck (eds) *Developmental Psychology of Personal Relationships*. Chichester: Wiley, pp. 199–218.

Crittenden, P.M. (2003) A guide to expansions and modifications of the Ainsworth Infant Strange Situation. Miami, FL (on file with author).

Crittenden, P.M. (2004) The Preschool Assessment of Attachment: coding manual using the dynamic matura-tional method. Miami, FL (on file with author).

Crittenden, P.M. (2005) The transition to adulthood attachment interview. Miami, FL (on file with author).

Crittenden, P.M. (2007a) Care-index: toddlers coding manual. Miami, FL (on file with author).

Crittenden, P.M. (2007b) Care-index: infant coding manual. Miami, FL (on file with author).

Crittenden, P.M. (ed.) (2008) *Raising Parents: Attachment, Parenting and Child Safety*. Portland, OR: Willan.

Crittenden, P.M. and Ainsworth, M.D.S. (1989) Child maltreatment and attachment theory, in D. Cicchetti and V. Carlson (eds) *Handbook of Child Maltreatment*. New York: Cambridge University Press.

Crittenden, P.M., Claussen, A. and Kozlowska, K. (2007) Choosing a valid assessment of attachment for clinical use: a comparative study. *Australian and New Zealand Journal of Family Therapy*, 28: 78–87.

Crittenden, P.M. and Craig S. (1990) Developmental trends in child homicide. *Journal of Interpersonal Violence*, 5: 202–16.

Crittenden, P.M., and DiLalla, D.L. (1989) Compulsive compliance: the development of an inhibitory coping strategy in infancy. *Journal of Abnormal Child Psychology*, 16(5): 585–99.

Crittenden, P.M. and Farnfield, S. (2007) Fostering families: an integrative approach involving the biological and foster family systems, in R.E. Lee and J.B. Whiting (eds) *Handbook of Relational Therapy for Foster Children and Their Families*. Washington, DC: Child Welfare League of America.

Crittenden, P.M., Kozlowska, K. and Landini, A. (2010) Assessing attachment in school-age children. *Clinical Child Psychology and Psychiatry*, 15(2): 185–208.

Crittenden, P.M. and Kulbotton, G.R. (2007) Familial contributions to ADHD: an attachment perspective. *Tidsskrift for Norsk Psykologorening*, 10: 1220–9.

Crittenden, P. M. and Landini, A. (1999) Administering the school-age assessment of attachment. Miami, FL (on file with author).

Crittenden, P.M. and Landini, A. (2011) *Assessing Adult Attachment: A Dynamic-Maturational Approach to Discourse Analysis*. New York: Norton.

Crittenden, P.M. and Morrison, A.K. (1988) Preventing maltreatment of infants: a hospital screening procedure. *Pediatric Nursing*, 14: 415–17.

Crittenden, P.M., Partridge, M.F. and Claussen, A.H. (1991) Family patterns of relationship in normative and dysfunctional families. *Development and Psychopathology*, 3: 491–512.

Croen, L.A., Grether, J.K., Yoshida, C.K., Odouli, R. and Hendrick, V. (2011) Antidepressant use during pregnancy and childhood autism spectrum disorders. *Archives of General Psychiatry*, 68(11): 1104–12.

Crosier, T., Butterworth P. and Rodgers, B. (2007) Mental health problems among single and partnered mothers: the role of financial hardship and social support. *Social Psychiatry and Psychiatric Epidemiology*, 42(1): 6–13.

Cunningham, C.E. and Barkley, R. (1979) The interactions of normal and hyperactive children and their mothers in free play and structured tasks. *Child Development*, 50: 217–24.

Cunningham, C.E., Benness, B.B. and Siegel, L.S. (1988) Family functioning, time allocation, and parental depression in the families of normal and ADDH children. *Journal of Clinical Child Psychology*, 17: 169–77.

Dallos, R. (1991) *Family Belief Systems, Therapy and Change: A Constructional Approach*. Milton Keynes: Open University Press.

Dallos, R. (2006) *Attachment Narrative Therapy*. Maidenhead: McGraw-Hill.

Dallos, R. and Draper, R. (2009) *Introduction to Systemic Family Therapy*. Maidenhead: McGraw-Hill.

Dallos, R. and Draper, R. (2010) *An Introduction to Family Therapy*. Maidenhead: McGraw-Hill.

Dallos, R. and McLaughlin. (1992) *Social Problems and the Family*. London: Sage.

Dallos, R. and Vetere, A. (2009) *Systemic Therapy and Attachment Narratives: Applications in a Range of Clinical Settings*. London: Routledge.

Damasio, A.R. (1994) *Descartes' Error: Emotion, Reason, and the Human Brain*. New York: Putnam.

Damasio, A.R. (1999) *The Feeling of What Happens: Body and Emotion in the Making of Consciousness*. New York: Harcourt Brace.

Damasio, A.R. (2003) *Looking for Spinoza: Joy, Sorrow, and the Feeling Brain*. Orlando, FL: Harcourt.

Darwin, C. (1925) *On the Origin of Species by Means of Natural Selection or the Preservation of Favoured Races in the Struggle for Life*. London: Oxford University Press.

Davidson, R.J., Jackson, D.C. and Kalin, N.H. (2000) Emotion, plasticity, context, and regulation: perspectives from affective neuroscience. *Psychological Bulletin*, 126(6): 890–909.

Dawson, G., Osterling, J., Meltzoff, A., and Kuhl, P. (2000) Case study of the development of an infant with autism from birth to two years of age. *Journal of Applied Developmental Psychology*, 21: 299–313.

de Gelder, B. (2006) Towards the neurobiology of emotional body language. *Nature Reviews. Neuroscience*, 7: 242–9.

de Gelder, B., Snyder, J., Greve, D., Gerard, G. and Hadjikhani, N. (2004) Fear fosters flight: a mechanism for fear contagion when perceiving emotion expressed by a whole body. *Proceedings of the National*

Academy of Sciences of the United States of America, 101(47): 16701–6.

Delgado, M.R., Jou, R.L., LeDoux, J.E. and Phelps, E.A. (2009) Avoiding negative outcomes: tracking the mechanisms of avoidance learning in humans during fear conditioning. *Frontiers in Behavioral Neuroscience*, 3: 33.

de Maat, S., de Jonghe, F., de Kraker, R., et al. (2013) The current state of the empirical evidence for psychoanalysis: a meta-analytic approach. *Harvard Review of Psychiatry*, 21(3): 107–37.

de Maat, S., de Jonghe, F., Schoevers, R. and Dekker, J. (2009) The effectiveness of long-term psychoanalytic therapy: a systematic review of empirical studies. *Harvard Review of Psychiatry*, 17(1): 1–23.

De Wall, C.N. and Bushman, B.J. (2011) Social acceptance and rejection: the sweet and the bitter. *Current Directions in Psychological Science*, 20: 256–60.

Dimidjian, S. and Hollon, S.D. (2010) How would we know if psychotherapy were harmful? *American Psychologist*, 65(1): 21–33.

Division of Clinical Psychology, British Psychological Society. (2013) Division of Clinical Psychology position statement on the classification of behaviour and experience in relation to functional psychiatric diagnoses: time for a paradigm shift. Available at: http://dxrevisionwatch.files.wordpress.com/2013/05/position-statement-on-diagnosis-masterdoc.pdf (accessed 10 Sept. 2013).

Doshi, J.A., Hodgkins, P., Kahle, J., et al. (2012) Economic impact of childhood and adult attention-deficit/hyperactivity disorder in the United States. *Journal of the American Academy of Child and Adolescent Psychiatry*, 51(10): 990–1002.

Ducharme, S., Hudziak, J.J., Botteron, P. et al. (2012) Decreased regional cortical thickness and thinning rate are associated with inattention symptoms in healthy children. *Journal of the American*

Academy of Child and Adolescent Psychiatry, 51(1): 18–27.

Dunn, J.P.R. (1991) Why are siblings so different? The significance of differences in sibling experiences within the family. *Family Process*, 30(3): 271–83.

Durston, S., Thomas, K.M., Worden, M.S., Yang, Y. and Casey, B.J. (2002) The effect of preceding context on inhibition: an event-related FMRI study. *Neuroimage*, 16(2): 449–53.

Eagleman, D. (2011) *Incognito: The Secret Lives of the Brain*. New York: Pantheon.

Ecker, C., Suckling, J., Deoni, S.C., et al. (2012) Brain anatomy and its relationship to behavior in adults with autism spectrum disorder: a multicenter magnetic resonance imaging study. *Archives of General Psychiatry*, 69(2): 195–209.

Eibl-Eibesfeldt, I. (1979) Human ethology: concepts and implications for the sciences of man. *Behavioral and Brain Sciences*, 2: 1–57.

Eisenberger, N.I., Lieberman, M.D. and Williams, K.D. (2003) Does rejection hurt? An FMRI study of social exclusion. *Science*, 302(5643): 290–2.

Elsabbagh, M., Mercure, E., Hudry, K., et al. (2012) Infant neural sensitivity to dynamic eye gaze is associated with later emerging autism. [Research Support, Non-U.S. Gov't]. *Current Biology*, 22(4): 338–342, doi:10.1016/j.cub.2011.12.056.

El-Sayed, E., Larsson, J.O., Persson, H.E., Santosh, P.J. and Rydelius, P.A. (2003) 'Maturational lag' hypothesis of attention deficit hyperactivity disorder: an update. *Acta Paediatrica*, 92(7): 776–84.

Epstein, N.B., Bishop, D.S. and Levin, S. (1978) The McMaster Model of Family Functioning. *Journal of Marital and Family Therapy*, 4(4): 19–31.

Fair, D.A., Bathula, D., Nikolas, M.A., and Nigg, J.T. (2012) Distinct neuropsychological subgroups in typically developing youth inform heterogeneity in children with ADHD. *Proceedings of the National*

Academy of Sciences of the United States of America, 109(17): 6769–74.

Fairbanks, L.A., Breidenthal, S., Bailey, J.N. and Jorgensen, M.J. (2006) Effects of maternal genotype and offspring genotype on the quality of the mother-infant relationship in vervet monkeys (chlorocebus aethiops). *American Journal of Primatology*, 68(suppl. 1): 91.

Fairbanks, L.A., Way, B.M., Breidenthal, S.E., Bailey, J.N. and Jorgensen, M.J. (2012) Maternal and offspring dopamine D4 receptor genotypes interact to influence juvenile impulsivity in vervet monkeys. *Psychological Science*, 23(10): 1099–104.

Falb, K.L., McCauley, H.L., Decker, M.R., Gupta, J., Raj, A. and Silverman, J.G. (2011) School bullying perpetration and other childhood risk factors as predictors of adult intimate partner violence perpetration. *Archives of Pediatrics and Adolescent Medicine*, 165(10): 890–4.

Fanselow, M.S. (1994) Neural organisation of defensive behavioural system responsible for fear. *Psychonomic Bulletin and Review*, 1: 429–38.

Faraone, S.V., Biederman, J., Feighner, J.A. and Monuteaux, M.C. (2000) Assessing symptoms of attention deficit hyperactivity disorder in children and adults: which is more valid? *Journal of Consulting and Clinical Psychology*, 68(5): 830–42.

Faraone, S.V., Sergeant, J., Gillberg C, and Biederman, J. (2003) The worldwide prevalence of ADHD: is it an American condition? *World Psychiatry*, 2: 104–13.

Farnfield, S., Hautamäki, A., Norbech, P. and Sahhar, N. (2010) DMM assessments of attachment and adaptation: procedures, validity and utility. *Clinical Child Psychology and Psychiatry*, 15(3): 313–28.

Feldman, R., Gordon, I., Influs, M., Gutbir, T. and Ebstein, R.P. (2013) Parental oxytocin and early caregiving jointly shape children's oxytocin response and social reciprocity. *Neuropsychopharmacology*, 38(7): 1154–62.

Felitti, V.J. (2009) Adverse childhood experiences and adult health. *Academic Pediatric Association*, 9(3): 131–2.

Folstein, S. and Rutter, M. (1977) Genetic influences and infantile autism. *Nature*, 265(5596): 726–8.

Fonagy, P., Gergely, G., Jurist E., and Target, M. (2002) *Affect Regulation, Mentalization, and the Development of the Self*. New York: Other.

Fonagy, P. and Roth, A. (1997) *What Works for Whom?: A Critical Review of Psychotherapy Research*. London: Guilford.

Galiana, H.L. (1986) A new approach to understanding adaptive visual-vestibular interactions in the central nervous system. *Journal of Neurophysiology*, 55(2): 349–74.

Garcia, J.R., MacKillop, J., Aller, E.L., Merriwether, A.M., Wilson, D.S. and Lum, J.K. (2010) Associations between dopamine D4 receptor gene variation with both infidelity and sexual promiscuity. *Public Library of Science One*, 5(11): e14162.

Garfield, C.F., Dorsey, E.R., Zhu, S., et al. (2012) Trends in attention deficit hyperactivity disorder ambulatory diagnosis and medical treatment in the United States, 2000–2010. *Academic Pediatric Association*, 12(2): 110–16.

Gaub, M. and Carlson, C. L. (1997) Gender differences in ADHD: a meta-analysis and critical review. *Journal of the American Academy of Child and Adolescent Psychiatry*, 36: 1036–45.

George, C., Kaplan, N. and Main, M. (1985–1996) *Adult Attachment Interview* (3rd edn). Berkeley, CA: Department of Psychology, University of California.

Gergely, G. (2001) The obscure object of desire: 'Nearly, but clearly not, like me': contingency preference in normal children versus children with autism. *Bulletin of the Menninger Clinic*, 65(3): 411–26.

Gernsbacher, M.A. (2010) Stigma from psychological science: group differences, not deficits. Introduction to stigma special section. *Psychological Science*, 5(6): 687.

Glaser, D. (2000) Child abuse and neglect and the brain: a review. *Journal of Child Psychology and Psychiatry*, 41(1): 97–116.

Golan, O., Ashwin, E., Granader, Y., et al. (2010) Enhancing emotion recognition in children with autism spectrum conditions: an intervention using animated vehicles with real emotional faces. *Journal of Autism and Developmental Disorders*, 40(3): 269–79.

Goldin-Meadow, S. and Beilock, S.L. (2010) Action's influence on thought: the case of gesture. *Perspectives on Psychological Science*, 5(6): 664–74.

Gordon, I., Bennett, R.H., Cordeaux, C., et al. (2013) Oxytocin's impact on core brain and behavioral features of ASD in children. Paper presented at the International Meeting for Autism Research, San Sebastian, Spain, May.

Gottman, J.M. (1993) The roles of conflict engagement, escalation, and avoidance in marital interaction: a longitudinal view of five types of couples. *Journal of Consulting and Clinical Psychology*, 61: 6–15.

Gray, D.E. (2003) Gender and coping: the parents of children with high functioning autism. *Social Science and Medicine*, 56(3): 631–42.

Green, J., Charman, T., McConachie, H., et al. (2010) Parent-mediated communication-focused treatment in children with autism (PACT): a randomised controlled trial. *Lancet*, 375(9732): 2152–60.

Grinder, J. and Bandler (1975) *The Structure of Magic II: A Book about Communication and Change*. Palo Alto, CA: Science and Behavior.

Haley, M. (1976) Management for mental health. *Mental Hygiene*, 60(1): 29–30.

Hallmayer, J., Cleveland, S., Torres, A., et al. (2011) Genetic heritability and shared environmental factors among twin pairs with autism. *Archives of General Psychiatry*, 68(11): 1095–102.

Hastings, R.P. and Johnson, E. (2001) Stress in UK families conducting intensive home-based behavioral intervention for their young child with autism. *Journal of Autism and Developmental Disorders*, 31: 327–36.

Hautamäki, A., Hautamäki, L., Neuvonen, L. and Maliniemi-Piispanen, S. (2010) Transmission of attachment across three generations: continuity and reversal. *Clinical Child Psychology and Psychiatry*, 15(3): 347–54.

Hechtman, L. (1996) Families of children with attention deficit hyperactivity disorder: a review. *Canadian Journal of Psychiatry*, 41(6): 350–60.

Higgins, D.J., Bailey, S.R. and Pearce, J.C. (2005) Factors associated with functioning style and coping strategies of families with a child with an autism spectrum disorder. *Autism*, 9: 125–37.

Hill, J.C. and Schoener, E. (1996) Age-dependent decline of attention-deficit hyperactive disorder. *American Journal of Psychiatry*, 153: 1143–6.

Hinshaw, S.P. and McHale, J.P. (1991) Stimulant medication and the social interactions of hyperactive children, in D.G. Gilbert and J.J. Connolly (eds) *Personality, Social Skills, and Psychopathology: An Individual Differences Approach*. New York: Plenum, pp. 229–53.

Hinshaw, S.P., Scheffler, R.M., Fulton, B.D., et al. (2011) International variation in treatment procedures for ADHD: social context and recent trends. *Psychiatric Services*, 62(5): 459–64.

Hoffmeyer, J. (2008) *Biosemiotics: An Examination into the Signs of Life and the Life of Signs*. Scranton, PA: University of Scranton Press.

Holden, E.W., Deichmann, M.M. and Levy, A.D. (1999) Empirically supported treatments in pediatric psychology: recurrent pediatric headache. *Journal of Pediatric Psychology*, 24(2): 91–109.

Howard, A.L., Robinson, M., Smith, G.J., Ambrosini, G.L., Piek, J.P. and Oddy, W.H. (2011) ADHD is associated with a 'western' dietary pattern in adolescents. *Journal of Attention Disorders*, 15(5): 403–11.

Howe, D. (2011) *Attachment Across the Lifecourse*. London: Palgrave.

Huggenberger, H.J., Suter, S.E., Blumenthal, T.D. and Schachinger, H. (2013) Maternal social stress modulates the development of prepulse inhibition of startle in infants. *Developmental Cognitive Neuroscience*, 3: 84–90.

Insel, T.R. and Wang, P.S. (2010) Rethinking mental illness. *Journal of the American Medical Association*, 303(19): 1970–1.

Jean-Gilles, M. and Crittenden, P.M. (1990) Maltreating families: a look at siblings. *Family Relations*, 39: 323–9.

Jensen, P.S., Mrazek, D., Knapp, P.K., et al. (1997) Evolution and revolution in child psychiatry: ADHD as a disorder of adaptation. *Journal of the American Academy of Child and Adolescent Psychiatry*, 36(12): 1672–9.

Jones, J. and Passey, J. (2004) Family adaptation, coping and resources: parents of children with developmental disabilities and behavior problems. *Journal on Developmental Disabilities and Behavior Problems*, 11: 31–46.

Jurkovic, G.J. (1998) Destructive parentification in families: causes and consequences, in L. L'Abate (ed.) *Family Psychopathology*. New York: Guilford, pp. 237–55.

Kahl, K.G., Winter, L. and Schweiger, U. (2012) The third wave of cognitive behavioural therapies: what is new and what is effective? *Current Opinions in Psychiatry*, 25(6): 522–8.

Kanner, L. (1949) Problems of nosology and psychodynamics of early infantile autism. *American Journal of Orthopsychiatry*, 19(3): 416–26.

Kazdin, A.E. and Blasé, S.L. (2011) Rebooting psychotherapy research and practice to reduce the burden of mental illness. *Perspectives on Psychological Science*, 6(1): 21–37.

Kent, L. (2004) Recent advances in the genetics of attention deficit hyperactivity disorder. *Current Psychiatry Reports*, 6(2): 143–8.

Kent, L., Green, E., Hawi, Z., et al. (2005) Association of the paternally transmitted copy of common valine allele of the val-66met polymorphism of the brain-derived neurotrophic factor (BDNF) gene with susceptibility to ADHD. *Molecular Psychiatry*, 10: 939–43.

Kerr, M.E. and Bowen, M. (1988) *Family Evaluation: An Approach Based on Bowen's Theory*. New York: Norton

Kindlon, D. and Thompson, M. (1999) *Raising Cain: Protecting the Emotional Lives of Boys*. New York: Ballantine.

Kozlowska, K. (2007) The developmental origins of conversion disorders. *Clinical Child Psychology and Psychiatry*, 12(4): 487–510.

Kozlowska, K. (2009) Attachment relationships shape pain-signaling behavior. *Journal of Pain*, 10(10): 1020–8.

Kozlowska, K. (2013) Stress, distress and bodytalk: co-constructing formulations with patients who present with somatic symptoms. *Harvard Review of Psychiatry*, 21(6): 314–33.

Kozlowska, K., Foley, S. and Savage,B. (2012) Fabricated illness: working within the family system to find a pathway to health. *Family Process*, 51(4): 570–87.

Kozlowska, K. and Hanney, L. (1999) Family assessment and intervention using an interactive art exercise. *The Australian and New Zealand Journal of Family Therapy*, 20: 61–96.

Kozlowska, K., Scher, S., and Williams, L.M. (2011) Patterns of emotional-cognitive functioning in pediatric conversion patients: implications for the conceptualization of conversion disorders. *Psychosomatic Medicine*, 73(9): 775–88.

Kozlowska, K. and Williams, L.M. (2009) Self-protective organization in children with conversion and somatoform disorders. *Journal of Psychosomatic Research*, 67(3): 223–33.

Kramer, P. (1993) *Listening to Prozac*. New York: Penguin.

Kuhn, D. and Franklin, S. (2008) The second decade: what develops (and how)?, in W. Damon, R.M. Leaner, D. Kuhn, R. Siegler and N. Eisenburg (eds) *Child and Adolescent Development: An Advanced Course*. Hoboken, NJ: Wiley.

Kuhn, T. (1962) *The Structure of Scientific Revolutions*. Chicago: University of Chicago Press.

Kunster, A.K., Fegert, J.M. and Ziegenhain, U. (2010) Assessing parent-child interaction in the preschool years: a pilot study on the psychometric properties of the Toddler Care-Index. *Clinical Child Psychology Psychiatry*, 15(3): 379–89.

Kwako, L.E., Noll, J.G., Putnam, F.W. and Trickett, P.K. (2010) Childhood sexual abuse and attachment: an intergenerational perspective. *Clinical Child Psychology and Psychiatry*, 15(3): 407–22.

Lahey, B., Piacentini J., McBurnett, M., Stone, P., Hartolagen, S. and Hynd, G. (1988) Psychopathology in the parents of children with conduct disorder and hyperactivity. *Journal of the American Academy of Child and Adolescent Psychiatry*, 27: 163–70.

Lampi, K.M., Lehtonen, L., Tran, P.L., et al. (2012) Risk of autism spectrum disorders in low birth weight and small for gestational age infants. *Journal of Pediatrics*, 161(5): 830–6.

Landa, R.J., Holman, K.C., O'Neill, A.H. and Stuart, E.A. (2011) Intervention targeting development of socially synchronous engagement in toddlers with autism spectrum disorder: a randomized controlled trial. *Journal of Child Psychology and Psychiatry*, 52(1): 13–21.

Lanphear, B.P. (2012) Attention-deficit/hyperactivity disorder: a preventable epidemic? *Archives of Pediatrics and Adolescent Medicine*, 166(12): 1182–4.

Lewis, M. (1990) The development of intentionality and the role of consciousness. *Psychological Inquiry*, 1: 231–47.

Li, X., Sroubek, A., Kelly, M.S., et al. (2012) Atypical pulvinar-cortical pathways during sustained attention performance in children with attention-deficit/hyperactivity disorder. *Journal of the American Academy of Child and Adolescent Psychiatry*, 51(11): 1197–207.

Lilienfeld, S.O. (2007) Psychological treatments that cause harm. *Perspectives on Psychological Science*, 2: 53–70.

Linehan, M.M. (1993) *Skills Training Manual for Treating Borderline Personality Disorder*. New York: Guilford.

Lipman, E.L., Offord, D.R. and Boyle, M.H. (1997) Single mothers in Ontario: sociodemographic, physical and mental health characteristics. *Canadian Medical Association Journal*, 156(5): 639–45.

Little, M. (1998) Cosmetic surgery, suspect norms, and complicity, in E. Parens (ed.) *Enhancing Human Traits: Conceptual Complexities and Ethical Implications*. Washington, DC: Georgetown University Press, pp. 162–76.

Lobo, I. and Zhaurova, K. (2008) Birth defects: causes and statistics. *Nature Education*, 1(1): 18.

Lord, C., Luyster, R., Guthrie, W. and Pickles, A. (2012) Patterns of developmental trajectories in toddlers with autism spectrum disorder. *Journal of Consulting and Clinical Psychology*, 80(3): 477–89.

Lupien, S.J., Parent, S., Evans, A.C., et al. (2011) Larger amygdala but no change in hippocampal volume in 10-year-old children exposed to maternal depressive symptomatology since birth. *Proceedings of the National Academy of Sciences of the United States of America*, 108(34): 14324–9.

Lynn, D.E., Lubke, G., Yang, M., et al. (2005) Temperament and character profiles and the dopamine D4 receptor gene in ADHD. *American Journal of Psychiatry*, 162: 906–13.

Macdonald, K. and Macdonald, T.M. (2010) The peptide that binds: a systematic review of oxytocin and its prosocial effects in humans. *Harvard Review of Psychiatry*, 18(1): 1–21.

Mackie, S., Shaw, P., Lenroot, R., et al. (2007) Cerebellar development and clinical outcome in attention deficit hyperactivity disorder. *American Journal of Psychiatry*, 164(4): 647–55.

Main, M., Kaplan, N. and Cassidy, J. (1985) Security in infancy, childhood and adulthood: a move to the level of representation. *Monographs for the Society for Research on Child Development*, 50: 66–104.

Marcu, I., Oppenheim, D., Koren-Karie, N., Dolev, S. and Yirmiya, N. (2009) Attachment and symbolic play in preschoolers with autism spectrum disorders. *Journal of Autism and Developmental Disorders*, 39(9): 1321–8.

Martel, M.M., Gobrogge, K.L., Breedlove, S.M. and Nigg J.T. (2008) Masculinized finger-length ratios of boys, but not girls, are associated with attention-deficit/hyperactivity disorder. *Behavioral Neuroscience*, 122(2): 273–81.

Marvin, R.S. and Mossler, D.G. (1976) A methodological paradigm for describing and analyzing complex non-verbal expressions: coy expressions in preschool children. *Representative Research in Social Psychology*, 7: 133–9.

Mash, E.J. and Johnston, C. (1983) Parental perceptions of child behavior problems, parenting, self-esteem, and mothers' reported stress in younger and older hyperactives and normal children. *Journal of Consulting and Clinical Psychology*, 51: 86–99.

McCleery, J.P., Akshoomoff, N., Dobkins, K.R. and Carver, L.J. (2009) Atypical face versus object processing and hemispheric asymmetries in 10-month-old infants at risk for autism. *Biological Psychiatry*, 66(10): 950–7.

McEwen, B.S. (1998) Protective and damaging effects of stress mediators. *New England Journal of Medicine*, 338(3): 171–9.

McGeary, J. (2009) The DRD4 exon 3 polymorphism and addiction related phenotypes: a review. *Pharmacology, Biochemistry and Behavior*, 93: 222–9.

McLaughlin, K.A., Fox, N.A., Zeanah, C.H., et al. (2010) Delayed maturation in brain electrical activity partially explains the association between early environmental deprivation and symptoms of attention-deficit/hyperactivity disorder. *Biological Psychiatry*, 68(4): 329–36.

McMain, S.F., Guimond, T., Streiner, D.L., Cardish, R.J. and Links, P.S. (2012) Dialectical behavior therapy compared with general psychiatric management for borderline personality disorder: clinical outcomes and functioning over a 2-year follow-up. *American Journal of Psychiatry*, 169(6): 650–61.

Mikulincer, M., Shaver, P.R. and Pereg, D. (2003) Attachment theory and affect regulation: the dynamic, development, and cognitive consequences of attachment related strategies. *Motivation and Emotion*, 27(2): 77–102.

Millichap, J.G. and Yee, M.M. (2012) The diet factor in attention-deficit/hyperactivity disorder. *Pediatrics*, 129(2): 330–7.

Minuchin, S. (1974) *Families and Family Therapy*. Cambridge, MA: Harvard University Press.

Mottron, L. (2011) Changing perceptions: the power of autism. *Nature*, 479(7371): 33–5.

Muhamedrahimov, R.J. (2000) New attitudes: infant care facilities in St. Petersburg, Russia, in J.D. Osofsky and H.E. Fitzgerald (eds) *WAIMH Handbook of Infant Mental Health*. New York: Wiley, pp. 245–94.

Muhamedrahimov, R.J., Konkova, M.J. and Vershinina, E.A. (2008) The age dynamics of emotions on infants' faces, in R.J. Muhamedrahimov (ed.) *Emotions and Relationships at Early Stages of Development*. St. Petersburg, Russia: St. Petersburg State University, pp. 13–34.

Naber, F.B., Bakermans-Kranenburg, M.J., van Ijzendoorn, M.H., et al. (2008) Play behavior and attachment in toddlers with autism. *Journal of Autism and Developmental Disorders*, 38(5): 857–66.

Naber, F.B., Swinkels, S.H., Buitelaar, J.K., et al. (2007) Attachment in toddlers with autism and other developmental disorders. *Journal of Autism and Developmental Disorders*, 37(6): 1123–38.

Nakao, T., Radua, J., Rubia, K. and Mataix-Cols, D. (2011) Gray matter volume abnormalities in ADHD: voxel-based meta-analysis exploring the effects of age and stimulant medication. *American Journal of Psychiatry*, 168(11): 1154–63.

Neale, B. and Flowerdew, J. (2007) New structures, new agency: the dynamics of child-parent relationships. *International Journal of Children's Rights*, 15(1): 25–42.

Nigg, J.T. (2010) Attention-deficit/hyperactivity disorder: endophenotypes, structure and etiological pathways. *Current Directions in Psychological Science*, 19: 24–9.

Nigg, J.T., Blaskey, L.G., Stawicki, J.A. and Sachek, J. (2004) Evaluating the endophenotype model of ADHD neuropsychological deficit: results for parents and siblings of children with ADHD combined and inattentive subtypes. *Journal of Abnormal Psychology*, 113(4): 614–25.

Nikolas, M.A. and Burt, S.A. (2010) Genetic and environmental influences on ADHD symptom dimensions of inattention and hyperactivity: a meta-analysis. *Journal of Abnormal Psychology*, 119(1): 1–17.

Nix, R.L., Bierman, K.L. and McMahon, R.J. (2009) How attendance and quality of participation affect treatment response to parent management training. *Journal of Consulting and Clinical Psychology*, 77: 429–38.

Nomura, Y., Marks, D.J., Grossman, B., et al. (2012) Exposure to gestational diabetes mellitus and low socioeconomic status: effects on neurocognitive development and risk of attention-deficit/hyperactivity disorder in offspring. *Archives of Pediatrics and Adolescent Medicine*, 166(4): 337–43.

Nylund, D. (2000) *Treating Huckleberry Finn: A Narrative Approach to Working with Kids*. London: Jossey-Bass.

Ochsner, K.N., Ray, R.D., Cooper, J.C., et al. (2004) For better or for worse: neural systems supporting the cognitive down- and up-regulation of negative emotion. *Neuroimage*, 23(2): 483–99.

Olson, D.H.L., Russell, C.S. and Sprenkle, D.H. (1989) *Circumplex Model: Systemic Assessment and Treatment of Families*. New York: Haworth.

Oppenheim, D., Koren-Karie, N., Dolev, S., and Yirmiya, N. (2009) Maternal insightfulness and resolution of the diagnosis are associated with secure attachment in preschoolers with autism spectrum disorders. *Child Development*, 80(2): 519–27.

Palazzoli, M., Boscolo, L., Cecchin, G. and Prata, G. (1978) Hypothesising-circularity-neutrality: three guidelines for the conductor of the session. *Family Process*, 19: 3–12.

Palazzoli, M., Cirillo, S., Selvini, M., and Sorrentino, A.M. (1989) *Family Games: General Models of Psychotic Processes in the Family*. (V. Kleiber, trans.). New York: Norton.

Palomo, R., Belinchon, M. and Ozonoff, S. (2006) Autism and family home movies: a comprehensive review. *Journal of Developmental and Behavioral Pediatrics*, 27(2 Suppl.): S59–68.

Parens, E. (1998) Is better always good? The enhancement project, in E. Parens (ed.) *Enhancing Human Traits: Ethical and Social Implications*. Washington, DC: Georgetown University Press, pp. 1–28.

Pastor, P.N. and Reuben, C.A. (2008) Diagnosed attention deficit hyperactivity disorder and learning disability: United States, 2004–2006. *Vital and Health Statistics* 10(237): 1–14.

Pauli-Pott, U. and Beckmann, D. (2007) On the association of interparental conflict with developing behavioral inhibition and behavior problems in early childhood. *Journal of Family Psychology*, 21: 529–32.

Pennington, B.F., McGrath, L., Smith, S.D., et al. (2009) Gene x environment interactions in reading disability and attention-deficit/hyperactivity disorder. *Developmental Psychology*, 45(1): 77–89.

Perry, B.D. (2009) Examining child maltreatment through a neurodevelopmental lens: clinical applications of the neurosequential model of therapeutics. *Journal of Loss and Trauma*, 14: 240–55.

Perry, B.D. and Pollard, R. (1998) Homeostasis, stress, trauma, and adaptation: a neurodevelopmental view of childhood trauma. *Child and Adolescent Psychiatric Clinics of North America*, 7(1): 33–51.

Piaget, J. (1932) *The Language and Thought of the Child* (2nd edn) New York: Harcourt Brace; London: Kegan Paul Trench Trubner.

Piaget, J. (1970) Piaget's theory, in L. Carmichael and P.H. Mussen (eds) *Carmichael's Manual of Child Psychology* (3rd edn, Vol. 1). New York: Wiley.

Plomin, R., DeFries, J.C., McClearn, G.E. and Rutter, M. (2001) *Behavioural Genetics*. (4th edn). New York: Freeman.

Politte, L.C., Henry, C.A. and McDougle, C.J. (2014) Psychopharmacological interventions in autism spectrum disorders. *Harvard Review of Psychiatry*, 22(2): 76–92.

Pollak, S.D., Cicchetti, D., Hornung, K. and Reed, A. (2000) Recognizing emotion in faces: developmental effects of child abuse and neglect. *Developmental Psychology*, 36(5): 679–88.

Popper, K. (1963) *Conjectures and Refutation*. London: Routledge.

Porges, S.W. (2011) *The Polyvagal Theory: Neurophysiological Foundations of Emotions, Attachment, Communication, and Self-Regulation*. New York: Norton.

Rapport, M.D., Bolden, J., Kofler, M.J., Sarver, D.E., Raiker, J.S. and Alderson, R.M. (2009) Hyperactivity in boys with attention-deficit/hyperactivity disorder (ADHD): a ubiquitous core symptom or manifestation of working memory deficits? *Journal of Abnormal Child Psychology*, 37(4): 521–34.

Rask, C.U., Ornbol, E., Olsen, E.M., Fink, P. and Skovgaard, A.M. (2013) Infant behaviors are predictive of functional somatic symptoms at ages 5–7 years: results from the Copenhagen child cohort CCC2000 *Journal of Pediatrics*, 162(2): 335–42.

Regal, D.M., Ashmead, D.H. and Salapatek, P. (1983) The coordination of eye and head movements during early infancy: a selective review. *Behavioural Brain Research*, 10(1): 125–32.

Reiner, I. and Spangler, G. (2011) Dopamine D4 receptor exon III polymorphism, adverse life events and personality traits in a nonclinical German adult sample. *Neuropsychobiology*, 63: 52–8.

Rimland, B. (1964) *The Syndrome and Its Implications for a Neural Theory of Behavior*. New York: Appleton-Century-Crofts.

Ringer, F. and Crittenden, P.M. (2007) Eating disorders and attachment: the effects of hidden family processes on eating disorders. *European Eating Disorders Review*, 15(2): 119–30.

Roberts, A.L., Lyall, K., Rich-Edwards, J.W., Ascherio, A., and Weisskopf, M.G. (2013) Association of maternal exposure to childhood abuse with elevated risk for autism in offspring. *Journal of the American Medical Association Psychiatry*, 70(5): 508–15.

Robinson, E.B., Koenen, K.C., McCormick, J. et al. (2011) Evidence that autistic traits show the same etiology in the general population and at the quantitative extremes (5%, 2.5%, and 1%). *Archives of General Psychiatry*, 68(11): 1113–21.

Robson, C. (2002) *Real World Research: A Resource for Social Scientists and Practitioner-Researchers* (2nd edn). Malden, MA: Blackwell.

Rubia, K., Halari, R., Cubillo, A., Mohammad, A.M., Brammer, M., and Taylor, E. (2009) Methylphenidate normalises activation and functional connectivity deficits in attention and motivation networks in medication-naive children with ADHD during a rewarded continuous performance task. *Neuropharmacology*, 57(7–8): 640–52.

Rubia, K., Taylor, E., Smith, A.B., Oksanen, H., Overmeyer, S. and Newman, S. (2001) Neuropsychological analyses of impulsiveness in childhood hyperactivity. *British Journal of Psychiatry*, 179: 138–43.

Rutter, M. (2009) Commentary: fact and artefact in the secular increase in the rate of autism. *International Journal of Epidemiology*, 38(5): 1238–39; author reply 1243–34.

Rutter, M., Kreppner, J., Croft, T. et al. (2007) Early adolescent outcomes of institutionally deprived and non-deprived adoptees. III: Quasi-autism. *Journal of Child Psychology and Psychiatry*, 48(12): 1200–7.

Samson, A.C., Huber, O. and Gross, J.J. (2012) Emotion regulation in Asperger's syndrome and high-functioning autism. *Emotion*, 12(4): 659–65.

Satir, V. (1972) *Peoplemaking*. Palo Alto, CA: Science and Behavior.

Say, L., Donner, A., Gulmezoglu, A.M., Taljaard, M. and Piaggio, G. (2006) The prevalence of stillbirths: a systematic review. *Reproductive Health*, 3: 1.

Sayers, W.M. and Sayette, M.A. (2013) Suppression on your own terms: internally generated displays of craving suppression predict rebound effects. *Psychological Science*, 24(9): 740 –6.

Schmitt, J. and Romanos, M. (2012) Prenatal and perinatal risk factors for attention-deficit/hyperactivity disorder. *Archives of Pediatrics and Adolescent Medicine*, 166(11): 1074–5.

Seligman, M.E.P. (1975) *Helplessness: On Depression, Development and Death*. San Francisco: Freeman.

Selvini, M.P., Boscolo, L., Cecchin, G. and Prata, G. (1980) Hypothesizing—circularity—neutrality: three guidelines for the conductor of the session. *Family Process*, 19(1): 3–12.

Semin, G.R. and Papadopoulou, K. (1990) The acquisition of reflexive social emotions, in G. Duveen and B. Lloyd (eds) *Social Representations and the Development of Knowledge*. New York: Cambridge University Press, pp. 107–25.

Seskin, L., Feliciano, E., Tippy, G., Yedloutschnig, R., Sossin, K.M. and Yasik, A. (2010) Attachment and autism: parental attachment representations and relational behaviors in the parent-child dyad. *Journal of Abnormal Child Psychology*, 38(7): 949–60.

Shah, P.E., Fonagy, P. and Strathearn, L. (2010) Is attachment transmitted across generations? The plot thickens. *Clinical Child Psychology and Psychiatry*, 15(3): 329–45.

Shaw, P., Gilliam, M., Liverpool, M., et al. (2011) Cortical development in typically developing children with symptoms of hyperactivity and impulsivity: support for a dimensional view of attention deficit hyperactivity disorder. *American Journal of Psychiatry*, 168(2): 143–51.

Shedler, J. (2011) The efficacy of psychodynamic psychotherapy. *American Psychologist*, 65(2): 98–109.

Siegel, D.J. (2012) *Pocket Guide to Interpersonal Neurobiology: An Integrative Handbook of the Mind*. New York: Norton.

Sigman, M. and Ungerer, J.A. (1984) Attachment behaviors in autistic children.

Journal of Autism and Developmental Disorders, 14(3): 231–44.

Siller, M. and Sigman, M. (2008) Modeling longitudinal change in the language abilities of children with autism: parent behaviors and child characteristics as predictors of change. *Developmental Psychology*, 44(6): 1691–704.

Simonff, E., Pickles, A., Charman, T., Chandler, S., Loucas, T. and Baird G. (2008) Psychiatric disorders in children with autism spectrum disorders: prevalence, comorbidity, and associated factors in a population-derived sample. *Journal of the American Academy of Child and Adolescent Psychiatry*, 47: 921–9.

Singh, I. (2002) Biology in context: social and cultural perspectives on ADHD. *Children and Society*, 16: 360–7.

Slavich, G.M. and Cole, S.W. (2013) The emerging field of human social genomics. *Clinical Psychological Science*, 1(3): 331–48.

Sluzki, C.E. and Ransom, D.D. (1976) *Double Bind: The Foundation of the Communicational Approach to the Family*. New York: Grune and Stratton.

So, M., Yamaguchi, S., Hashimoto, S., Sado, M., Furukawa, T.A. and McCrone, P. (2013) Is computerised CBT really helpful for adult depression? A meta-analytic re-evaluation of CCBT for adult depression in terms of clinical implementation and methodological validity. *BioMed Central Psychiatry*, 13: 113.

Social Justice Policy Group (2007) *Breakthough Britain: Ending the Costs of Social Breakdown. Vol. 2: Economic Dependency and Worklessness*. Available at: http://www.centreforsocialjustice.org.uk/UserStorage/pdf/Pdf%20reports/BB_economic.pdf (accessed 10 Sept. 2013).

Spezio, M.L., Adolphs, R., Hurley, R.S. and Piven, J. (2007) Abnormal use of facial information in high-functioning autism. *Journal of Autism and Developmental Disorders*, 37(5): 929–39.

Spieker, S.J. and Crittenden, P.M. (2010) Comparing the validity of two approaches to attachment theory: disorganization versus danger-informed organization in the preschool years. *Clinical Child Psychology and Psychiatry*, 15: 97–120.

Spitz, R.A. (1946) Hospitalism; a follow-up report. *Psychoanalytic Study of the Child*, 2: 113–17.

Stern, D. (2000) *The Interpersonal World of the Infant. A View from Psychoanalysis and Developmental Psychology*. New York: Basic Books.

Strathearn, L., Fonagy, P., Amico, J. and Montague, P.R. (2009) Adult attachment predicts maternal brain and oxytocin response to infant cues. *Neuropsychopharmacology*, 34(13); 2655–66.

Strathearn, L., Li, J., Fonagy, P., and Montague, P.R. (2008) What's in a smile? Maternal brain responses to infant facial cues. *Pediatrics*, 122(1): 40–51.

Swain, J.E., Lorberbaum, J.P., Kose, S. and Strathearn, L. (2007) Brain basis of early parent-infant interactions: psychology, physiology, and in vivo functional neuroimaging studies. *Journal of Child Psychology and Psychiatry*, 48(3–4): 262–87.

Tamm, L., Menon, V. and Reiss, A.L. (2006) Parietal attentional system aberrations during target detection in adolescents with attention deficit hyperactivity disorder: event-related fMRI evidence. *American Journal of Psychiatry*, 163(6): 1033–43.

Tarren-Sweeney, M. (2008) Retrospective and concurrent predictors of the mental health of children in care. *Children and Youth Services Review*, 30: 1–25.

Taylor, M.J., Edmonds, G.E., McCarthy, G. and Allison, T. (2001) Eyes first! Eye processing develops before face processing in children. *Neuroreport*, 12: 1671–6.

Thoma, N.C., McKay, D., Gerber, A.J., Milrod, B.L., Edwards, A.R. and Kocsis, J.H. (2012) A quality-based review of randomized controlled trials of cognitive-behavioral therapy for depression: an assessment and metaregression. *American Journal of Psychiatry*, 169(1): 22–30.

Thompson, A., Hollis, C. and Dagger, D.R. (2003) Authoritarian parenting attitudes as a risk for conduct problems. Results from a British national cohort study. *European Child and Adolescent Psychiatry*, 12: 84–91.

Tottenham, N., Hare, T.A., Quinn, B.T., et al. (2010) Prolonged institutional rearing is associated with atypically large amygdala volume and difficulties in emotion regulation. *Developmental Science*, 13(1): 46–61.

Trivers, R. and Burt, A. (1999) Kinship and genomic imprinting. *Results and Problems in Cell Differentiation*, 25: 1–21.

van Ijzendoorn, M.H., Rutgers, A.H., Bakermans-Kranenburg, M.J., et al. (2007) Parental sensitivity and attachment in children with autism spectrum disorder: comparison with children with mental retardation, with language delays, and with typical development. *Child Development*, 78(2): 597–608.

Venuti, P., de Falco, S., Esposito, G., Zaninelli, M. and Bornstein, M.H. (2012) Maternal functional speech to children: a comparison of autism spectrum disorder, Down syndrome, and typical development. *Research in Developmental Disabilities*, 33(2): 506–17.

Volkmar, F.R., Hoder, E.L. and Siegel, A.E. (1980) Discrepant social communications. *Developmental Psychology*, 16: 495–505.

von Bertalanffy, L. (1968) *General Systems Theory*. New York: Braziller.

Vygotsky, L.S. (1962) *Thought and Language*. Cambridge, MA: MIT.

Vygotsky, L.S. (1978) *Mind and Society: The Development of Higher Psychological Processes*. Cambridge, MA: Harvard University Press.

Walker, P. and Carrive, P. (2003) Role of ventrolateral periaqueductal gray neurons in the behavioral and cardiovascular responses to contextual conditioned fear and poststress recovery. *Neuroscience*, 116(3): 897–912.

Wallien, S.C.M., Veenstra, R., Kreukels, B.P. C. and Cohen-Kettenis, P.T. (2010) Peer group status of gender dysphoric children: a sociometric study. *Archives of Sexual Behavior*, 39(2): 553–60.

Wan, M.W., Green, J., Elsabbagh, M., Johnson, M., Charman, T. and Plummer, F. (2012) Parent-infant interaction in infant siblings at risk of autism. *Research in Developmental Disabilities*, 33(3): 924–32.

Wang, P.S. and Insel, T.R. (2010) NIMH-funded pragmatic trials: moving on. *Neuropsychopharmacology*, 35(13): 2489–90.

Watanabe, H., Homae F. and Taga G. (2011) Developmental emergence of self-referential and inhibition mechanisms of body movements underling felicitous behaviors. *Journal of Experimental Psychology. Human Perception and Performance*, 37(4): 1157–73.

Watzlawick, P., Beavin, J. and Jackson, D. (1967) *Pragmatics of Human Communication*. New York: Norton.

Webb, E. (2013) Poverty, maltreatment and attention deficit hyperactivity disorder. *Archives of Disease in Childhood*, 98(6): 397–400.

Whittingham, K., Sofronoff, K., Sheffield, J. and Sanders, M.R. (2009) Do parental attributions affect treatment outcome in a parenting program? An exploration of the effects of parental attributions in an RCT of Stepping Stones Triple P for the ASD population. *Research in Autism Spectrum Disorders* 3: 129–44.

Wilensky, A.E., Schafe, G.E. and LeDoux, J.E. (2000) The amygdala modulates memory consolidation of fear-motivated inhibitory avoidance learning but not classical fear conditioning. *Journal of Neuroscience*, 20(18): 7059–66.

Willcutt, E., Sonuga-Barke, E.J., Nigg, J.T. and Sergeant, J.A. (2008) Neuropsychology of childhood disorders, in T. Banashewski and L. Rohde (eds) *Biological Child Psychiatry: Recent Trends and Developments*. Basel, Switzerland: Karger, pp. 195–226.

Williams, B.T., Gray, K.M. and Tonge, B.J. (2012) Teaching emotion recognition skills to young children with autism: a randomised controlled trial of an emotion training programme. *Journal of Child Psychology and Psychiatry*, 53: 1268–76.

Yin, R.K. (1994) *Case Study Research: Design and Methods* (2nd edn). Thousand Oaks, CA: Sage.

Index

79764272R00125

Made in the USA
Lexington, KY
25 January 2018